THE RHETORIC OF SOCIAL RESEARCH

THE RHETORIC OF SOCIAL RESEARCH

UNDERSTOOD AND BELIEVED

EDITED BY
ALBERT HUNTER

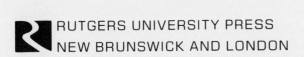
RUTGERS UNIVERSITY PRESS
NEW BRUNSWICK AND LONDON

Library of Congress Cataloging-in-Publication Data

The Rhetoric of social research : understood and believed / edited by
   Albert Hunter.
         p.   cm.
      Includes bibliographical references.
      ISBN 0-8135-1596-3 (cloth)   ISBN 0-8135-1597-1 (pbk.)
      1. Sociology—Methodology.   2. Rhetoric.   3. Communication in
   social sciences.   I. Hunter, Albert.
   HM24.R483   1990
   301'.072—dc20   90-31076
                         CIP

British Cataloging-in-Publication information available

For ALLYSON and ANDREW

Contents

THE RHETORIC OF SOCIAL RESEARCH

Epigram to

AN OBSCURE WRITER

Philo with twelve years study hath been griev'd
  To b'understood. When will he be believ'd?

John Donne

ALBERT HUNTER

Introduction

Rhetoric in Research, Networks of Knowledge

To be understood requires careful communication, to be believed demands persuasive argument. The first task of the social scientist is to observe and to report on social phenomena in a clear and understandable fashion. The second task is to convince others that what one says is true. From the seventeenth century to the present, when Sir Francis Bacon took the traditional questions rhetoricians posed to one another, and instead turned them outward and posed them to nature itself, modern science was born in this empirical dialogue between scientists and the natural world. Reporting back the answers to those questions has always required a convincing language so that the answers will be accepted after careful scrutiny by astute skeptics. While the methods of scientific research, narrowly construed, seem to involve a simple dyadic interaction between the scientist and the real world, most scientists are aware, sometimes painfully, that the reporting of research is a social and rhetorical interaction between speaker and listener, author and reader. The role of rhetoric in science is now being extended, however, to include the empirical methods themselves, to the social processes involved in the initial formulation of the questions, and to the social context of the extremely complex and collective dialogues of empirical research (Collins, 1985; Mulkay 1979).

An additional question that is posed by rhetoric uniquely to the social versus the natural sciences is that the phenomena studied are themselves the actions of conscious human beings. This further expands the complex web of social relationships involved in social science research to include three-way interactions among researchers, subjects, and audiences. A fourth element tying these relationships together involves the various media of the interactions—the texts. In this book—which is about, for, and by sociologists—we explore these interactions as symbolic communication expressed in research texts. The chapters present grounded analyses of sociological research that draw from or are, in part, informed by recent developments in "the new rhetoric," and various other disciplines that deal with "texts" (Nelson et al. 1987). We are not, however, rhetoricians. We are less concerned with elaborating or refining rhetorical categories and concepts than with showing how a rhetorical perspective can be used to inform our understanding of social research. This book's authors are practicing sociological researchers who share an interest in questions of how we present, and represent, our research. The ultimate goal is to produce better social science research.

This book deals with three levels of sociological "writing." The first and most often criticized level is that of the grammar, language, and "jargon" of sociologists. Beyond the bad sentence structure and excessive use of the passive voice, which any high school English teacher with a sharp red pencil would quickly correct, lie the dense, convoluted, polysyllabic conceptual inventions of the discipline that nonsociologists enjoy reducing to a single sentence, such as "sociologists write poorly." The book briefly looks at this more narrow topic of "writing" per se, and we note that a number of excellent books have recently appeared that more directly deal with it, such as Howard Becker's *Writing for Social Scientists* (1986) and Friedman and Steinberg's *Writing and Thinking in the Social Sciences* (1989). But this book is not so much a normative statement of "how to write" as an analysis of how and why we write the way we do.

Our interest in sociological texts extends beyond "words" and the act of writing in two directions. First, we define "text" broadly to include, in addition to the more traditional scholarly articles and academic texts, other representational materials such as maps and statistical tables, and also other forms or "genres" in which the words of sociology may appear, such as the mass media and student papers. Our second extension beyond the "words" of texts lies in our committed and enduring interest in the social organization of sociology and the social processes of interaction and communication that texts represent. Sociology, like any science and like all productive human endeavors from making art (Becker 1982) to waging war (Janowitz 1960), involves a complex web of social relationships for its production and distribution. We are interested in exploring how this social organization of social science both affects and is, reflexively, affected by sociological texts.

Beyond our inherent interest in sociologial "texts"—that is, what sociologists write—lie broader teleologial interests both generic and specific. The generic interest lies in a consideration of what are claimed as "sociological truths," the manner in which such claims are made, and the basis of such claims (see Fleck 1979 for a detailed analysis of the complex processes involved in establishing a single scientific fact). As sociologists we cannot but see truth claims as examples of social interaction, and their refutation or acceptance is an inherently social process. The social production of knowledge may or may not reflect some ultimate epistemological claim to "the truth." As sociologists, however, our bias is in seeing truths as beliefs that are socially constructed, constructions that in themselves contain various epistemological assumptions about the central conception of a science of society. In recent decades this line of inquiry about the role of rhetoric in social science has been openly pursued in both the United States (see Brown 1977, 1987; McCloskey 1985; and Simons 1988) and in the British Stong Programme (see Bloor 1976; Collins 1981; Edmondson 1984; and Mulkay 1979, 1985, among others). Though the implications of such inquiry for the conduct of science in general, and the social sciences in particular, are still emerging, the very posing of these questions about the role of rhetoric in science is a value in and of itself that cannot be ignored, refuted, or closed prematurely by any epistemology that adheres to the central scientific spirit of free inquiry.

Our more specific teleological interest is the desire to understand and historically bracket the positivistic scientism so prevalent today in the social sciences generally, and in sociology specifically. By referring to this as "scientism" we do not mean to reject quantification, mathematical modeling, or other "operational indicators" of modern positivism out of hand. Many of the authors of this text have and will continue to employ such "techniques" and "styles" in their research. We do, however, contend that science, as individual and collective thought and behavior, is a much more complex social phenomenon than such a narrow positivist conception connotes. Narrow positivist claims have a ring of "modernism," but an unreflective stylistic pursuit of "modernity" may do more disservice to sociology's aspirations to become a science of human behavior than any humanist's defensive exhortation on the indeterminate, liberated free will of the human spirit (see DiTomasso, 1982).

Positivistic proselytizing may have been a particularly appropriate strategic stance for the youthful social sciences to assume as they sought to define a discipline and demarcate a domain of activity. Over the years, however, we have won that battle. In the glimmering of what some see as the dawn of a "postmodernist" age positivism is not rejected but absorbed, encapsulated, or subsumed (McCloskey 1985, xix–xx). Dialectically, this new movement, by whatever name we call it, is not simply an antipositivist, knee-jerk reaction, but a thoughtful synthetic incorporation that reexplores "modernism's" intellectual origins and, after a stormy divorce of several centuries, remarries them to rhetorical analysis. Sociology as a discipline need no longer be seen dialectically as a perpetual battleground of humanism versus science, but rather as an encompassing discipline in which science and rhetoric are rejoined as interdependent human endeavors.

Freeman Dyson, a physicist at the Institute for Advanced Study, wrote in his autobiographical book *Disturbing the Universe* (1979):

> For insight into human affairs I turn to stories and poems rather than to sociology. This is the result of my upbringing and background. I am not able to make use of the wisdom of the sociologists because I do not speak their language. (4)

With a more conscious concern for rhetoric, sociologists can learn to speak a language that will allow their insights and wisdom to join those of mathematicians, physicists, poets, and storytellers alike.

Rhetoric, Science, and a Rhetoric of Science

Rhetoric is the systematic study of the acts of communication by which people convince others of the reality of truth of their assertions. To quote Aristotle's most succinct phrasing "Rhetoric is the faculty of observing in any given case the available means of persuasion" (1984, p. 24). Rhetoric historically precedes and categorically incorporates science. It was reduced to the limited domain of superfluous and emotive speech—"mere rhetoric"—by modern science, which claimed it had a better method of understanding the reality of the world in its objective essence. Science, in contrast to rhetoric, it was argued, could present self-evident facts, bare-boned observables that would appeal to reason not emotion. The neutral language of mathematics could express this assumed and discoverable order of the world more succinctly than any metaphor or catchy phrase of rhetoricians. Bacon above all expressed it most succinctly when he said that he took the forms and questions of rhetoric, and rather than ask them of another, turned and posed them to nature itself.

The contemporary sociological study of science, which views science as an organized social process, has called this hypothesized simple dyadic dialogue between the scientist and nature into question. When we look at what scientists do, and not merely at what they say they do (Latour and Woolgar 1979), then we have a standard against which to judge their reports of nature's answers. It is ironic, and perhaps dialectic, that the rhetorical questioning of the overly simple view of science as a dyadic dialogue should be done in the name of improving science itself.

Facts and Truth: Scientific and Rhetorical

A common conception of what scientists do is that they discover and report facts. The issue of whether scientists discover or construct truth will be dealt with momentarily, but first we pose a few questions about the scientific rhetoric of "truth" itself. Science begins from the assumption of physicalism, positing a real world, a physical world that exists out there independent of the observer. Even here, however, in modern quantum physics, for example, such a dualism is questioned, for the observer is seen as a necessary part of scientific truths. The inseparability of the observer and the observed is clearly stated in the paradox of Schroedinger's Cat, and in Stephen Hawking's discussion of the "anthropic principle," which states that the properties of this universe exist as they do only because these properties are those necessary to create beings capable of knowing it (Hawking 1988, 124–126).

Science as a human activity involves fallible human beings with their limited senses actually doing things in interaction with the real world to find out what that world is *like*. It is not a raw reality, but a metaphoric reality in that we attempt to understand it in terms of what we already know, whether what we already know is a mathematical model, other research, or personal experience. Given the fallibility of these interactions (and the limitations of various instruments that may be used to assist scientists in their sensing of the real world, from subatomic supercolliders to social surveys), scientists acknowledge that their knowledge and their facts are imperfect. The scientific process and the "truths" it produces are often idealized abstractions resulting from best approximations and sometimes bumbling activities—accidents of serendipity, false starts, wild guesses, and outright mistakes. The changing technology of science itself leads scientists to anticipate that theirs is at best a momentary approximation to the "truth." Facts are not simply "out there" waiting to be picked up, but instead are the manufactured products of scientific activity. Most competent scientists readily acknowledge this (Polanyi 1958; Chandrasekhar 1987), and yet this key understanding of imperfect, constructed knowledge rarely finds its way into the modern discourse and rhetoric of science (Bazerman 1981; Cartwright 1983; Collins 1985; Galison 1987; Hesse 1972).

The logic of science is a logic of "truth claims." Its statements of truth appeal to the credulity, the beliefs, of some audiences. These truth claims are historically and technologically bound—that is, given the technology available at the moment, the facts we know today are what we currently believe to be true. The rhetoric of science, however, still tends toward a generalized universalism. This ahistoricity of scientific claims to truth is paralleled by the depersonalization of science. Truth claims are rendered not as my truth claim as of today, but nature itself is given voice, and the truth is represented as speaking for itself (Mulkay 1985, 44–45). Immutable and immortal truth speaks pure and simple. Why has this universal, depersonalized conception of science emerged?

First, science is increasingly seen as a collective enterprise of a growing number of highly organized and specialized scientist-worker-technicians producing research products. The individual scientist disappears within the collective enterprise of science. Second, in an attempt to heighten the rhetorical credibility of research, scientists only report that which "works." The false starts, the personal chance hunches, the trail of "trial and error" are missing from scientific reports (Lakatos 1976, 143). To present these might call into question the competency of the researcher and the pristine precision of the research reported. Post hoc research reports therefore tend to portray linear and logical omniscience that when aggregated over time suggests a progressive accumulation of knowledge (Kuhn 1962). The normative structuring of how the scientific paper should be written, what should be both included and excluded, was itself a product of the new Newtonian science and has crystallized into the genre of the modern research report (Bazerman 1981).

The above is not to suggest that truth does not have an independent ontological status, that one cannot look at a piece of research and say, "That's wrong." To say something is wrong, however, is to question its truth claim on one of two levels: (1)wrong because the procedures used to generate that "truth " were faulty, an internal criticism of "methods" often framed in terms of internal validity; or (2) wrong compared to some other contradictory knowledge external to the research and to which one gives greater credence or external validity. Either way, to say something is wrong is to assert ultimately, "I don't believe it." Therefore, the belief that any one fact or proposition is true is based on much other knowledge, some stated some implied, and on assumptions about the world, not only the scientific world of existing theory and research, but assumptions, too, about the common world of the everyday.

In spite of the elaboration of rules of "method," scientists, like people in general, often rely on intuition in making judgments—the intuitive "sense" that something feels right. Touching this resonant chord produces a harmony, a shared community of discourse; while a discordant note may be rejected because it just doesn't sound right. (To continue the metaphor, the instrument of the discordant note may be "retuned," or if it continues to sound its egregious note, to be banished from the symphony of accepted truth making.) Intuition is the point at which both mathematicians and physicists often invoke a sense of "beauty" as a critical criterion of believing a truth claim (Chandrasekhar 1987). Appeals to intuition and beauty are perhaps nothing more than attempts to articulate and label all of the numerous subtle influences of socializaiton and personality that are a part of the unexamined, taken-for-granted rules that remain unexpressed in the more consciously articulated rules of scientific method. The power of rhetorical analysis in science can be used precisely at this point to elucidate the social context of justification by opening the unexplored black box of why it is that certain arguments "feel right." When confronted with the hard choice between beauty and truth—truth as it is known, given the limited instrumentality of the time—scientists will often opt for beauty (Chandrasekhar 1987). Such scientific beauty itself is often expressed as elegance and, furthermore, as a simple elegance with all of the random variation and disparate facts summarized into an abstracted simplicity. In the rhetoric of science facts may be irrefutable, but beauty is compelling.

Methods of Truth

Aristotle's *Rhetoric* suggests three domains of rhetorical discourse and persuasion: forensic (legal), political (deliberative), and epideictic (ceremonial). While the latter two are usually (though erroneously) considered irrelevant in the domain of scientific discourse, the first may be seen as the direct precursor of both modern rational law and the dialectic of modern rational science. Both domains are predicated on rational thought and the role of reason in adjudicating among facts as to "what really happened in the past" and "what is likely to happen in the future." Both legal and scientific discourse abound in questions about the nature of evidence, the rules for gathering evidence, and the relevance of the evidence to a given argument. Translate evidence to data and one has the three scientific domains of epistemology, methodology, and theoretical verification.

With the triumph of the age of reason in both legal and scientific scholarship a set of procedural rules shifted the agency of discovery from human actors to the structure of the rational rules themselves. Scientific method not scientists, and the rule of law not lawyers, would decide the relevance and the validity of the facts of a case. In short, procedures ensured reliability, which reasonably applied would ensure validity. The legal equivalent of a strict operationalism within the sciences, that scientific truth is what the measurements of science produce, is the assertion that legal truth is what the procedures in courts of law produce. Larger epistemological claims to "the real truth" are in both cases reduced to "available," "legitimate," and "presentable" facts. In both science and law, "findings" are judgments. There are of course significant differences between legal and scientific rationality, and for a fuller comparison one should consult the work of Vernon Dibble (1972), who explores differing claims and approaches to truth between these two rational discourses. The central point, however, is that the parallels noted between scientific and legal reasoning are not mere metaphor but reflect a common genetic ancestry.

With the triumph of its procedural methods, modern science did not merely distance itself from its parent, rhetoric, but turned and ferociously attacked it (a dialectic of differentiation often found in closely allied ideas that take on the character of internecine warfare, or more Freudianly, a ritual murder of one's parent). The attack on the emotive and irrational aspects of rhetoric succeeded in reducing it to the superfluous category of "mere rhetoric." Rhetoricians themselves, as David Zarefsky notes, contributed to this image with a scholastic elaboration of rules of presentation that read like books of etiquette for successful argumentation.

Science's continued distancing from the subjective "words" of rhetoric was aided by its increasing use of mathematics. Numbers, quantification, and equations increasingly replaced Aristotelian categorization as the mode of presenting scientific knowledge. As the famous quote by Lord Kelvin carved on the social science building at the University of Chicago states, "If you cannot measure your knowledge is meagre and unsatisfactory." The claim of objectivity through mathematical measurement implied that numbers, as distinct from words, are precisely and objectively denotative, not ambiguously and subjectively connotative. Again, by an appearance of removing human agency, the decisions and acts of humans in generating the numbers could more readily be overlooked or ignored, and the numbers assumed an objectivity that did not merely "map" reality but become reality itself (Dantzig 1954, 231). Though people might deceive or be deceived, the procedures of science and the numbers generated from nature could not. To paraphrase Einstein, nature may be subtle, but not devious. Hence, the facts, ideally, would bespeak their own truth if only the right questions were asked. To ask the right questions, however, usually means that one has some hint, some inkling of what form the answer might take to a given question. It is here, again, that the "black box" of intuition is often invoked. Mathematical intuition, for example, involves sensing the final form of a solution to a problem, and by working backward from the answer, one figures out the right way to pose the question to arrive at the desired result.

Early premodern science was not disconnected from many of the basic philosophical issues we have raised above, such as epistemology, teleology, aesthetics, ethics, logic, and rhetoric. Aristotle perhaps best exemplifies this epitome of a pre-Renaissance mind that addressed all of these domains of knowledge. Not that all of these issues of necessity produced a unified schema, but their interlinkage within the synapses of a single mind attest to the interrelatedness of the questions posed and the answers sought. Our concern is not, however, with all of these issues but primarily with the linkage between epistemology and rhetoric, the ways of scientific knowing and how we express that knowledge convincingly. Where to the early Greek philosophers rhetoric was an essential and necessary part of the development of ideas, the age of scholasticism witnessed both the triumph and eventual trivialization of rhetoric as a degenerate and narrowing road to truth. Rhetoricians wandered in their own world of words, forgetting the purpose of understanding the external world that lay around them.

There is the threat of a parallel closure within modern science, a hyperpositivism, a scientism, an inherent fascination with models that may or may not have any bearing on the reality they purport to model. This elaboration of arcane complexities runs the risk of transforming elegant, penetrating sophistication into a veiling and murky sophistry. A return to rhetoric, or the cultivation of a rhetorical sensitivity, may lead to a more appropriate reassertion of the means and ends of science as a way to understand, not overstep, reality. Science must remain open to the telling reality of the world, including the social world of which it is a part. Science is one of the more significant human endeavors and cannot become divorced from its humanity. A rhetorical perspective above all reasserts this essential humanity of science.

The significance of the new rhetoric is that it does in fact incorporate rather than dismiss the scientific method and its rules of evidence. It is neither the use of mere rhetoric nor a return to classical rhetoric, but rather a reconstituted scientific rhetoric that can be used to study both the process and the products of science. This joint focus constitutes a rhetoric of science. The postmodern approach to science is also neither antipositivist nor antiquantitative. It is also why, perhaps, the social sciences are uniquely poised to raise the questions posed by a postmodern perspective (Brown 1977, 231–234). On the one hand, they view the sciences not simply as ideological epiphenomena, disembodied "findings" or quantitative "truths," but as grounded social institutions whose "knowledge" and "ways of knowing" are legitimately subject to their analyses. On the other hand, the social sciences do not dismiss science from some humanistic or philosophical perspective, for they do claim, after all, to be sciences. But above all, the postmodern rhetoric of science sees the rules and procedures of science as normative claims guiding complex social processes. Invoking the rules of science is both a methodological and rhetorical strategy used to persuade an audience that appropriate behaviors were used to generate the "findings" or content of one's empirical research. To remove human agency is to talk about the discovery or finding of patterns out there, in nature; and debates about findings center on competing substantive claims about what patterns capture more of that reality (Mulkay 1985, 19–78). To reinsert human agency is to talk about humanly generated patterns that are claimed to parallel patterns in nature; and debates about the patterns may also include questioning the thoughts and actions of the agent. Scientists do not find truth; they generate it. Try as they might, scientists cannot remove themselves from science.

The Uses of a Rhetorical Perspective

If nothing else, viewing science from a rhetorical perspective is somewhat novel and interesting. If it is to have a larger claim on our interests than a mere curiosity, however, it must in some way be useful in generating better science generally, and better social science and sociology in particular. Framed more pragmatically, the question to ask of the rhetorical perspective is "What can you do with it?" or perhaps most succinctly, "So what?"

If, as I have claimed, the new rhetoric does not necessarily imply a revolutionary negation of modern science but rather a mutual incorporation of the two, then the important question to answer is "How can a rhetorical perspective benefit social science research?" Rhetorical framing will not necessarily lead to better research by producing new techniques, procedures, or rules for scientific inquiry. Rather, it is more likely to affect the behavior of scientists more indirectly by first making them more self-conscious in their use of existing techniques and procedures. It can be especially important in making them more self-conscious of the ways in which they present, and represent, in their writings their scientific results to others. Furthermore, though it may not necessarily cause scientists to pose their existing questions in new and better ways, it may cause them to ask new questions that have been relatively ignored. Questions about the social context of science that the rhetorical perspective brings to center stage become important to the degree that they can be shown to influence the conduct of inquiry and the claims of truth. This indirect effect of the rhetorical perspective is even more powerful than a self-conscious, correcting criticism of existing scientific techniques or a simple call for a more graceful and convincing writing style. A rhetorical view need not directly question or challenge the questions scientists are currently asking nor the answers they are generating; but it does ask why questions and answers are posed as they are and, perhaps more profoundly, what questions are left unasked and remain, therefore, unanswered. In short, the rhetorical perspective speaks to the question of cultural hegemony and provides an opening crack in the door to stepping outside of the edifice of contemporary ideas (Brown 1987, 118). By clearly showing that the edifice itself is historically and socially constructed, rhetoric provides a potential for deconstructing the edifice and reconstructing it in new ways.

This power for deconstruction and potential for reconstruction is again, however, not simply a celebration of new ideas for their novelty alone. There is a more morally empowering objective, that of providing people with the capacity to join scientific reasoning to moral and political action. This is the perennial problem of intellectual praxis (Brown 1977, 227). Joining rhetoric to science can be used where necessary to unmask the often hidden personal and political agenda of social research, and alternatively, this joining can legitimate the need for and use of existing facts of social science research as a basis for informing rational debates about public policies and social action. Rhetoric is the art of persuasion, and as Kenneth Burke (1969, 50) has noted, persuasion is needed only when individuals have freedom of choice and action. Where constraint and coercion reign, one need not be concerned about rhetoric. A rhetorical view of the social sciences can be used, therefore, to join knowledge to power, and it is especially needed if we are to join the freedom of inquiry to the freedom of action.

Rhetorical and Research Relationships

Methodolgical questions of how sociologists do their research cannot be divorced from rhetorical questions of how they represent their research results. If the different methods of sociology are seen as normative styles of research (Brewer and Hunter 1989, 25–26), there are direct parallels in the normative styles by which research is represented in texts. Through texts social scientists establish a communication relationship with their colleagues about subjects in which they have a mutual interest. The researcher-subject-colleague set of relationships is paralleled by the rhetorical relationships of author-argument-audience. We will briefly look at some elements of the interplay of these two sets of triadic relationships.

Author and Subject:
Authenticity, Truth, and the Question of Voice

One of the central ways of viewing the link between author and subject in the social sciences, where the subject is one's fellow human beings, is to see research as a social relationship. What Norman Denzin (1978) calls "the research act" is perhaps more aptly called research interaction, for all scientific measurement involves some type of interaction. As researchers our goal is to come to know our subjects; yet in the process our subjects will, to varying degrees, also come to know us. The central rhetorical question of this relationship as expressed in social science texts is one of voice—who is speaking and with what veracity (see Booth 1961, for a discussion of rhetorical voice). Is it the authenticity of the subject's voice, as in the field worker's use of judicious quotes informed by Weber's empathetic *verstehen?* Or is it the objective, distant, and ominiscient authorial scientific voice offering analytical insights, revealing latent structures, or debunking some cherished false consciousness?

The rhetoric of science views the scientist as an active agent in the production of scientific "truths"—that is, science is a human process and a human product. This runs counter to the dominant normative position of positivistic modern science, which tends to render any particular scientist irrelevant, for the rules of procedure are designed to ensure a universalistic mind of reasonable competency. Reliability of results can be assured among all reasonable people who follow the same procedures. In the written language of science the ego disappears, the scientist is rendered transparent, and the active creative agency of the scientist's "I found" is rendered as the more passive discovery of received truth, "It is found."

Try as hard as they might, however, scientists are never transparent. Not only is this evident from a careful reading of their scientific texts or within the writing itself, but it is most clearly opaque in the reward system of modern science, which attaches ego to ideas. Few scientific articles are submitted or published anonymously (though, interestingly, reports do exist of some being published under pseudonyms). The fixing of ego to ideas and the credit and reputations that are the currency of the scientist assure a personalized competitiveness in the marketplace of ideas. Though truth may be posited as "out there," to be acknowledged as "the discoverer" of any particular truth enables one to add to one's vita, one's salary, and one's reputation. In short, to Thomas Kuhn's "exemplars," the celebrated models of scientific research, must be added the celebrated model makers, the "exemplarers."

Social science has become stylized in the form of its presentation. The use of the passive voice, for example, is a stylization that tends to highlight the argument over the arguer. Even the mode of the argument itself, however, usually takes on the stylized form of a readily recognized commonplace. Many writers have suggested that the major type of argument made by social scientists is that of irony (Berger 1963; Brown 1977; Burke 1941; Edmonson 1984; Nisbet 1976). The social scientist as ironic observer and analyst presents an explanation of subjects' behaviors that are unrecognized and often at odds with the understanding of the subjects themselves. The ironic stance is one that crosscuts methodological and theoretical predilections from the structural functionalist's distinction between "manifest and latent functions," to the Marxian conception of "false consciousness," to the ethnomethodologists's idea of "taken-for-granted rules." To engage in ironic analysis requires a dynamic tension between coming to know one's subjects well and distancing oneself from them. In field research, for example, this tension is expressed in the role of "participant-observer," and for the social sciences in general its counterpart is the transformation of "subjects" into "objects." The manipulation of data is a set of procedures, intervening mechanisms that distance oneself as researcher from observed subjects. As a researcher one relates to data, to units of analysis, variables, categories, and classes of phenomena. This is the nomothetic thrust of the social sciences. The contrast in its extreme would be the most subjective "autobiography," something closely approached in the social sciences by the genre of the "life history" (Bennett 1983) or presented in prefaces and appendices or occasional revelations of the backstage of science (Hammond 1964).

There is, however, a double irony for social scientists, because as authors and researchers they must deal with two voices—their own and their subjects'. Both subjective interpretation and objective description are therefore combined in social science texts. Relative positionings and the rules of rhetoric dictate the degree to which one is submerged to the other. Since a text is an attempt to communicate and to persuade others, the social scientist must assume a dual voice of subjectivity and objectivity. Attempts to bury subjectivity—either the author's or the subject's voice—would depersonalize the social sciences at multiple levels. Subjects are devocalized, turned into data, and the author's voice is also silent, data demonstrate , tables show, no people speak. It is at this point that the intricacies of sophisticated analyses may operate more like the layered and obscuring veils of sophistry. The double irony is strikingly evident in the social sciences even for those who claim they are allowing the subjects to speak for themselves. Such analysts often claim in a louder voice than the more distanced, quantitative data manipulators that they have removed themselves from the analysis. Data, however, are never raw but must be prepared for consumption, if only in the selective picking and transporting to consumers (Krieger 1983). Highly sophisticated quantitative data manipulators may in fact be less deceptive in consciously presenting the intricate recipes they have used to cook their data. In sum, authorial voice is always present, and subjective interpretation is an inherent part of analysis. What varies are the rhetorical mechanisms of how authors' interpretations of their subjects are persuasively presented.

Subject and Audience:
The Text in the Context of Prior Knowledge

Just as authors are selective in their exposition, so audiences are selective in their exposure. We all find it difficult to deal with "cognitive dissonance" or the scientific disconfirmation of preconceptions. When the data or conclusions of a colleague's research do not fit a treasured hypothesis we are likely, as sophisticated, skeptical scientists, to scrutinize and critique the methods of the research, hunting for ways to dismiss it. Less scrutiny and skepticism are usually applied to results that are confirming. We are inherently more skeptical of arguments whose conclusions diverge from rather than converge with our own. This sets up a peculiar tension in reading texts. On the one hand, the reader reads for new knowledge, and yet on the other, for that knowledge to be comprehended or grasped it must fit at some minimal level into the cognitive structure of what the reader already knows. Sociology in the United States has a long history of exploring attitudes and attitude change and the process of persuasion as it is affected by structural positions and personal predispositions of consumers (readers). From voting studies (Bereleson, et al. 1954), to a physician's adoption of a new drug (Coleman et al. 1966), to religous conversion by cults (Lofland 1966), sociologists have explored the central rhetorical process of persuasion (Fuller 1988). By focusing on social and personal predispositions of potential audiences, these researchers have been following the old rhetorical admonition to "know your audience."

The audience almost always has some prior link to the argument, to the subject of the discussion either through their own research and experience, or through knowledge of others' research experiences. Within the social sciences the subject of a study is likely to be a group or groups familiar to a reader who consciously or unconsciously draws on personal experience as a basis of evaluating the research. A study of academicians (e.g., Ladd and Lipset 1973) may prompt an unparalleled scrutiny, because the audience is reading about themselves (see Lang 1981 for a particularly powerful case in point). The infinite regress of a "science of science" is that it self-reflectively studies itself as a subject.

The relationship of a reading audience to the subject involves a continuum of varying degrees of prior knowledge and interpersonal linkage, from "being one" themselves (where identity is one pole of a continuum) to "some of their best friends are . . ." or they have "talked to a cabby who said . . ." Toward the other end of the continuum they may only have read or been exposed to others' accounts—from more general, public accounts such as news stories to more specific scientific research reports. Only on rare occasions is the subject totally new, something the audience has no prior knowledge of whatsoever. But if totally new, the subject must be seen to be of import and must therefore be able to be placed in either a comparative or theoretical context. For example, if one is writing about a poor slum community to a middle-class, educated audience, the implicit if not explicit comparison is to middle-class communities; or if writing about a foreign political system, then the implicit comparison is most likely to one's own. This contextual comparison demonstrates that the particular subject or case is usually indicative of or exemplary of a larger set of issues or cases, for no research stands alone apart from other knowledge.

As we have seen, social scientists often adopt the neutral role of recorder and reporter, that of a copying scriber not a selective describer. The author attempts to become transparent and to place the audience in "direct contact" with the experience, not secondhand experience filtered through the author. The aim is to provide, in short, what Clifford Geertz (1985) calls "local knowledge" through "thick description." As we have seen, however, an author's claims to transparency are obviously limited. The experience of the audience is in fact that of "reading an account," not "experience" itself. In order to be able to accept an account of someone else's experience as credible an audience must have enough prior knowledge to be able to fill in the gaps, the unreported experiences of the author as researcher. The degree to which the audience can do this depends on their own familiarity with these research experiences, because they have read other accounts in sufficient detail, or because they too at some point have engaged in and are knowledgeable about the techniques of the research (whether the techniques are so mundane as watching a titration reach its endpoint in a chemistry lab or watching analytical results being printed out on a computer after controlling a regression equation for heteroscedasticity). Audiences vary in the degree of prior knowledge that any argument can and must assume about the methods of the research experience itself. As a consequence, audiences evaluate the credibility of research, in part, based on their comparison of the present text's account of its methods versus prior knowledge of those methods.

Within sociology the subject matter usually consists of people in a particular time and place, their organizations, institutions, actions, and events. Depending on how widely the circle of the subject matter is drawn, the reader usually has some prior knowledge of the subject directly through personal experience or more indirectly through other texts. Therefore, any given reading is in fact a dialogue, a trialogue, or perhaps more accurately a chorus of numerous other authors whispering offstage in the wings through the reader's mind. No text stands alone, rather, a text is positioned amid other texts, other arguments, other voices. There are texts the reader has read of which the author is unaware, just as there are texts the author has read of which the reader is unaware. The degree to which the experiences and texts of writer and reader are shared and overlap define the parameters of a community of discourse. Similar to Goffman's argument about the process of establishing an "authentic self" in *The Presentation of Self in Everyday Life* (1959), the reader is constantly judging the veracity, authenticity, or truth claims of the author's argument in a given text over and against other knowledge the reader possesses. Within literary analyses these issues are central to the discussion of what is called "reader-response criticism" (Tompkins 1980).

Audiences may orient themselves to particular topics, commonplaces of content, the tags and labels of discourse that define specialties, subspecialties, and professional and personal identities—high-energy physics versus low-temperature physics, recombinant DNA versus morphological zoology, or social stratification versus formal organizations. In parallel with selective exposure to particular topics readers may orient themselves to particular channels of communication—articles, books, working papers, seminars, the top journal in the field, a few specialty journals, a working paper series from a particular lab or research center, or more generic outlets such as *Science* magazine. Readers may also orient themselves to particular methods or styles of research—qualitative versus quantitative—and within each to a variety of stylistic variations from ethnomethodology to symbolic interaction, from path-analytic-regression analysis to smallest-space analysis and blockmodeling. Overall, the questions become, most generically: What texts are read? How are they read? Are they believed?

Ultimately, the reader's belief in the account rendered in any single scientific text depends on a complex calculus of evaluation of the text in comparison with a broad array of prior knowledge about the subject taken from the reader's context. This comparative context includes prior knowledge of social groups and the behaviors or events reported on, familiarity with the methods of research, and the reader's position in social networks and selective exposure to certain channels of communication.

Author and Audience:
The Social Organization of Communities of Discourse

A central way of viewing the author-audience relationship is as a community of discourse with a shared language and the shared perspective it implies. The boundaries of this community may be narrow or broad, circumscribed by the jargon of an esoteric academic subdiscipline or encompassing a wider literate and reflective public. Different texts have different functions or purposes intended by a text's producer (author plus all others involved in its production), and these purposes may reflexively define the language used. This seems to imply a relatively passive role for producers of texts to the degree that they attempt to read what the potential market may be and produce an appropriate text to match. Texts, however, may not only aim for a given community but, to parallel the marketing metaphor (and the reality of publishing texts in a competitive market), a text may attempt to create its own market, to create a community of discourse. Often an author is writing for an unknown, hypothetical, or assumed community. A community of discourse, therefore, is variable in its vagueness or clarity and is defined by multiple dimensions (for example, it may be a small and personally known potential market of researchers in paleolithic, comparative, vertebrate embryology versus a larger, literate public defined by the readers of the *New York Review of Books*).

As we have seen, all arguments are embedded in a taken-for-granted world view of numerous assumed understandings about what the world is and how it works. No author in a single "text" can retrace all of these embedded assumptions, which include, among other things, the very language being used to state the argument, the historical background of the argument, the socialization of individuals into the nature of the argument, or the comtemporary social context. Therefore, every argument is bracketed in a broadly assumed set of shared understandings. Only on occasion are surface disagreements pushed to the point where these assumed understandings may reveal very different ontological assumptions. More often surface disagreements and scholarly debates suggest an underlying agreement among protagonists that the hotly debated point is in fact of significance, at least of sufficient significance to command resources ranging from public attention and research grants to publishing space.

As we have suggested, however, texts are not solely a passive response to a preexisting community of discourse; they also serve to create or construct communities of discourse. Specific texts, their ideas, and their authors become the content of discourse, and communities of discourse are constantly reconstituted by texts. Texts are not only read but are talked and written about, and therefore serve a dual function as both mechanism and material for communities of discourse. Texts and communities of discourse, in short, interactively reconstruct one another (Fish 1980; McCloskey 1985). The dynamics of this process can lead to varying evaluations of texts over time, shifts in salient issues, and shifting boundaries for a community of discourse. Two features of this dynamic are of particular interest. First, communities of discourse become organized and structured horizontally with a division of labor and vertically with respect to power and prestige. Therefore, rather than the rhetorician's traditional "community of discourse" one might more aptly refer to the "social organization of discourse." Second, the dynamics of discourse result from the fact that there are multiple audiences or multiple communities of discourse that an author and a text must address.

Where a community of discourse implies an equality among interacting individuals, the social organization of discourse implies differentiation, stratification, and hierarchy. Take for example how much information about the social organization of discourse is readily conveyed on the title page of a book. First is the title of the text. The producer wants the reader to extract both meaning *and* remembrance from the title. The title (or more often the subtitle) must descriptively define the content of the book and yet be sufficiently catchy for later recall and referencing. Next comes the name of the author, who may be unknown or known to varying degrees from personal acquaintance, through networks of reputation, or from prior work. From the author's name we may readily infer gender and sometimes ethnicity. Often an institutional affiliation appears beneath the author's name, with all the reputational connotations such an affiliation conveys. Other questions about the author are usually more fully "fleshed out" in a brief "bio" somewhere on the flyleaf or the back of the book. We of course know the "publisher," which connotes content and quality linked to the publisher's reputation and prestige (Coser et al. 1982; Powell 1985). On the copyright page we find date of publication, copyright and publishing history, and Library of Congress classification. All of these communicate the social position of the text in a complex web of social organization. We leave aside the process—part chance, part purpose— by which the text and the reader have come together. Here I simply refer one to the introduction of Italo Calvino's "postmodernist" novel *If on a Winter's Night a Traveler* (1981), the first "chapter" of which elaborates at length the vagaries of decision and chance that enter into a given text's coming before the eyes of a reader.

Differentiated networks of interaction and discourse result in selective channels of communication, subgroups, and invisible colleges that become stratified within discipines. Awards are granted to certain texts and their authors, singled out as exemplars and exemplarers, and through the test of time selected texts become heralded as classics. Such recognition may lead to repeated referencing over time within a community of discourse vaguely alluding to an illusion of immortality. Debates and competition for resources ensue among subgroups, and ecological hierarchies of differing ideologies evolve. Numerous back channels of communication exist between author and audience that lie beyond the link established by a single text. The social relations of author and audience in organized social networks may be direct and involve personal acquaintance or more indirect, but these are significant for the construction of the argument itself, its communication, and ultimately its reception as a credible piece of research.

There are of course multiple audiences for science, and especially for the social sciences potential audiences may be multiplied ranging from particular disciplines to a more general public discourse. Such audiences may reflect preexisting social categories and groups, women and men, blacks and whites, liberals or conservatives. Multiple audiences may reflect various combinations of such overlapping social circles, and the appropriate rhetoric for convincing arguments will vary and multiply accordingly. Within any single social science text multiple audiences are usually addressed. Sometimes these are clearly indicated in distinct sections such as the "acknowledgments," where one both thanks the specific individuals named in a personal communication and does so publicly to a larger audience. Acknowledgments may also be interpreted as a positioning of the author within a network of named and known scholars, a further claim to validation if not validity. Even in a seemingly seamless "text" multiple audiences may appear from paragraph to paragraph or sentence to sentence. For example, Erikson in *Everything in Its Path* (1976) introduces certain concepts with the phrase "what sociologists call," indicating that sociologists are not the primary audience.

One true test of rhetorical rigor lies not in convincing the like-minded of the wisdom of their thoughts, but in convincing one's opponents of the error of theirs. The former, to harken back to Aristotle's tripartite distinction, is "ceremonial rhetoric," a celebration of shared values. How much of science, and social science in particular, is an expression of mutual celebration, the "elaboration of ritual" within "normal science," a speaking to friends rather than opponents, thereby avoiding the confrontation of "opposing facts" or contrary "representations of reality"? The rhetorical purpose of "carrying the day," of convincing an audience of the reality from which they should operate (namely, one's own), requires a knowledge of the positions of one's audience, both their ideological or intellectual positions and their correlated social positions. Just as the author is seldom a transparent embodiment of rational scientific procedure, so especially, as Mannheim (1936) powerfully argued, are the audiences of scientific discourse socially situated and selective recipients of "truth." Aristotle's admonition to "know one's audience" may be interpreted narrowly as a challenge to know one's intellectual adversaries, but most significantly and in its broadest form it may be interpreted as a call for a disciplined study of society itself. The ultimate rhetorical challenge for "the calling of sociology" (Shils 1961; Weber 1958) is to present convincing arguments about the operations of society that will be both accepted and acted on by society itself.

The Contents of the Book

The difficulty of organizing a wide-ranging set of essays into a coherent sequence of chapters is itself a difficult rhetorical task of an editor. The three elements or nodes of a rhetorical analysis—author, argument, and audience—and the reflexive and reciprocal relationships among the three are all to be found in varying degrees in each of the following chapters. Though each chapter contains elements of all three, my editorial interpretation of the relative emphasis of each chapter led me to categorize and sequence the chapters as found. More prosaically and pragmatically, someone had to do it some way.

The first set of chapters (those by Kai Erikson and Carl Milofsky) deal with writing per se and the significance of writing to the sociological imagination. We then move into two chapters (by Claude Fischer and Joseph Gusfield) that deal with different forms, styles, or genres of sociological writing and the important question of audiences. The next chapters (by Majorie DeVault, myself, and Lawrence McGill) look at the rhetoric of methods and the methods of rhetoric employed by sociologists as these relate to the issues of validity and credibility. Finally, we conclude with two chapters (by James Bennett and David Zarefsky) that stress how rhetoric itself can contribute to greater understanding of the sociological imagination.

Kal Erikson begins our grounded look at rhetoric in sociology by examining how sociologists write. He acknowledges, as many outside the discipline have readily observed, that sociologists write poorly. He goes beyond this criticism, however, to critique the critics and to offer an explanation of what it is sociologist are trying to do (observe, understand, and write about society) and how the communication of the sociological perspective differs from the everyday experience of social life. He in turn offers sociologists an approach to writing that is a challenge to retain its "scientific" objective, while combining it with a style of simple elegance that is both graceful and convincing. Erikson's own work is a model of this fusion.

We then turn to a chapter by Carl Milofsky, which explores how the sociological perspective is itself learned by students through their writing. Specifically, Milofsky describes how the teaching of fieldwork through an ongoing critique of students' field notes brings about an increasingly objective observation of social life. Field notes are the interactive text through and by which students learn to see and express their emerging sociological imagination. Writing and seeing are not separate activities, but mututally interactive.

Claude Fischer then explores the important question of how sociology's findings about social life enter into public discourse, and he uses as a case in point the book by Robert Bellah and his associates, *Habits of the Heart* (1985). Fischer raises the important rhetorical question not only of how we write, but of the audiences we write for. This question of the breadth of sociology's community of discourse and of the need to write for multiple audiences goes beyond writing per se to explore the social organization of the discipline and its relation to the media. Assuming that the results of sociological research are of value, the question becomes one of how to ensure that these results enter into and inform public debate.

Pursuing the question of multiple audiences, Joseph Gusfield develops the idea that there are different genres of sociological writing that are geared to different audiences. He compares two works that address inequality in America, Elliot Liebow's *Tally's Corner* (1967) and Peter Blau and Otis Duncan's *American Occupational Structure* (1967). He details how the forms of these two works represent two distinct genres that have implications for their varying accessibility and credibility to different audiences.

We then turn to a set of chapters that focus on the craft of sociology and the ways in which the methods of doing sociology are intimately tied to the writing of sociology. Marjorie DeVault compares two books written by women—Rosabeth Moss Kanter's *Men and Women of the Corporation* (1977) and Susan Krieger's *Mirror Dance: Identity in a Women's Community* (1983). Somewhat in parallel to Gusfield's use of the idea of different "genres," DeVault analyzes the different rhetorical strategies used by these women authors as examples of a dominant masculine objectivist voice versus a more feminist subjective understanding. This introduces the key question of how different rhetorics may be linked to the question of power relations between groups. I then look at a selected number of case studies, such as Robert and Helen Lynd's *Middletown* (1929), Herbert Gans's *Urban Villagers* (1982), and Kai Erikson's *Everything in Its Path* (1976), to show how the rhetorical contexting of case studies, "setting the scene," has important implications for the generalizability and credibility of field research. Lawrence McGill then raises the important question of how tables and other modes of representing quantitative data are used by readers of texts, and the role such data presentation plays in readers' assessments of the scientific rigor and credibility of research texts.

Finally, we conclude with two chapters that more explicitly explore relationships between the rhetorical perspective and the sociological imagination. James Bennett takes Robert Merton's landmark article, "Social Structure and Anomie" (1938), and shows how a close rhetorical reading of the text, a more explicitly hermeneutic approach, can elucidate the nature of Merton's argument and the place of the text in a larger body of social thought. David Zarefsky concludes with a brief historical overview of how the disciplines of rhetoric and sociology have come to "discover" each other. He explicitly looks at how Alvin Gouldner's early call for a "reflexive sociology" to solve *The Coming Crisis of Western Sociology* (1966) was a solution that presaged today's merger of sociology and rhetoric.

KAI ERIKSON
On Sociological Prose

IT HAS BEEN widely agreed both inside and outside the profession that sociologists do not express themselves very gracefully. Malcolm Cowley complained years ago that the wisdoms of sociology, such as they are, tend to be conveyed "in a language that has to be learned almost like Esperanto" (1956, 41). And Edmund Wilson (1956), who once toyed with the idea that the writing of every specialist in the university should be reviewed by professors of English, feared that sociology could not survive such a requirement at all. Exposing the defects of sociological writing is a literary sport of long standing.

The editor of Fowler's *Modern English Usage* (1965), in an entry on "sociologese," thought he knew why:

> We live in a scientific age, and like to show, by the words we use, that we think in a scientific way. . . . Sociology is a new science concerning itself not with esoteric matters outside the comprehension of the layman, as the older sciences do, but with the ordinary affairs of ordinary people. This seems to engender in those who write about it a feeling that the lack of any abstruseness in their subject demands a compensatory abstruseness in their language. . . . There are of course writers on sociological subjects who express themselves clearly and simply; that makes it all the more deplorable that such books are often written in a jargon which one is almost tempted to believe is deliberately employed for the purpose of making what is simple appear complicated, exhibiting in an extreme form the common vice . . . of preferring pretentious abstract words to simple concrete ones. (569–570)

Sociologists are of course aware that the abuse we attract is often justified. We are not sure that our prose suffers greatly from comparison with that of other social scientists, mind you—nor, for that matter, do we always blush with embarrassment when we read what professors of English have to say. Still, we often wonder in the quiet of our own counsels what there is about us or about the sociological project in general that seems to produce such murky writing.

The lines a person composes, obviously, reflect the furnishings of the

An earlier version of this essay appeared in *The Yale Review* 78 (1989):525–538.

mind that fashioned them, and in that sense a prose style is an individual thing like a signature or a voice. It is important to note right away, then, that sociologists are for the most part recruited from those corners of the academic world where people are neither trained in nor committed to the literary graces. We tend to regard good writing as an ornament rather than as an important professional tool, and while many of us honor and appreciate it, we do not often reward it in the coin of advancement.

So our students are not chosen in the first place for the sweetness of their voices. But that may not be the root of the matter anyway, for a great many seem to feel that whatever writing skills they brought with them into the field began to erode the minute they entered a professional apprenticeship in earnest. The lines people compose are not only a reflection of their individual imaginations, then, but of the discipline to which those imaginations are being tuned— those habits of mind and temper that are among the intellectual reflexes of the field. And that complicates any inquiry into the state of our prose.

What *is* the charge against our language anyway? Here are three samples of sociological writing selected by writers anxious to point out its faults. Jacques Barzun and Henry F. Graff, in *The Modern Researcher* (1970), were impressed by the scholar who wrote: "a highly consistent structuration of the external stimulus world may, at times, be experienced with sufficient intensity because of its personal implications to inhibit the operation of usually applicable internal structurations or standards of judgement." Hanan C. Selvin and Everett Wilson (1984), uncommonly literate sociologists themselves, contributed this scrap: "The impression is commonplace that a family system marked by such factors as late-age-at-marriage, a high degree of nonmarriage, a high incidence of marital disruption, and a low marital fertility schedule is conductive to the high involvement of women in economic activities outside the home" (212). And Sir Ernest Gowers, author of the entry on "sociologese" in *Fowler's* (1965) cited earlier, thought the following worth adding to the gallery: "The home then is the specific zone of functional potency that grows about a live parenthood; a zone at the periphery of which is an active interfacial mambrane or surface furthering exchange—from within outwards and from without inwards—a mutualizing membrane between the family and the society in which it lives" (70).

Passages such as these—I could have used scores of others collected by alert critics both inside and outside the field—would pain the most obdurately tone-deaf of sociologists. They are awful. No argument there. Now the fact that these specimens have been so carefully singled out should suggest that they need not read as ordinary, workaday offenses, drawn at random from the many millions of sentences that together constitute the sociological literature. They stood out even in what the critics already saw as a wasteland of inert prose. They are not representative misdemeanors, then, but high crimes.

Yet what makes them so bad? An uncommon number of these words have several syllables, of course, but they can be found in the working vocabularies of most educated speakers of English, and the sentences themselves are loyal to all of the published rules of composition. So the problem is not one of technical inaccessibility, as is often the case in professional papers by physicists or economists. The problem is that these sentences lumber painfully across the page, bent low by the weight of all the unnecessary syllables and complex locutions they are being asked to carry. They are ponderous, convoluted, hulking, bovine, full of a contrived profundity. The passage quoted by Barzun and Graff means something like "a plausible enough stimulus [a hoax, in this case] can throw you off stride so completely that you lose your ability to judge it correctly." The Selvin and Wilson sample really says: "Women who marry late, who remain single, who are separated from their husbands, or who have fewer children to take care of are more likely to have jobs away from home." And the Gowers selection: "A home can be seen as a contained space in which parents raise their children, but it is a space that both influences and is influenced by the social world around it."

The passages held up here for exhibit presumably contain ideas necessary to the larger arguments of which they are a part, but, sitting alone on the page, those ideas seem to be modest ones by any standard. And that is Gower's charge exactly—that sociologists so often convey a thought of slim dimension in the most pretentious and abstract language they can devise. It is an effort to lend a kind of technical authority to what are otherwise simple and even quite obvious observations.

Howard S. Becker (1986), author of a wonderful treatise on sociological writing, argues convincingly that such habits run deep in the intellectual grain of the discipline. They include a remarkable ability to coin neologisms, to slip into the passive voice, and, in general, to erect complex scaffoldings of words in the hope that the thought will seem wiser and more scientific than common sense would otherwise suggest. Mervyn Jones (1966), writing in the *New Stateman,* clipped the following from a report that happened to cross his desk: "In the London Traffic Survey, future traffic flows are seen to depend more than anything else on car ownership, and that in turn is shown to be a function of household income" (313). Simple words, each of them; two out of three, in fact, have a single syllable. But what does the phrase mean? "Cars are driven by people who own them," is Jones's way of decoding it, "and bought by people who have enough money." Well, that may not quite be it. Better to say: "When incomes go up, people buy cars, and that of course means heavier traffic." But the author's point, if a bit more complex, is no more profound than the translation by Jones gives it credit for being.

The grouchiest of our critics, then, sometimes conclude from the sheer opaqueness of our language that sociology is a kind of confidence game, an effort, as George Orwell (1946) put it, to give "an appearance of solidity to pure wind" (156). That strikes close to home. But it will not serve as an answer.

Most critics of sociology come from fields where things do not need to be stated very precisely and where the need for specialized vocabularies and specialized ways of presenting information tends to be small. In that sense sociologists occupy a kind of border territory, positioned between the holdings of historians and literary critics, say, who often use language to reach out to larger audiences, and the holdings of economists and statisticians who circulate material to one another written (if that is the right word) in a species of code. To the first set of neighbors we look inelegant; to the second we look inexact.

George Orwell (1946) once translated a familiar passage from Ecclesiastes into what he took to be a sample of modern sociologese. The original reads: "I returned and saw under the sun, that the race is not to the swift, nor the battle to the strong, neither yet bread to the wise, nor yet riches to men of understanding, or yet favor to men of skill; but time and chance happeneth to them all." And Orwell's parody reads: "Objective consideration of contemporary phenomena compels the conclusion that success or failure in competitive activities exhibits no tendency to be commensurate with innate capacity, but that a considerable element of the unpredictable must invariably be taken into account" (153).

Now Orwell wants us to note that the language of the first passage is incomparably richer than the language of the second, and who would argue with that? The original is wondrous poetry, the translation as labored and dreary as the cunning of a fine writer could make it. Yet there is another moral here as well, one that Orwell did not intend for even a moment. The poetry is enchanting. It bathes one in its warmth. But it does not ask to be read critically, which the parody, for all its deliberate clumsiness, does. And that really matters, too, for once readers are invited to listen to the *thought* rather than the language, the *logic* rather than the mood, they may more easily notice that the passage is full of the most doubtful conclusions. The facts are that the race usually *does* go to the swift, the battle to the strong, the advantage to people of knowledge and skill; and while time and chance may now and then supply exceptions to those rules, no sensible person would dream of living by so contigent a philosophy. What government would make it the basis of a defense system? What brokerage the basis of an investment portfolio? Damon Runyan understood: "The race may not be to the swift nor the victory to the strong, but that's how you bet."

H. L. Mencken (1955) made largely the same point in an essay on Abraham Lincoln:

> The Gettysburg speech is at once the shortest and the most famous oration in American history. . . . Nothing else precisely like it is to be found in the whole range of oratory. Lincoln himself never even remotely approached it. It is genuinely stupendous.
>
> But let us not forget that it is poetry, not logic; beauty, not sense. Think of the argument in it. Put it in the cold words of everyday. The doctrine is simply this: that the Union soldiers who died at Gettysburg sacrificed their lives to the cause of self-determination—"that government of the people, by the people, and for the people," shall not perish from the earth. It is difficult to imagine anything more untrue. The Union soldiers in that battle actually fought self-determination; it was the Confederates who fought for the right of the people to govern themselves. (179–180)

Mencken may have misread the speech himself, but that does not matter for our purposes now. The point is that hundreds of millions of Americans have read the Gettysburg Address and tens of millions have memorized all or parts of it, but it is reasonable to guess that no more than a few have ever been moved to "think of the argument in it."

The challenge for sociological prose, then, is to convey ideas and information with enough clarity to be understood outside the narrow precincts of the field and yet with enough precision to allow for careful inspection and evaluation within it. We would be quite right to dismiss the rebukes of a Cowley or an Orwell out of hand, since they have no idea what sociology is all about and, moreover, are simply wrong to think that social life must be easy to understand and write about because it involves "the ordinary affairs of ordinary people." None of them would argue, presumably, that physics ought to come easily to us because we are subject to the laws of motion, or that physiology ought to come easily to us because we occupy living bodies. Why is it so much easier to suppose that the ways of human culture are simple and well within the grasp of anyone who lives in society?

Sociological prose is responsible to a particular disciplinary vision, and it is not possible to assess the one justly without taking the other into account. How might that vision be described?

Most sociologists think of their discipline as an *approach* rather than a subject matter, a *perspective* rather than a body of knowledge. What distinguishes us from other observers of the human scene is the manner in which we look at the world—the way our eyes are focused, the way our minds are tuned, the way our intellectual reflexes are set. Sociologists peer out at the same landscapes as historians or poets or philosophers, but we select different details out of those scenes to attend closely, and we sort those details in different ways. So it is not *what* sociologists see but the *way* they look that gives the field its special distinction.

I suggest to my students: Imagine that you are walking down a sidewalk at rush hour in New York. You pass thousands of people in the space of a few moments, all of them intent on their own personal errands, absorbed in their own private thoughts, making their own individual way through the crowd. Every face is different. Every gait is different. It is difficult to sense any pattern or order in that scene, for what the eye sees down there at ground level is an immense scatter of individuals who are moving to their own rhythms and living out their own lives. If you were looking for an element of human drama in that scene, you would probably find your attention drawn to certain of the people passing by—that woman over there who seems to be in such an urgent hurry, that man who seems to be talking crazily to himself, that child who looks as though she is about to do something very special. A thousand different people. A thousand different stories.

Imagine, however, that you climbed to the twelfth floor of a building nearby and looked down on that same sidewalk. At that elevation, you are too far away to see the expressions on those faces, too far away to make any guesses about the motives that impel those people along their individual paths. From that vantage point, the eye sees a mass of humanity in motion, a swarm of particles that weave in and out as if moving along invisible tracks. A hundred thousand persons may pass down that thin strip of pavement in a matter of minutes without so much as a single collision, flowing in currents that no one seems aware of. And if you are looking for drama in *that* scene, it may occur to you that you are witnessing a remarkable act of coordination. The movement on the sidewalk seems patterned, governed by rules, choreographed; and the wonder of it is that no one down there can tell you how the trick is done. Chances are, in fact, that if you asked a few of those passersby to think about what they are doing—to concentrate on their own maneuvering—they would become self-conscious, lose their bearings, perhaps even stumble into one another.

Sociologists can be said to look at social life from the vantage one gains at a twelfth floor. The particular qualities of individuals seem less distinct and even less compelling at that height, for one can sense that there are forces out there in the world that give shape and direction to the flows of everyday behavior in much the same way that they give shape and direction to the flows of traffic on a sidewalk. When sociologists refer to "society," then, they are speaking of tides, currents, forces, pulls—something in the organization of human life that causes people to behave in reasonably predictable ways. It becomes apparent when one views the world from a twelfth floor that there are consistencies in the way people think and act; consistencies in the way they move from place to place; consistencies in the way they see the universe around them, relate to one another, and even find their way through moving swarms of pedestrians. Human life is subject to social forces that give it form and pattern.

Sociologists view those forces as real *things*. One cannot see them, of course, or reach out and touch them. But we infer that they exist because we observe what happens to the people caught in them— which is exactly how physicists infer the existence of gravity. Human life takes place in a field of force, and sociologists try to learn the secrets of that field in much the same way that other specialists study a galaxy, an organism, a molecular structure, or any kind of organized matter. No sociologist would suggest that human groups are *like* galaxies or molecules. They are more diverse, more volatile, and (most sociologists feel) more interesting. We would argue, though, and properly so, that the eye one trains on human society is disciplined in the same way as the eye one trains on the things of the physical world.

There is pattern in the way human beings grow up, become adults, choose occupations, form families, raise children. There is pattern in the way people become ill or commit crimes or write poetry or think thoughts. Now sociologists are certainly aware that societies are composed of individuals who carve their own separate path through life and are moved by their own private visions. Everyone who lives is a singular personality, a rare and special being. But the view from the twelfth floor suggests that there are commonalities in the midst of all that uniqueness that give social life its distinctive design. Every individual biography is at the same time a part of some larger historical sweep, and is, to some extent, caught up in it; every person is connected by ten thousand invisible threads to every other. The poet Stanley Kunitz put the matter wonderfully: "The supreme awareness we can have is that all existence is continuous tissue, a gigantic web of interconnected filaments, so delicately woven that if touched at any point the whole web trembles."

Those patterns, those filaments, are the subject matter of sociology. They are its challenge as well as the source of its intellectual excitement. But they are also a source of our difficulty in communicating to readers outside the discipline whose good opinion we would very much like to have, because our vocubulary can seem so opaque and our syntax so convoluted when we look for ways to speak of those filaments. We put the language to quite a different set of tasks than is the case for most of those who elect to become our critics.

To begin with, we sociologists are invited by the logic of our perspective to be more concerned with *general tendencies* than with *particular events*. Our assignment in the world of scholarship is to move up onto the plane of generality as soon as our data permit (if not a good deal sooner), attending to those regularities that are the substance of everyday human experience rather than those unique persons and unique moments that stand out as special (and for that very reason attract the interest of journalists and dramatists and historians). Dennis Wrong (1983) writes of "the intense straining" among sociologists "for universality, for a language that transcends the particular and the commonplace by breaking through its own limits" (7). And, indeed, sociologists are wisest when they distrust the individual case as being too idiosyncratic and unrepresentative. Journalists often begin their stories with profiles of particular individuals, asking them in effect to portray, represent, even act out the lives of larger populations. This is a way of focusing attention and establishing a tone—of giving the problem at hand a kind of personality and texture—and it is a rhetorical strategy found in virtually every form of expository writing. But it offers few opportunities to the sociologist, whose task it is to draw group profiles with a distinct accent on numbers, percentages, tendencies, and underlying structural forces. We like to say that ours is a nomothetic science rather than an idiographic one, and that distinction speaks volumes not only about the epistemological boundaries within which we work but about the languages we are fated to use in doing so. For our pursuit of the general has given most sociologists the feeling that we have had to more or less abandon the arts of portraiture and description, of painting landscapes, so to speak, with words. Not for us the lavish cadences of Johan Huizinga (1954), even though he is engaged here in a task that can only be called ethnographic:

To the world when it was a half a thousand years younger, the outlines of all things seemed more clearly marked than to us. The contrast between suffering and joy, between adversity and happiness,

appeared more striking. All experience had yet to the minds of men
the directness and absoluteness of the pleasure and pain of child-life.
Every event, every action, was still embodied in expressive and sol-
emn forms, which raised them to the dignity of ritual. . . . Calamities
and indigence were more afflicting than at present; it was more difficult to guard against them, and to find solace. Illness and health presented a more striking contrast; the cold and darkness of winter were
more real evils. Honours and riches were relished with greater avidity
and contrasted more vividly with surrounding misery. We, at the
present day, can hardly understand the keenness at which a fur coat,
a good fire on the hearth, a soft bed, a glass of wine, were formerly
enjoyed. . . . The contrast between silence and sound, darkness and
light, like that between summer and winter, was more strongly
marked than it is in our lives. The modern town hardly knows silence
or darkness in their purity, nor the effect of a solitary light or a single
distant cry. (18–19)

It might be noted, too, that sociologists are invited by the logic of
their perspective to think in terms of *collateral* arrangements rather
than *sequential* ones. Our stock in trade has normally been the relations that obtain at any given point in time among people and events
and institutions—the way income relates to voting, the way working
helps shape personality, the way migration affects the urban land-
scape, the way poverty influences household composition, and, in all
such instances, vice versa. Ours is the language of concomitance. This
means that sociologists are rarely in a position to use a narrative line,
to tell a story. And that's a real loss, because one of the surest ways to
sort out one's thoughts and organize one's materials is to arrange them
in chronologies. Malcolm Cowley (1956), in the same article cited earlier, complained that the sociologist "seldom uses transitive verbs of
action, like 'break,' 'injure,' 'help,' and 'adore.' Instead he uses verbs of
relation, verbs which imply that one set of nouns and adjectives, used
as compound subject of sentence, is larger or smaller than, dominant
over, subordinate to, causative of, or resultant from another series of
nouns and adjectives." (41). Well, sure! What did he expect? Relations
between things and changes in those relations are what sociologists
write about; and should our repertoire seem meager to someone who
likes the sound of such verbs as *break* and *adore,* that is the product
of our craft and not of our prose style.

And it might be noted, to offer a final example, that when sociologists contemplate a conversation between two persons or a wider interaction involving several, they are invited by the logic of their
perspective to attend to the pattern that ensues rather than the contributions of the individual participants. A distinguished law professor
of a generation ago is supposed to have said to his students: "If you
can think of the relationship between two objects without thinking

about the objects themselves, then maybe you have a legal mind." That certainly fits sociology. Our eyes are trained on the *spaces between* intersecting individuals—on the shape of their conversation, the architecture of their transaction, the way the words spoken and the gestures enacted form a composition independent of the persons who contributed to it.

There are many similar matters one might raise, but the chief point is that the languages of sociology tend toward the abstract at least in part because the perspectives of sociology tend toward the abstract. The realities we study are a prospect unique to those who look out at the world through a special disciplinary lens, and the languages we use need to be able to capture that marvelous, peculiar vision. Joseph Wood Krutch (1963) may have been closer to the mark than he knew when he suggested that "the war between science and religion will be settled long before that between literature and sociology. The proponents of each were born under different stars and are equally incapable of seeing the same things as either significant or interesting" (69–72). Take out the tone of annoyance and the exaggeration that follows from it, and you have here a very shrewd observation.

It is important, then, to begin with the context in which sociology is written, for one of our tasks as a discipline is to distinguish between those of our usages that are an inevitable result of the sociological way of looking at things and those usages that are really no more than casual habits that have drifted in among the other conventions of the field.

There is no escaping the fact, though, that a good many of the infelicities of sociological prose are of the latter kind. So let me shift from defense to offense as I bring these comments to a close and note that once sufficient allowance is made for the special character of our vision, we can the more easily see all the lazy addictions and mindless routines that form like a crust over so much sociological writing. The "verbal folkways of sociology," Cowley called them. Most of these folkways seem to have found their way into the intellectual weave of the field without any deliberation at all. Our habit of avoiding the pronouns *I* or *me* in the most ordinary of sentences, for example, has to be read as a kind of conceit—a sample, to give Gowers his due, of trying to sound scientific. To write "it is thought" when one means "I think" has the effect of removing the writer from the field of action and giving the utterance to follow a hint of distance and universality for which there is no warrant in reality: it is as if nature had made the point and the writer is only serving as its scribe. Others of these folkways are the product of ancient instructions, their origins long forgotten. William

Fielding Ogburn (1930), one of the most honored of our tribal elders, asked his fellow social scientists in 1930 to work toward "the writing of wholly colorless articles"—a necessary "antidote," he thought, to the "bad legacy" of scholars like Thomas Huxley and William James who wrote with personality, vigor, and occasional moments of passion (301).

The question, then, is whether the languages of sociology can reflect the specialness of our disciplinary vision and yet reflect the grace and clarity and sense of craft critics so often miss in our prose. And the answer to that question can only be yes.

In *Life on the Mississippi,* Mark Twain (1967, 69–72) described his apprenticeship in another trade that involves a special way of perceiving the world. He asked a wily old riverboat pilot one day how one should tell the difference between a bluff reef and a wind reef—the one as dangerous as a charge of explosive and the other little more than a slight tremor on the surface of the water—and the old pilot could only say: "I can't tell you. It's an instinct. By and by you will just naturally *know* one from the other, but you never will be able to explain why or how you know them apart."

> It turned out to be true. The face of the water, in time became a wonderful book—a book that was a dead language to the uneducated passenger, but which told its mind to me without reserve, delivering its most cherished secrets as clearly as if it uttered them with a voice. And it was not a book to be read once and thrown aside, for it had a new story to tell every day. Throughout the long twelve hundred miles there was never a page that was void of interest, never one that you could leave unread without loss, never one that you would want to skip, thinking you could find higher enjoyment in some other thing. There never was so wonderful a book written by man . . .
>
> Now when I had mastered the language of this water, and had come to know every trifling feature that bordered the great river as familiarly as I knew the letters of the alphabet, I had made a valuable acquisition. But I had lost something, too. I had lost something which could never be restored to me while I lived. All the grace, the beauty, the poetry, had gone out of this majestic river!

Twain goes on to describe a "wonderful sunset" he had witnessed when steamboating was still new to him—a scene in which the shifting colors of the sky lent a new cast and texture to everything, in which the shadows of rocks and trees slanted across the moving surfaces of the water like delicate tracings. "There were graceful curves, reflected images, woody heights, soft distances; and over the whole scene, far and near, the dissolving lights drifted steadily, enriching it every passing moment with new marvels of coloring." A picture of extraordinary beauty.

But Twain then tells us what the eye of an experienced riverman sees in such a scene: the reflected colors of the sun and the dark shadows of the forest and the shimmers of the water had become something else—signs of danger, forewarnings of bad weather yet to come, symptoms of some deep disturbance in the order of the river. The eye had been disciplined to see that which is the pilot's special business to know.

> No, the romance and the beauty were all gone from the river. All the value any feature of it had for me now was the amount of usefulness it could furnish toward compassing the safe piloting of a steamboat. Since those days, I have pitied doctors from my heart. What does the lovely flush in a beauty's cheek mean to a doctor but a "break" that ripples above some deadly disease? Are not all her visible charms sown thick with what are to him the signs and symbols of hidden decay? Does he ever see her beauty at all, or doesn't he simply view her professionally, and comment upon her unwholesome condition all to himself? And doesn't he sometimes wonder whether he has gained most or lost most by learning his trade?

The problem for any professional, then—river pilot, doctor, sociologist—is how to train one's eye to read the whorls and ripples and boils on the surface of one's subject and then to find a conceptual vocabulary that can portray them accurately to others. That is what Cowley and the others fail to see. Sociologists look out at the same human scene as poets, exactly as river pilots look out at the same body of water as their passengers, but their professional business is to see it and describe it in a special way.

At the same time, however, one need only read the above lines to learn that the beauty and the poetry of the river did not really desert Twain at all, even if they were distant from his thoughts while he was actively plying his trade. And that is the project we should be pursuing—to combine the eye of a river pilot and the voice of a Mark Twain.

CARL MILOFSKY

Writing and Seeing

Is There Any Sociology Here?

WHEN PRESENTING the discipline to newcomers, sociologists often describe their approach as a new way of "seeing" reality. One thinks of C. Wright Mills's *Sociological Imagination* (1959); a chapter in Peter Berger's *Invitation to Sociology* (1963, 25–53) titled "Sociology as a Form of Consciousness"; Randall Collins's *Sociological Insight: An Introduction to Nonobvious Sociology* (1982); and Richard Benkin's introductory text *Sociology: A Way of Seeing* (1981). Why do sociologists think the discipline offers a way of seeing that is any newer than what other disciplines offer? I can well imagine a text titled *Physics: A New Way of Seeing* or *English Criticism: A New Way of Reading*. Any discipline offers a new way of seeing or it would not long be in business. Academics justify their existence by being able to surprise and enlighten people, shedding new light on things other people thought were commonsense and ordinary. Are those who advertise this sociological vision simply talking about the "ordinary" insight and clarity that analytic rigor provides?

Without claiming to answer for sociology, this chapter explores some distinctive aspects of the sociological perspective by taking a developmental perspective. If there is a uniquely sociological way of seeing, then one way of describing its nature is to look at what happens to students as they progress through a course of study and become more like sociologists. The course of study I will talk about is rather narrow and specific. It involves an exercise in field research over one or two semesters in which students work for three to six hours in a social service agency and then write field notes about their experience. I write detailed comments on each of their five sets of field notes. My comments often are about as long as their notes—roughly four double-spaced pages. What impresses me about this exercise is that over the course of a semester there nearly always is a dramatic change in students' papers. At the beginning papers are organized around conventional assumptions about what they are seeing and what is important in the field settings. Their writing is constrained, bland, and boring.

By the end, people are writing lively material full of provocative, counterintuitive insights about the institutions they are studying. While they are not yet producing theoretical sociology, their writing is recognizably more sophisticated and informed by a sociological viewpoint. What does this mean? What happened?

One of the things that has troubled me over the years is that perhaps my style of teaching and the gains students make has nothing particularly to do with sociology. It might be that nothing at all meaningful is happening. While students are clearly doing something different by the end of the term, it might be that they just improve at guessing what I want them to write, and their products might, thus, only reflect my own idiosyncratic tastes. On the other hand, it might be that the gains are real but the students are only reflecting the generalized effects of education. School effects always seem to show that no single intervention has any predictable impact on students. The experience of going to school, however, improves intellectual performance. Perhaps intensive writing in any subject would cause students to develop. The gains they make in my class are picked up and then advanced further in some French class or course in art history. In either case it would not be the sociological emphasis that made a difference.

I argue here that it is the sociology that matters. The sociological perspective as I teach it presents all knowledge as a form of argument. Students learn to abandon the notion that there are right or wrong ways to describe or analyze a setting or a social process or a social problem. They learn that in any setting there are myriad ways of describing the same concrete events and many possible explanations for any problematic occurrence. They learn that a key part of sociological understanding is knowing how to ask questions and formulate alternative interpretations. They also learn that collecting additional data is necessary if one is to fill in one's understanding of the things one has seen.

These are habits of mind that students develop through specific instruction. We can trace the principles that underlie this methodology to master theorists of qualitative observation such as Mead (*Mind, Self, and Society,* 1962) and Merton ("Manifest and Latent Functions," 1949). To my continual amazement students move from finding these theoretical writings obtuse and dry to finding them gripping and full of detailed suggestions about how to observe social settings. Students learn some specific, concrete skills, and those skills were discovered and articulated by some of the people we identify as the architects of the discipline.

While the habits of mind are characteristically sociological and rep resent what Collins and Makowsky (1984, 3–17) correctly believe is the major technical contribution sociology has made to modern scientific knowledge, the perspective students adopt is not owned exclusively by sociology. The perspective brings to self-consciousness some ways of perceiving social reality that are inherently human and thus not new or introduced to the culture by sociology. The perspective is one that many people spontaneously discover as a useful and necessary part of their personal intellectual equipment. I have met quite a few public school teachers, for example, who have discovered a sociological perspective through their work.

The perspective may be spontaneously discovered by people in lay society, but what makes it sociological is its union with theory. Theorizing involves integrating many observations into a comprehensive system of propositions and using that system to define and explore problematic issues. These problematic issues are linked to comprehensive understandings or explanatory systems about society. Particular case studies are at once illustrations of these comprehensive theories and means of extending, testing, and fine tuning those theories by holding them accountable to concrete experience. I am thinking here of Stinchcombe's (1983) critique of Marxist social science for being insufficiently attentive to the difficulties case study data pose for Marxism. Macrotheory needs to be at once general and disciplined by facts. Case study data must push to build theory and avoid contentment with telling a good (but limited) story.

Although the theory linkage makes this style of observation sociological, I do not mean to suggest that a global theory, in the style of Parsons or Marx, is the likely outcome. The style of observation I teach helps people discover nonobvious or counterintuitive processes and relationships. It encourages them to avoid closed, unidimensional understandings about *settings* and to seek instead a kaleidoscopic view of social reality (Geertz 1973; Sarason 1972). This means there is no single or correct way to view any social setting. The way one views or perceives a setting is conditioned by the point one wishes to make. That point is partly discovered as one observes and partly defined by one's broader theoretical agenda.

Thus, any given setting can give rise to many different observational studies and many different, perhaps contradictory, theoretical conclusions. Creating a field study has continuities with fiction writing as well as with experimental science. Because field observers accept the constraint that their writing will derive from actually observed events and efforts to test hypotheses against data, their work is scientific. Because observers make selections among many available interpretations and seek out a "plot" that will make their observations hang together, storytelling is an important part of the art. Field researchers must not only collect "the facts." They must also find ways of making their description compelling. They must find ways of convincing their audience that their depiction is real and true. It is the narrative that makes the account convincing, not the facts.

Requiring that there be a dialogue between the vast complexity of settings and the simplifying, organizing propositions of theory limits the latter. It is hard to produce theories that go much beyond the middle range (Merton 1967) without sacrificing fidelity to the setting. This is a pragmatic issue, not an ideological challenge to metatheory. If we take seriously the complex reality field research finds to be primary, then theories by their nature will be limited and fragmentary. Even metatheories are limited because of their inability to capture the complexity of settings.

If theories are fragmentary, then we have to see them as tools rather than as revelations of objective truth or of the lawfulness of the universe. This, of course, is no more than Mead (1962, 61–99) argued. But it is important to keep in mind in an age when measurement and quantitative analysis have become sophisticated and dominant. We create theories to serve purposes. Those purposes involve social and political goals. Theories and systematic observation are rooted in empirical reality. They are driven, however, by argument and artful presentation.

Theorizing in this sense rests on a base of sensitivity to the complex reality of settings. Without such a sensitivity I suspect one too easily is convinced that theories can be truly comprehensive or that statistical data is something other than an approximation of truth. That sensitivity is the sociological perspective I mentioned earlier and it is a distinct skill that can be taught. It seems to be separate from theorizing ability, although you cannot have the latter without the former. The sociological perspective is a grammar for our discipline where theorizing is our poetry. With this in mind, allow me to describe what my students learn. From this description perhaps we can learn what makes up this sociological perspective.

What I Do and What They Learn

As I said above, my students come to write strikingly different field notes after receiving my criticisms on four or five sets of notes. I do not claim that my way of doing field observation or of coaching students is right in any absolute sense. There are many philosophies of field observation and longstanding battles between the proponents of different approaches. I am not interested in entering those battles here.

Suffice it to say that my style is most based on a Mertonian sort of structural functionalism. That is to say, I do not worry much about generating hard data out of field observation. In my own work (Milofsky 1974, 1976, 1989), I do not use video cameras or tape recorders. I do not amass mountains of note cards to be organized on the dining room floor. Rather, field observation for me is a process of interpreting social life by guessing about what motivations, dilemmas, and conflicts might be driving the actors in front of me. I do build up a mass of field notes as I observe, but usually these just represent successive refinements of my ideas about what problems are worth discussing and what interpretations best explain why people act as they do. The field notes themselves enter my final writing only as illustrations of ideas already worked out through successive rewritings of the same ideas during the months of my fieldwork.

I say this approach is Mertonian because it emphasizes his contrast between the manifest and latent dimensions of social structure (Merton 1949). More specifically, when I criticize student papers I try primarily to have students recognize what Merton (1976) calls "coordinate norms." He suggests that *structure* in institutions is a variable. It may or may not be present and it may be more or less crystallized. When it is strong, it often is organized around characteristic value dilemmas that confront actors. These value dilemmas are similar to the role conflicts described by organizational role theorists such as Katz and Kahn (1966). But where role theorists see role conflicts as problems to be overcome, Merton sees them as the main source of energy and creativity in organizational and professional work. Structure evolves not to eliminate dilemmas. Rather, workers use formal organizational arrangements to legitimate the fact that certain dilemmas are necessary and central to their work. Institutionalized roles represent acknowledgment in a social system that certain dilemmas must be addressed and resolved and that specific named actors have the obligation and the privilege to achieve those resolutions.

Thus, when Skolnick (1967) explains that police must juggle conflicting demands that they maintain order while obeying the rule of law, he is talking both about an irritant to police and the primary cause of "police culture." When Merton (1976) talks about the struggle many physicians face between their need to be scientific problem solvers while also being sensitive to the psychological needs of patients, he is not only talking about reasons members of the public sue doctors for malpractice. He is also explaining why doctoring is a difficult, rewarding, and highly paid job in our society. In both of these cases, the secretive, intense, creative worlds intrinsic to these occupational cultures derive from the central value dilemmas and the efforts of practitioners to gain respect, autonomy, and privilege.

My students, of course, do not develop the sort of sophisticated institutional understanding Skolnick has of the police or Merton has of doctors. This is partly because they do not have the time required to complete the studies they begin in my class (although I have had students who took the time and completed "the book"). It also is because what Skolnick and Merton have done requires theoretical sophistication, a talent few undergraduates have even begun to develop.

What I do teach my students is to use the methodology implicit in these studies to penetrate the ideological facade that cloaks most of the settings they observe. One might just as well say that I am teaching them to use a dialectic approach to observation as that I am teaching structural functionalism. Contradictions, oppositions, value conflicts—whatever we call them—are a powerful way to help them "pry open" social structure so that they can see existing arrangements as conditional rather than as inevitable. The task is to lead them to see alternative possibilities. Once they see these, we can talk about the causes of existing arrangements and ways alternatives might come to pass.

Allow me now to describe the process by which they learn to "see" social structure. As I said earlier, students go through a remarkably regular process as they acquire this vision. What is more, because the developmental stages I shall describe are so clear-cut, it proves possible to teach student assistants to criticize student papers about as effectively as I do. In other words, I do not think the teaching that happens is a product of my idiosyncratic qualities as an instructor. After I talk about the learning process, I shall return to the question of what it is that students seem to be learning.

Description

When students turn in their first set of field notes their presentations of people and events are usually so vague that it is hard to understand what they saw or what interpretations of events might work as alternatives to those they offer. Thus, my first object in commenting on their papers is to convince students to write in a concrete, cinematic way that as much as possible divorces their depictions from their interpretations. Of course, it is impossible to completely separate description from definitions of the situation—axiomatic concepts. I do not want to enter into elaborate arguments here about the philosophy of knowledge. My goal is to push students to describe events richly enough so that when they offer interpretations, readers will have enough material to evaluate them and to offer alternative frames. Thus, description is the process of presenting events in ways that allow readers to visualize the people and the settings as ones that are concrete, unique, and individual.

Students have three problems with description. First, they do not write passages that are long, full, and complete. Description needs to be written as though it were important in and of itself. Writers should enjoy the people, appreciate the peculiarities of the physical space, reflect on their reactions to things, and generally work to create a round, full, complex image. It also helps if students write informally, as though they were having a conversation with a friend.

Second, students are too goal-oriented. They think that because they are visiting a public school classroom and our course is concerned with, say, the institutional problems of schools, that the only appropriate subject matter for them to write about has to do with the work people do in schools. I try to convince students that their eyes and their imaginations must wander. They should pay attention to: students flirting, to the way janitors seem to be "above the struggle," to the way teachers dress and the way students dress, to the way space is used in the school, and so on. Such an "undisciplined" approach to observation makes field notes *grounded* (Glaser and Strauss 1967) rather than goal-oriented.

Grounded observation is essential if students are to break out of the ideological prison created when they feel that they must decide whether teachers are doing a good or a bad job of teaching reading. I say this is an ideological prison because when one accepts the job of evaluating organizational practices one usually accepts implicitly the social and cultural premises of the institution. One of the primary goals of field observation is to question those premises. To do so one has to break out of the institutionalized myth or viewpoint of the organization one is studying and question its social, political, and cultural assumptions.

The third, and probably most subtle, problem students have is that statements they mean to be descriptive are in fact *summary* statements that interpret a whole sequence of events. One way they do this is by talking about what all the people in a category are doing: "The students came into the classroom like a thundering herd and did not settle down all morning." Another way is to talk about places or times in general terms: "Fridays are always a drag at the office." In both of these examples, there are many individual exceptions to what the authors are describing. By cutting these out, the narrators prevent readers from asking why the class seemed like a thundering herd when, in fact, one-third of the students were being quiet and orderly. Asking a question like that can open up a complex discussion. When description closes off such questions it also closes off our opportunity to generate insights.

Contradiction

Contradictions are events that observers find surprising, troubling, or conflict-filled. I call them contradictions because to have such a reaction implies that one has brought to the field setting certain expectations that now are being violated. Contradictions are not "bad practices." They may be little, peripheral things such as how people dress, unexpected courtesies, or times when someone treats you differently than they have in the past. They may also be conflicts among people in one's field setting where two sets of expectations are being violated, the observer's anticipation of orderliness and the combatants' ideas of how their opponents ought to behave. By asking students to flag contradictions I try to force them to recognize clashes of values, world views, or expectations and to see that such clashes are inherent in most situations. Since one of the ways U.S. ideologies close off inquiry is by presenting people as like-minded and cooperative (Bloom 1987; Weiss 1987), a focus on these value conflicts leads students to recognize the multifaceted nature of reality.

Contradictions are not important in themselves. Rather they are tools that help students gain leverage on a situation. *Leverage* is the capacity to find multiple definitions of a situation that one initially finds seamless and opaque. One of the main challenges of this exercise is to get students to write interesting, insightful papers. One cannot simply command another to be interesting when that person has no idea how to achieve insight. Consequently, I have to give students concrete, specific instructions about how they can produce interesting insights. This is important mainly so that they get the feeling of what it is like to write interesting material. Once they gain this feeling, they may find techniques for generating fascination that are very different from those I present them with. Finding contradictions is not the only way to generate insights. It is just a trick that is easy to describe and that works.

Once students find contradictions, I tell them they must convince the reader that the contradiction is indeed contradictory, explain what their expectations were, and then describe the events they found surprising clearly enough so that a reader will be convinced that those events do, in fact, violate expectations. As they do this, students often begin to question their own preconceptions and recognize that the problematic behavior they have seen is reasonable given the situation and experiences of those they are observing. This does not always happen right away, however, and quite often students are angry, disgusted, or appalled by what they have seen. It can be a major project to convince them to back off from their anger enough to give the benefit of the doubt to those they are observing.

Explanation

Contradictions raise questions. Explanations are answers to those questions.

An explanation is an attempt to account for the events one has found surprising so that they seem understandable and reasonable. Usually I ask students to begin by relating the expectations they had and how they were violated. Then I ask them to offer a rationale that makes the event seem plausible and reasonable.

Students often complain that they do not know why others have acted as they have or why the behavior they have seen might be reasonable or how it might be made explicable. One of my main projects, then, becomes convincing them to speculate and write a little fiction about how that troublesome behavior could be reasonable. One always can come up with some outlandish plot to make the worst outrages understandable. I tell students that they ought to be able to come up with four or five similarly outrageous plots. With this encouragement, students usually begin offering interpretations that are far from outlandish. In fact, their explanations usually seem pretty plausible.

The biggest growth step for students in the whole field notes writing exercise is learning to generate multiple explanations for a single phenomenon. To do so they have to develop a cynical, playful, or appreciative attitude about watching the social world. Many students are especially reluctant to be relaxed, irreverent, and potentially wrong when they write papers in academic settings. Many have a normal academic writing style that is formal, general, and impersonal. What makes much student writing hard for me to stomach is that I get little feeling of individuality. My task is to let students know that individuality and freshness is what I expect and what will be rewarded.

Since this *is* an academic setting and since I do write long, critical comments on their paper justifying a grade, a big problem to overcome is the sense of threat students feel in response to my power in this setting. I may talk about the importance of originality, but they still feel safest if they use familiar defensive writing techniques that have kept them out of trouble in other classes (see Becker 1986).

When commenting on student writing, I find it important to emphasize possibilities rather than limitations. When they receive a steady diet of criticism, students look for evidence that they have done it wrong and that therefore I think they are stupid. I try to show them that their problems have to do with not telling me enough about what must be happening in their settings. I avoid telling them that what they have seen is wrong since, after all, it is they who have seen it not I. In other words, from the outset I try to convince them to speculate and to free themselves up in the hope that they will eventually be able to think up explanations.

Choosing Explanations

As time passes, the speculations students offer to explain the strange behavior of people they observe builds up into a collection of brief stories about settings. As vignettes accumulate, it becomes increasingly clear to students that explanations they used in one setting help make sense of new things they are seeing. If they do not see these connections, I try to point these continuities out to them. When I asked them to explain contradictions they may have complained that they could not explain the behavior of others. With the accumulation of vignettes we see that certain explanations seem to account adequately for many sequences of behavior. I point out that this convergence of explanations is a form of proof. That suspicions and unlikely explanations turn out to be predictive is one of the things that makes this approach exciting. I encourage students to speculate about things that ought to be true in their settings if certain of their favored explanations are correct. Then I encourage them to talk to people or to seek access to new settings that will allow them to test their ideas. As their suspicions are borne out, the speculations they formulated gain new support and come to seem more like truth than fiction.

What are some examples of converging explanations? Consider these:

1. A student is working in a high school and finds that the office staff is rude on a few occasions early in the school year. Thinking back to past experiences in the school (the student had worked there the previous year as an aide), she remembered her impression that the secretaries in the office had seemed to run the place. Part of their efficiency then was friendliness to everyone. They encouraged people to come to them for help and seemed to know how to solve any bureacratic complexity without requiring that one bother the principal or assistant principal. This year, there is a new superintendent. As the student spends time in the teachers' room, she hears that the superintendent has been meeting with teachers, administrators, and parents around the school.

Writing her field notes, the student speculates about the unfriendli-

ness of the secretaries. Maybe they had forgotten her from the previous
year. Maybe the leader of the secretary group was suffering from some
illness no one had told the student about. Maybe they really were
angry at her for the time she had laughed when a student spilled coke
all over the office. The explanation that makes the most sense to her,
however, is that the secretaries are mad that the superintendent has
not acknowledged their hidden importance to the school by having a
special meeting with them like the meetings he has had with others
in the district. With this favored hypothesis in mind, the student wat-
ches in later sessions to see whether the superintendent favors the secretaries with a special audience, perhaps softening the chill in the
office. Or perhaps the secretaries will settle into some sort of long-
term, hostile posture. As time passes the student notes with satisfac-
tion that the secretaries seem to have found some allies in criticizing
the superintendent. Life begins to return to its old, friendly pace as a
culture of criticism and hostility to the superintendent builds in the
school.

2. A student working in the local family planning agency notices
that the sign in front of the office shows a seemingly happy family—
mother, father, and children holding hands. As she begins working in
the organization she notes that there is almost never a family among
the clientele. There seems to be nothing but single women with embar-
rassing sexual problems. As time passes, the student comes to recognize that the agency seems to serve as the community safety valve for
sexual difficulties. This is a small town with many residents who have
strong, fundamentalist religious beliefs. Open discussions of sexuality
are rare in town and there is frequent public opposition to frank sex
education programs either in town or on campus. Were there no
agency like family planning present, one might expect sexual scandals
to be more visible. Perhaps people in town would be forced to acknowledge that teenagers are sexually active, and however much adults
might disapprove, they would see that collective action needs to be
taken to protect children against sexually transmitted disease and un-
wanted pregnancy.

The student has seen a contradiction between the image of rational
reproductive planning in families and a clientele that comes in only
when they are too embarrassed to go to their family doctor—the person
who actually oversees "nice" family planning. There are a variety of
explanations for this observation. Perhaps young people come to the
agency because it is inexpensive. Perhaps they come because it is the
only place in town where they can receive really frank sex education.
Perhaps the clientele is affected by the location of the agency on a busy
highway near the high school. The student's preferred explanation is

that the family planning agency is performing a function many in town think is immoral and illegitimate but that it is necessary if that very value system is to be preserved. If the agency is helping to hide the sexual adventures of the young, then the old and the "moral" can pretend that sexuality is not common and that sexual misadventures represent deviance rather than normality. If the student's hypothesis is correct, then one ought to see town leaders criticizing loose sexual practices in public while they support the agency in private.

An episode occurs in the middle school: some liberal parents complain about a strong right-to-life theme in the sex education curriculum. The superintendent contacts the head of family planning and asks her to work quietly with the parents on a signature campaign demanding a change in school policy. He explains that he cannot take a leadership role and an overly visible parental campaign would probably bring a backlash reaction among religious conservatives. He nonetheless agrees that the curriculum should be reformed.

Few students actually master this final step of recognizing the power of their explanations. Usually, recognizing the superiority of certain explanations comes more out of my comments than out of the things the students themselves have written. But this does not bother me much. One of the things that is fun about this approach to teaching is that students and I are, in some ways, engaging in collaborative research. They observe and write while I look over their shoulders. They generally are happy for the opportunity to share, and I not infrequently stumble upon new research ideas.

One might say that I am plagiarizing my students' work. I do not think this is the case, however, because what I see in their writing primarily are opportunities to elaborate theoretical ideas I already am carrying around or using in other research. Students are not generally prepared to move their research onto a more analytic plane and most are not interested in doing so. One of the things that most impresses me is how difficult it is for students who have become good at writing field notes to move on to make a coherent sociological statement about their work. This is one of the things that convinces me that the sociological vision students develop through this exercise is limited and distinct from the theoretical sophistication put in play by a professional sociologist.

Sociological Vision?

This chapter has proceeded by assertion. Central to the discussion is my claim that over five sets of field notes students move from writing vague, stiff accounts to sharp, interesting, noticeably *sociological* accounts of their field experiences. Assuming that students progress as I claim they do, does this constitute some distinctive sort of vision sociologists have given to the world? Maybe. Students do learn that social reality always has hidden dimensions and they gain clearer ideas of what we mean by social structure. Certain kinds of ideological defenses against sociological arguments become harder to maintain after students have written field notes.

However, as I have talked to people who teach critical thinking in other disciplines using techniques that involve students and teachers in mutual discovery projects, some of the things I have attributed to sociological thinking seem part of general analytic sophistication. It is no easier to see the many levels of meaning in a piece of literature than it is to see them in a piece of social life. It is no easier to be playful and speculative with mathematics problems than it is to be speculative about why social contradictions occur.

Exercises such as field notes are unusual in the classroom because the material we use is accessible to students rather than hidden behind esoteric vocabulary or an archaic, stylized method of writing. Because students select the things they will talk about they also have control or ownership of the subject matter. They are slower to be alienated by professorial demands that they be thoughtful.

This sort of sociological exercise is also powerful because people in most other disciplines avoid the sort of discovery teaching I have described here. Sociologists, meanwhile, use techniques like the ones I have described quite often. Others could use this method of teaching and achieve some of the same results. I took a course in biophysics as an undergraduate that convinced me this was the way to teach. Because few people in other disciplines teach this way, we might gain a distorted sense that what we are doing is distinctively sociological when in fact all that we have is a curricular innovation that happens to be popular with sociologists.

With these caveats in mind, let me now argue that my students really are gaining something distinctively sociological. When people in other disciplines use similar teaching techniques, they are just capitalizing on sociological insights that have percolated out into the broader culture. The thing that makes these observation techniques sociological is that they can and should progress in a seamless, logical way into the main business of sociological theorizing.

One can teach biophysics using discovery methods, but there comes a point at which students must have specific technical skills to do the work. One of the problems my undergraduate biophysics teacher faced was that we nonscience majors had to be "cooled out" (Clark 1960) of a serious interest in science. He would explain that you have to want to do it from the time you are twelve. He might be wrong. Kuhn (1970) seems to suggest that you could teach science up to the Ph.D. level using discovery methods. But he probably is right that scientific ability is like musical ability. It is something you cultivate from an early age and either have or do not have. Amateurs cannot wander in off the street and begin practicing the art at the level of proficiency enjoyed by the prodigies that make up the main body of practitioners.

My impression is that sociology is made of different stuff. While we have some prodigies to spring, intellectually mature, from adolescence and others whose insights stun us with their power and beauty (Collins 1975, 24–36), they do not dominate the discipline. The main task of the discipline is to synthesize and integrate massively complex bodies of information. People come to sociology as adults because they need to appreciate the multidimensionality and conditional nature of reality before they can understand what it is the discipline really studies. Without that recognition, people tend to confuse sociology with the study of social problems and social reforms. The latter may be part of sociology, but sociology does not stop with those concerns.

The exercise I have described in this chapter is distinctively sociological because what it produces in students is an awareness of the multidimensional and conditional nature of reality, the qualities that provide a jumping-off point for theoretical sociology. I suggested at the outset that through field observation students gain a distinct skill. It is useful in many other institutional settings (as in teaching biophysics), and it stands on its own as something distinct from sociological theorizing. At the same time, skill at field observation poses metaphysical problems for most people. If the world is theatrical, relativistic, and conditional rather than morally clear, concrete, and dominated by clear causal relationships, then how can one gain a secure sense of reality? How can one decide how to act?

One might ignore these issues and settle into contented (anesthetized?) anomie. Alternatively, one might acknowledge that these represent the great moral and intellectual questions of our time and begin exploring what social science has to say about them. That begins moving one into a new level of analytic sophistication, the level of social theory. I do not pretend that social theory has answers to the tough questions of being and action presented by a relativistic way of viewing the world. But this way of viewing the world is, I think, the gateway to social theory. One might deny the complexity of everyday life, as Bloom (1987) seems to want us to do. Once one acknowledges it, however, it seems one is stuck with a world where the abstractions of social structure, culture, and class conflict become *the* transcendent reality and where all theoretical or moral understandings of the world are conditional, fragmentary, and rhetorical. Because the observations students learn to make through field research seem to me locked together with the world of social theory, I think they are indeed learning sociological vision.

CLAUDE S. FISCHER
Entering Sociology into Public Discourse

SOCIOLOGY is poorly represented in U.S. media and public discourse, with lamentable consequences for both the discipline and the discourse. Sociology *ought* to be more often and better reported (Dunwoody and Ryan 1985). We have self-serving goals for publicizing our work—higher salaries, more research funding, more students, more esteem, perhaps more power—but we also have a moral obligation to disseminate our studies. We are supported as scholars and faculty in great measure by the public purse, and unlike most arts and humanities, the justification for the money is largely that our activities inform public action. More important, we know much that is vital to national decisions and ought, as citizens, to contribute our knowledge—both detailed social facts and general social perspectives—to public discourse.

In this chapter I first explore sociology's current role, or lack thereof, in U.S. media; second, I put forward some speculations about the causes of the situation; and third, I present some suggestions for moving sociology further into public discourse.

The Problem

Concern over sociology's paltry role in American media is not new; several committees have studied the issue (Gollin 1984). But neither is there sign of much progress. The high points of sociological influence in national debate are dated. One thinks of the 1933 Recent Social Trends panel headed by William F. Ogburn; of the American Soldier studies; and of sociologists' participation in the 1950s and 1960s debates over racial integration. Recent years have probably seen a smaller public role, if any change at all, for sociology.

Thousands of pages of sociological reports do appear on the shelves of policy makers. But even when staff actually dust off and use the studies—let us not ask how often that happens—the reports become technical tools for policies shaped by others. Those policies rest in significant measure on popular assumptions and on consensus influenced, in turn, by public discourse. The arena of that public discourse is the media.

Our discipline is currently either invisible or embarrassingly too visible in the U.S. media. It is invisible in that relatively little sociological research per se is reported and that little sociological commentary is included in topical stories. Of "social science" studies appearing in the media in 1982, according to a systematic review, less than a fifth originated in university research. Most empirical claims came from government, partisans, or the media itself (as in their call-in "polls"; Singer 1986). Even within academia, sociology's presence appears small compared to that of psychology, medicine, or economics. (Indeed, the last has advanced far recently, even intruding into sociology's traditional topical domains, such as crime and family life.) And sociology's presence is minor in U.S. media compared to its role abroad, where sociologists are visible and respected participants in public debate. (I am thinking of people such as Aron and Dahrendorf.) Sociology's invisibility leaves a vacuum in public discourse (more on this below) and leaves sociologists with only a vague public definition: are we social workers, socialists, socializers, or what?

When sociology does appear in the press, we often wish it hadn't. Too frequently, the research reported is exotica—particularly sexual exotica—or it is a well-publicized but poorly done study, or it is the work of mountebanks masquerading as sociologists (for example, "pollsters" working on behalf of a lobbying group). Even straightforward reports of "human interest"—for example, one on whether lottery winners quit their jobs (CBS Radio News, 12 September 1985)—are denuded of sociological content (in this case, the motivations for work) and presented as entertaining trivia. Too often, the sociological commentary that appears is inexpert, vacuous, and obviously self-promotional.

One consequence of this kind of visibility is that sociology is subjected to ridicule. Senators favor us with "Golden Fleece" awards; journalists such as Eric Severeid sneer that "sociology is slow journalism"; and television commentators use "sociologist" with the same condescending chuckle they apply to bueaucrats, politicians, and other pompous fools. Unfortunate publicity seems inevitable if the discipline leaves press coverage to chance. A variant of Gresham's Law applies— a lack of the good will invite the bad.

Take as an illustration of what can happen the controversy during 1986 over what the likelihood was for college-educated women over thirty years of age eventually to marry. Taking off from a sociologist's informal remark about his preliminary research (rather than a report of a completed study), the media blared the notion that such women were doomed to spinsterhood, that, said *Newsweek,* they had a better chance of personally meeting a terrorist than a husband. The brouhaha raged for months and relatively little of the fuel was solid sociological research. The initial researchers despaired of clarifying the media's accounts. By the time the air had cleared, one of the victims was (yet again) sociology's reputation.[1]

Sociology is also swept onto the public stage by political winds. For many years, partisans marshaled sociologists and their studies on both sides of the busing issue: did or did not busing create "while flight"? Did or did it not aid minority students' school achievement? Although such dissensus among sociologists can be awkward, debate over substance and systematic studies is still far more desirable than haphazard coverage. Debate is part of scholarship itself and will never be eliminated. (Nor has lack of consensus undercut the authority of economists much.) What we would like, however, is for the audience to possess the minimal background to evaluate the debate. That preparation depends in part on steady exposure to more routine sociology. It is this that we sorely lack.

This vacuum embarrasses us, but more important, it impoverishes U.S. public discourse. Many simple social facts are absent in reports on issues of the day. Discussions of unwed mothers miss the point that rates of teenage pregnancy have not changed; what has changed is the likelihood of teenagers marrying after the pregnancy. The most effective cure for drug addiction is getting older; what does that imply for policy? Despite public scares, migrants and immigrants are more often the "cream of the crop" than they are the "bottom of the barrel." Surges in crime during the 1960s and early 1970s were aberrations in a generally downward trend during the century (Walker 1985). Industrial expansion in the nineteenth century depended greatly on government programs, such as subsidies to railroads, military support for new manufacturing processes, and direct aid for technology, rather than private entrepreneurial capital. The illustrations of policy-relevant "facts" largely ignored in public debate can be multiplied.

More profound than the absence of an empirical sociology in public discourse is the weakness of "popular sociological theory." Some scholarly perspectives on human action have entered public understanding. Medical models (germ theory, genetic transmission, and the like) and psychodynamic models (drives, repressions and sublimations, unconscious motives) are now part of folk biologies and psychologies, challenging older moral or spiritualist models. Teenagers are no longer considered to be drug users because they are "bad" or "possessed," but because they are depressed or self-destructive, in turn a result of mishandled childrearing, or hormonal imbalance, or the like. (The popularity of this folk psychology is evident in the mocking of "psychobabble.") Recently, economists have popularized concepts such as cost-benefit ratios and free-market models. Although folk versions of behavioral science are confused, they do establish a sympathetic and moderately comprehending audience for serious scholarship, and they provide an intuitive understanding of the world (intuitive in the sense that these ideas eventually become taken for granted and seemingly obvious) consistent with those disciplines.

A popular sociology would view human action as motivated and constrained by culture and social structure—not simply by internal states. For example, unemployment is not simply or even primarily a product of individual skill, will, or human capital as valued by market demand, but also a product of an occupational structure, economic institutions, political ground rules, and cultural standards concerning appropriate work. A popular sociology would comprehend collective phenomena as emergent and not reducible to individual states. "Collective irrationalities"—panics, escalations of conflict, bystander apathy, derelictions of social responsibility—are processess that occur almost irrespective of individuals' goodwill or psychic resources.[2] One irritation from the media frenzy about the marriage odds of women over thirty was journalists' phrasing of the issue as a problem of individual women (or men): why didn't they *want* to marry? What were *they* doing wrong? Little of the popular discussion focused on the demographic and economic structure unmarried women face.

(Similarly, during 1986, I was interviewed a few times by journalists on the subject of "friendship." I invariably found myself providing a minicourse in sociology over the telephone, trying to reorient their questions from "why does each of us *want* the friendships we have, or *want* to avoid having friends?" to "What is the culture and structure within which we can choose friends?" I found the journalists typically open and understanding. But a single conversation is unlikely to change the deeply ingrained psychological models journalists share with other Americans.)

Deepening the appreciation of a sociological perspective is in the long run probably more important than conveying specific research findings. Without it, findings are unabsorbed, sloughed off, or misappropriated.

A popular sociology would also attend to historical and cross-cultural comparisons. Medical, psychological, and market views of the world are largely insensitive to such variations, since they presume that bodies, psyches, and markets operate much the same way everywhere. But popular sociology would incorporate an appreciation of time-boundedness (for example, that what we consider the normal U.S. family was largely unique to the 1950s, or that urban disorder was greatest in the mid-nineteenth century) and an appreciation of international variations (for example, the relation between health systems and health levels cross-nationally, or the distinctiveness of the United States's violent crime). In its own right, a wider comparative perspective—one, I think, more common in Europe—would enrich policy discussions in the United States. Sociology could popularize such a structural and cultural perspective.

There is, then, a case for sociologists aggressively attempting to disseminate their work and views to the general public. But there is another, simpler argument. One way or another, pieces of sociology *will* be publicized; opinions about sociology will develop among at least the opinion elite. It is far better that we try to guide that process and shape those opinions that be subject to them.

Sources of the Problem

Why is it so difficult for sociology successfully to penetrate U.S. media and Americans' awareness. We might locate the barriers in three places: the wider U.S. society, U.S. media, and U.S. sociology.

U.S. society may be particularly resistant to a sociological perspective for a few reasons. One is the pervasive tradition of individualism. The mover of all action is the individual and individuals ultimately stand alone; society emerges from and exists for individuals. Ironically, modern psychodynamic perspectives reinforce this traditional individualism by explaining social phenomena in terms of aggregated psychologies—for example, that Nazism emerged from Germans' "authoritarian personalities," or that protests of the 1960s arose from the child rearing of the "Spock generation." While there may be some validity in these accounts, alone they are bare of social context. (There has been some, albeit modest, change in these assumptions. Americans have, according to Gallup Polls, become more willing over the last few decades to attribute crime to society rather than to the individual.) But an individualistic world view is not receptive to approaches that stress social structure and culture (Bellah et al. 1985; Gans 1979).

There is also political resistance. Sociology in some respects subverts established practice and belief by making the implicit explicit. That

can engender reaction. The Reagan administration's attack on research into the structural sources of poverty and mental illness illustrates such resistance. But conservatives have no monopoly on
resisting sociology. The liberal establishment in the 1960s resisted the
news that crime was increasing, and the black establishment long ignored news of the many broken black families. Sociology also suffered
a blacklash by its identification with the politics of "social engineer-
ing" in the 1960s and 1970s. The turmoil of that era and the elitist
quality of much social change—notably, enforced busing—linked sociology to "limousine liberals" and other populist villains.

For such reasons, Americans will not be receptive to sociology on
their own, but will need wooing and convincing.

Neither are the U.S. media especially receptive. And why should
they be? They face their own agendas and constraints (Gans 1979).
The media are not structured for reporting science. Rather, they are
largely in the business of telling stories: "news" stories about events
critical to readers' lives and "interesting" stories that contain dramatic
structure and often a moral. Science is rarely news, being neither critical to readers' lives nor a distinctive event (aside from startling "discoveries"). And science is rarely interesting, since its protagonists are
corporate or dull and there is little drama; science instead entails considerable background, details, complexity, and equivocation—and the
better the research the more of it. (Qualifications and contexts, so critical to good scholarship, are usually missing in media reports; Singer
1986).

Editors need stories that report the novel, but we typically work on
the mundane; they need to report action and change, but we study
structure and continuity; they need timely "pegs," we seek timeless
truths; they need simple stories simply told, but we dwell on complexity in life and in language. Salable stories have controversy and conflict rather than the bland consensus of scientific opinion. And here
lies a potential minefield for the sociologist: journalists may seek or
even stimulate contentiousness over a research report. Some of the
coverage, for example, of busing studies in the 1960s and 1970s and of
the research on college-educated women's chances for marriage in the
1980s took on the scent of battlefield gunsmoke. The danger of controversial entanglement is especially likely when, as in these two cases,
profound political or emotional concerns are aroused. In the swirl of
battle, it becomes exceedingly difficult to explain the technical bases
of one's work. But bemoaning the structural circumstances of the media that produce disregard or misuse of sociology will not change them.

The *social* sciences face some additional difficulties in the media.
Being about ourselves, sociology and its sisters lack the mystique of,

say, particle physics or dinosaur hunting and lack the eerie authority of "real" scientists. Similarly, many editors and reporters assume that any journalist can cover and interpret social science, while only expert reporters can cover the esoteric disciplines. Being about ourselves, sociology is vulnerable to oversimplification, trivialization, and a "Ho-hum, we knew it all the time" reaction.[3] (More about this later.) Being about social affairs, sociology is often weighted with political and moral implications, so that reports may be distorted by journalists or others with their own agendas. Journalists have few benchmarks to evaluate and locate sociological reports—no authority like the American Medical Association, whose endorsement would support or challenge a new finding; no Noble Prize winners to bless or damn a novel claim; no authoritative way to judge among the cacophony of voices.

Yet we also have some advantages over the so-called hard sciences. Being about ourselves, sociology is potentially interesting in ways that chemistry, mathematics, and entomology might never be. Sociology stories may not have the "sizzle" of those on cancer or manic depression, but reports concerning families, jobs, and communities have inherent appeal. And being about ourselves, sociology ought to be more easily comprehended than the physical sciences or, for that matter, than much of psychology and economics.[4] (This claim may be challenged; see more below.) We also have the advantage that our stories can be easily scheduled to fit publication needs. Finally, as professionals, we often travel in the same circles as journalists and can use social contacts to publicize our work.

We have an opportunity to make sociology more like news and to make it more interesting. If we do not popularize our work, almost all of it becomes scholastic footnotes. Other parts of our work become popularized anyway, in forms we do not appreciate. It is better that we do it.

And so the third barrier to popularizing sociology: sociologists. There seems to be some ambivalence about media in our profession (Gollin 1984). Some of us see ourselves as "pure" scientists and scholars who simply put the work "out there." We feel that our work is too specialized, that it would be distorted by journalists, or that popularization is distasteful. And, in fact, some of us have experienced distortions by reporters; but only a minority of social scientists have such complaints (Singer 1986). Nevertheless, we have an obligation to disseminate sociology, as well as self-serving reasons to do so, and much of it will be popularized *anyway,* but poorly so, if we stand aloof. Popular interest need not direct our work, but our work should be available.

One successful case of sociological visibility illustrates the value, or maybe the necessity, of purposeful publicity: *Habits of the Heart* (Bellah et al. 1985). *Habits* interpreted public ideology in the contemporary United States based on four depth-interview or participant-observation studies. It also conveyed a profound sociological perspective: that people's conceptions of their own lives are rooted in, and to be understood by, our society's cultural assumptions about the individual. The book was a commercial success. More important, columnists, churchpeople, and politicians debated its ideas in many forums. Quality was a necessary ingredient of the book's success, to be sure. But that was not enough. *Habits* was also widely promoted, through public channels (Bellah lectured across the nation on it even before the book was written) and through contacts with people in the media. If it were not a stimulating and valuable contribution, the publicity would probably not have helped. But without the publicity, it—like other worthy volumes—might not have entered public discourse.

Other sociologists reach out even farther. They disdain the ivory tower and immerse themselves in public life. But these scholars *engagé* typically also disdain the establishment media and usually end up addressing just one another and a few like-minded observers. (Their explicit political agendas may also distort their vision and alienate the media.) This sort of ambivalence about media involvement obviously undercuts efforts to communicate to the wider public.

I also detect insecurity among some sociologists, a fear that sociology may be revealed as common sense in jargon drag. There is, indeed, an obviousness about much of sociology. But the implication is not that we should cast about for counterintuitive discoveries—we certainly find many of these anyway and they are welcomed by the media—but to understand the nature of this apparent prosaism. In many and perhaps most cases, sociological findings appear obvious *after the fact,* because so-called common sense is contradictory. People believe, for example, that wealth is better than poverty *and* that rich people are secretly miserable; that women are submissive *and* that "hell hath no fury like a woman scorned"; that men must woo reticent maidens *and* that women snare their husbands. Whichever side of these and hundreds of similar oppositions a sociological study supports, it will be greeted as certifying the obvious. In a sense, that has to be so. In other cases, a finding is conventional, but the reasons for it far from evident. We may have always known that rich people are more politically powerful than poor people, but the how and why of it are more complex than just the direct purchase of influence; they include the effects of prestige, self-confidence, expertise, implicit power, agenda setting, and the like. Our job is more than to convey facts to the public—although we must do that first—but also explanations.

Sociologists also inhibit their communication with the public by failing to reward people who do it well. Sometimes popularizers earn monetary rewards, but not professional ones. Touching the masses is too often seen as pandering and contaminating. This ought not to be so. Our contempt ought to be saved for those who distort sociology in their popularizations, but we ought to applaud those who can present sociology accurately and engagingly at the same time. (An example here, I believe, is my colleague Harry Edwards's talks on the sociology of sport. A nonsociologist, Charles Silberman, has also done good work in interpreting social science for a wide audience.)

One more legitimate concern about popularization is that the reward system of the media will supplant that of the profession. Attention in the *New York Times* rather than solid scholarship will be the ticket to high academic position.[5] This already happens to a minor extent. A better safeguard than avoiding the media, however, is to convince it to incorporate some of the same standards that we apply.

Sociologists also undercut their popular appeal by their abysmal writing. This is an old complaint, inside and outside the profession. We might explore reasons for it: efforts to clothe ourselves in "science," insecurity about our contributions, a lack of training, and so on. There is no reason why we cannot write clearly and straightforwardly. Perhaps quantum physics can only be understood in the context of a mathematical language, but our work is not so technical or esoteric that it cannot be explained in prose to an educated lay audience. (Or, if it cannot, there is probably something wrong with the work.) Historians have been able to write enormous tomes—say, Stone's *Family, Marriage, and Sex in England*—that are read and respected by both scholars and the educated lay public. Sociologists may have some more technical tools than do historians, but we should be able to do much the same.

Another reason *Habits of the Heart* succeeded, I think, was its literacy. For example, the authors used the effective rhetorical device of personal portraits. Biographies of paradigmatic individuals dramatized cultural typologies and made vivid abstract analyses. Both in our own writing and in explaining difficult concepts to journalists we can promote a clearer language.

Proposals

Whom do we seek to address? And what do we seek to do? We should try to reach all audiences from high- to low-brow, if we can, but focus on the opinion-leader media—the major national newspapers, networks, news magazines, and magazines of opinion. These are the central forums of policy discourse and sources for stories in more peripheral outlets. We should publicize quality sociological studies of general interest and insert sociological commentary into discussions of topical issues. This participation in public discourse will yield as byproducts greater esteem and rewards for the profession and, over the longer run, an expanding "popular sociology."

Despite my bleak pronouncements, some activity is occuring along these lines. For example, Robert Crain's work on long-term effects of school integration has received reasonable coverage in the *New York Times* and on National Public Radio. Gerald Marwell had a public radio series in Wisconsin on sociology. Kristin Luker's book on pro- and antiabortion activists has enriched print discussion about the sources of those movements. *Habits of the Heart* has engaged political thinkers in active debate, cited, both approvingly and not, by writers of opinion from left to right. Arlie Hochschild's *Second Shift*, a study of the domestic pressures on working women, even made the pages of *People* magazine. The American Sociological Association's (ASA) *Footnotes* has been charting smaller versions of these activities around the nation. We need to multiply, organize, and energize such activities.

The major effort needs to be institutional, most likely based in the ASA. An institution can provide resources, structure, and legitimation for sociology in the media. Fortunately, some action is afoot. The 1985 ASA Committee on Public Information, chaired by Ray Milavsky of NBC, considered several steps to promote sociology's presence in the media, including the following.

The ASA should have a full-time, professional press office headed by someone with solid journalistic experience and contacts. Among the functions of the office would be:

- issuing press releases on new sociological reports of general interest;
- answering inquiries from journalists and referring them to appropriate sociologists listed in a data bank by specialty (since the early 1980s such a referral service has operated for the general sciences, with major attention, of course, on "hard science": the Media Resource Service of the Scientists' Institute for Public Information, New York, N.Y.);
- brokering between the media and sociologists by helping sociologists with topical essays in mind and editors seeking such essays to find one another, and even perhaps suggesting such essays to the two parties;
- educating journalists informally about sociology—for example, suggesting story lines over lunch dates;

- organizing more formal "miniconferences" for journalists on current topics with a panel of sociologists—for example, a panel on the sociology of epidemics;
- organizing spur-of-the-moment press conferences with a panel of sociologists on breaking stories, such as South Africa, dramatic economic news, or a crime wave; and
- administering "mini-Nieman Fellowships" for journalists to study graduate-level sociology for a year.

In pursuing these activities, the ASA press office would combine a journalistic sense with standards of scholarly excellence. For example, articles could be publicized that both would "sell" and had passed serious journal review; and sociologists invited to panels would be acknowledged experts.

These sorts of programs would aggressively enter sociology into public discourse, would make sociology more visible to the media and in the media, would legitimate under an official banner much of the sociology that did appear in the press, and would provide journalists with a reliable and authoritative source of news and confirmation.

The ASA should also establish an award that recognizes those sociologists and perhaps those nonsociologists who have best publicized sociology—best in the sense of reaching the public *and* accurately conveying sociological findings and perspectives.

A more ambitious and controversial step would be for the ASA to issue authoritative opinions, speaking for sociology on issues of controversy. The American Psychological Association has, I believe, issued opinions as to, for example, the "normality" of homosexuality. Our association could issue opinions—obviously based on scholarly review—about questions such as the effects of women's employment on family life, or whether racism is still a factor in black job opportunties.

Since 1985, the ASA has undertaken a few of these and some other steps in joining sociologists and journalism. What is certainly still needed are significantly resources. As of early 1987, the ASA had one-third of a professional staffperson to coordinate these tasks (compared to six for the American Psychological Association; Howery 1987).

At a local level, departments of sociology ought to recognize and reward accurate popularization by their faculty. They should consider providing—requiring?—courses for graduate students in writing both for other sociologists and for nonsociologists and perhaps give courses on public speaking as well. Departments should collaborate with university press offices in publicizing the work of their faculty. Here, as at the national level, attention must be paid to the scholarly quality of the popularization.

. Finally, one might address individual sociologists—although as sociologists we are skeptical of stimulating social change through individualistic means—and urge more activity in the public sphere. Where, one wonders, are sociology's Stephen Jay Goulds, Jane Goodalls, Lester Thurows, and Paul Samuelsons—scholars with solid credentials who also reach the lay public? Perhaps we could use a few entrepreneurs such as these, operating alongside the institutions. Even those who would prefer to avoid the limelight could help by educating journalists on background about various topics, thereby increasing the accuracy and clarity of the sociology that does get reported. At the same time, sociologists who present their work to the media need to be prepared and assisted to confront possible controversy over what they report.

This list of suggestions is certainly not exhaustive; others are welcome as additions or substitutions. But, in any case, we need to act—for our professional good and in our roles as citizens—to bring more of sociology into public discourse.

Notes

Materials from and conversation with members of the ASA Committee on Public Information helped inform this paper, and the comments of Ann Swidler, Elie Abel, Tom Debley, and of fellow contributors to this volume helped improve it, but the views expressed here are solely my own. Revision of this paper was assisted by a fellowship at the Center for Advanced Study in the Behavioral Sciences, Stanford, and support there from the Andrew W. Melton Foundation.
1. On this point, as on others in this chapter, I thank Neil Bennett for comments on his own media experiences.
2. The one emergent phenomenon vaguely appreciated today in U.S. folk understandings is the market: individual capacities and rewards are multiplied by engagement in a collective process of bidding. Few sociologists would concede that this model is satisfactory, applicable to more than a narrow range of social action, or accurate except under limited historical conditions.
3. Psychology, especially psychiatry, which is also about ourselves, has to some extent avoided this with the mystification the medical model provides.
4. To say that sociology stories ought to be easily *comprehended* does not imply that they could be easily *evaluated*. They do need expert reportage.
5. This point was suggested by Ann Swidler.

JOSEPH R. GUSFIELD

Two Genres of Sociology
A Literary Analysis of
The American Occupational Structure and *Tally's Corner*

IT IS APPROPRIATE that I begin with an apocryphal story. Some years ago a novelist responded to the review of his book with a letter to the journal. The reviewer had it all wrong, wrote the author. That was not what he had meant at all. The reviewer wrote back: "Sir, you do not understand what you have written."

The novelist's dilemma is no different than the sociologist's. What we come to know by our studies is only a step in the process of telling our tales of scholarship. The text we write is itself a stage in the process. What the reader does in the act of reading is still another. What is known, what is written, and what is conveyed are by no the means the same.

The movement toward the analysis of research as a text is now slightly more than a decade old (Brown 1977; Gusfield 1976; Latour and Woolgar 1979). It is congruent with the general movement in the humanities and the social sciences toward a self-reflexiveness that examines and questions the assumptions on which the methods of the discipline have been based. The rhetorical turn in sociology has meant that the reporting of research in books, monographs, and journal articles is not a neutral process. The act of writing is a further stage in the process of constructing scholarship. The written product is not a transparent window to a world outside but is instead colored and opaque, reflecting the language and organization of written work.

Sociological writing, like most of social science, is rhetorical in that it presents an argument; it is an effort to persuade (Perelman and Ol-brechts-Tyteca 1969; Toulmin 1958). How persuasion is accomplished is a legitimate inquiry. Style, structure, language, metaphors, visual material—all are germane to the analysis of "scientific" reports, as they have been to literary materials. The very style and organization of a discipline is itself an essential aspect of its conventional rhetoric (Gusfield 1981, chaps. 2–4; Bazerman 1989).

Rhetoric, like communication in general, is more than a one-sided affair. As Kenneth Burke recognized many years ago and as literary theory has come to realize in recent years, reading is a relationship between text and reader (Burke 1945; Iser 1978; Suleiman and Crosman 1980). The reader is not a passive slate on which the author may inscribe. I return to the story with which I began. The text that the novelist experienced was not the text that the reviewer experienced. What constitutes the text for any particular reader and in any particular context is not given by the search for a fixed meaning that has conventionally occupied professors of literature. Much depends on the interaction between the reader and the "text" (Iser 1978). The experience of the reader is constructed in the process of reading in a particular context (Fish 1980; Smith 1981).

The writer and others involved in the production of the product, such as publishers, editors, and designers, are aware of their audiences. Being aware, they are concerned with influencing the reception their work will have on their readers. The text can be examined as a means of potential control over how the reader will read. Does the text attempt to ready the reader for the nature of the argument that the author appears to be making?

"His [the interpreter's] object should therefore be, not to explain a work, but to reveal the conditions that bring about its various possible effects . . . [to clarify] the *potential* of text" (Iser 1978, 18).

There is an additional interest in this enterprise besides the joy of playful scholarship. How is it that scientific presentations gain the authority of certain fact? How are audiences and readers led to belief? How do they come to accept and trust the texts that purport to establish fact and to draw credible conclusions from facts?

The Rhetorical Problem of Sociological Texts

Perhaps it may be objected that the texts of sociological studies are not literary works and therefore are not rhetorical works. They are not products of creative imagination. They are attempts to represent a reality, a world of fact and not imagination. The stuff of literature is fictive. Social science, as a cultural product, is mimetic; it represents phenomena that are real.

But central to this paper is just that point. How to maintain the character of sociological work as *not imaginary* will be the crux of much of my examination of these texts. Most sociological texts with which I am familiar are organized to convince the reader that some state of affairs is so, and that alternative, imagined states are not so. Being efforts to persuade, they are analyzable as rhetoric. Being an organization of language, they are capable of being examined as literature.

In this light, most sociological arguments are ways of leading the reader to a conclusion that, given the means used to present the data and its analysis, cannot be denied by its audience. The reader is imagined as part of a universal audience for whom the diversities of interest and community are irrelevant. No matter what the reader desires, the argument will reach undeniable conclusions, will compel the reader to the author's persuasion (Perelman and Olbrechts-Tyteca 1969; Gusfield 1981, chap. 4).

It is this form of argument, and the deviations from it, that occupy my attention in this chapter. It too is an argument, and how successful it is in earning your assent is, ultimately, in your hands.

In one sense, no writing ever begins at the beginning. It must assume the readers' knowledge of the language and their literacy. It must assume some of the conventions of reading as well. In this essay I need to prevent readers from raising certain difficulties that will act as barriers to their willingness to follow the argument. Among these is a way of setting some matter outside of the text of the essay so that readers will not raise them or will not let them dominate their reading.

One is the question of evaluation. My intent is not to evaluate the adequacy of these documents by any criteria of adequacy. This, I know, would be a difficult and in the end an unsuccessful effort. But let me save for a later discussion that gnawing and important question. Let us put it, at least for the time being, outside the frame of this essay.

Let us also place the character of these two studies as truly representative of their respective genres outside the frame. *The American Occupational Structure* and *Tally's Corner* were both published in 1967. Each has become a "classic" example of method: *The American Occupational Structure* of census survey and quantitative analysis, and *Tally's Corner* of field observation and qualitative analysis. Both are still read by sociologists and used to train students, whatever the current acceptance or rejection of their conclusions. I treat each as typical of a genre in sociological writing, although I have no warrant resulting from a more thorough examination of other such works. In writing of these two works as examples of genres I recognize that such an assumption is substantiated only by impressions derived from my general experience in reading sociology.

The two genres have been described in various terms although no major effort has been made to define them clearly. The distinction has gone under a variety of terms. Among them are thin-thick description: quantitative-qualitative, experience-far and experience-near, etic-emic, objective-subjective, scientific-humanistic, generalizable-concrete.

Last, this is my interpretation and examination of two texts. While I write as if the authors intended the consequences I see, that is only a conceit, a metaphor for the analysis of the potential I discover in the text. My data is not the intentions of the authors but the texts as I examine them. The text, however, is available to all who care to examine it.

The American Occupational Structure and *Tally's Corner*

With this chapter's frame in place, I am ready to lead you onto the canvas. I chose these books for three reasons. First, each has become a "classic" in its field. Though published almost twenty-five years ago, they are still read and referred to. Second, each represents an example of a distinct and different model. *The American Occupational Structure* is a quantitative study in the mode I will call the experimental; it is analogous to what is often called the "scientific model." The data drawn on are from a survey of 25,000 persons planned by the authors and conducted by the U.S. Bureau of the Census. *Tally's Corner* is an observational, ethnographic account of the author's participation with a group of black men in a section of Washington, D.C. The data drawn on are the author's observations. Last, I was reasonably familiar with each of these books, having taught *Tally's Corner* several times and having conducted a study not unlike *The American Occupational Structure*, based on a survey of occupational careers and utilizing the quantitative method pioneered in this book.

Forming The Audience:
Controlling Access To Readership

For whom is a book meant and who is likely to read it? Not everyone is a likely reader of every book. Just as opera, by the expense of tickets and the formality of clothing required, tells many that it is not for them, so a book, even in its physical appearance, keeps the gates open and accessible to some and repels and rejects others. Granted that a text is a relationship between the author, text, and reader, what is done to influence the composition of the readership?

A folk adage asserts that "you can't judge a book by its cover." A more skeptical perspective suggests that the cover is the initial presentation the author makes to intended readers. It is the first evidence with which to answer the questions "What kind of book is this? Am I part of its readership?"

Three aspects of the physical structure of books are clues to their implied and potential readers. The size of a book and the shape of its contents are one form of presentation telling readers something of its accessibility. *The American Occupational Structure* is a big book: 18 pages of front matter, 442 pages of text, and 70 pages of appendices and index. Its type is elite and its paper glossy. *Tally's Corner* is a short book: 15 pages of front matter, 230 pages of text, a 25-page appendix, and 4 pages of references. The type is larger than in *The American Occupational Structure* and the paper thicker, of rag quality. Chapter 1 of *Tally's Corner* is 25 pages long and contains 40 paragraphs and approximately 5,000 lines. Chapter 1 of *The American Occupational Structure* is 21 pages long, contains 49 paragraphs, and is approximately 9,700 lines long. In physical structure *Tally's Corner* might be a novel. *The American Occupational Structure* would be hard to present as a novel, even if by Umberto Eco.

The same difference in accessibility appears in the titles. *The American Occupational Structure* announces its abstract character. "Structure" is a conceptual term, a metaphor suggesting the solidity and persistence of a building. It is not the ordinary language of most Americans. "The" gives the title a decontexualized appearance; the structure as distinguished from the individuals and individualized cases from which it is drawn (Gusfield 1986). This is not presented as a book calculated to interest the average reader, nor one likely to be understood without some special knowledge. The book jacket supports this. It is orange and blue. The orange part announces the title and the authors. The blue part seems to be an abstract form. On closer inspection the contours of human figures are discernible.

Tally's Corner announces its lesser technical, "serious" nature by its cover. I am comparing the original hardback copy of *The American Occupational Structure* and its jacket with the paperback *Tally's Corner*. (The paperback copy of *The American Occupational Structure* is unavailable to me.) The hardback copy of *Tally's Corner* is available and is beside me, but the jacket and original binding have been replaced by library binding. The size and shape of hardback and paperback copies of *Tally's Corner* are identical. The title is specific and uses the ordinary language of urban imagery—somebody's corner. The subtitle, "A Study of Streetcorner Men," testifies to its character as research. The front cover is black along one side and white along the other. The white side announces the full title and the author, the author's name in larger type than additional matter, including the subtitle. The frontcover also includes the information that there is a foreword by Hylan Lewis (a black sociologist) and there is a quote lauding the study by Daniel Patrick Moynihan, then director of the Joint Center for Urban Studies at MIT and Harvard University. The black side is a photo of blacks on a street. Three young men are standing around a mailbox, one reading a newspaper. A man some distance away is reading something, standing against a storefront. A fifth man is walking on the sidewalk between the man and the three youths. It is an ordinary moment caught by the camera.

The cover suggests a concrete character to the book. It is about specific people in specific places. The credibility of the author and the importance of the study are supported by the prestigious people (Hylan Lewis and Daniel Moynihan) who vouch for it even before the reader has opened the pages.

The authors, like the star system in movies, may influence the readers' belief that they are fit readers. Peter Blau and Otis D. Duncan, authors of *The American Occupational Structure,* were both well known to professional sociologists and were professors at major universities. The inside front flap of *The American Occupational Structure* jacket describes the authors, indicating their academic positions, including major awards, places taught, and books published. Their credentials are "hung on the wall." The back of the jacket describes the book, emphasizing the "most comprehensive set of facts and data on occupational mobility ever assembled for any nation." Elliot Liebow, author of *Tally's Corner,* was then unknown outside of a small circle of colleagues. The back cover of *Tally's Corner* presents quotes from reviews or blurbs praising the book. Three of these are identified by the newspaper in which they appeared: the *New York Times, Washington Star, Detroit Free Press.* Three are identified by the names and positions of the reviewers: special assistant to the secretary of Housing and Urban Development, psychiatrist-in-chief of MIT, and the quote and identification of Moynihan that appears on the front.

Even before readers open the books, they have seen the differences of access and credentials of its authors. The relation of *Tally's Corner* to policy questions connected with urban planning has already been suggested. The technical character of *The American Occupational Structure* has been presented, and the possible inaccessibility of the book for some audiences has been established. The high repute of its authors is presented. Liebow's book began as his doctoral thesis in anthropology at Catholic University in Washington, D.C. That fact is contained in his Acknowledgments, while the cover "sponsors" the work through the praise of eminent persons and institutions.

The table of contents is a second way for authors to reveal the level of accessibility of their books. The titles of chapters are ordinary language in *Tally's Corner* and the special vocabulary of sociology in *The American Occupational Structure*. Thus, chapter 2 in Liebow's study is "Men and Jobs." In Blau and Duncan it is "The Occupational Structure: Patterns of Movements." Despite these differences, however, both works are efforts to persuade readers to conclusions that explain some phenomena. In that respect they both have recourse to the cloak of science and use the lineaments of rhetoric to accomplish this.

The language used in the text is a third sign of how the audience of readers may be limited or expanded. Consider the following sentences, with which each book begins its first chapter:

The objective of this book is to present a systematic analysis of the American occupational structure, and thus of the major foundation of its stratification system. Processes of social mobility from one generation to the next and from career beginnings to occupational destination are considered to reflect the dynamics of the occupational structure. (Blau and Duncan 1967, 1)

Problems faced by and generated by low-income urban populations in general and low-income urban Negroes in particular have become one of the chief concerns of the nation. We have declared War on Poverty and mobilized public and private resources for a concerted effort to expunge delinquency and dependency from our national life. (Liebow 1967, 3)

The first is the language of the professional sociologist. The second is the language of the college-educated reader.

Implied in the opening of these books are particular kinds of readers and the particular communities in which they are found. *The American Occupational Structure* is aimed at a more technical audience than is *Tally's Corner*. Blau and Duncan require a reader who understands "sociologese," who knows some rudimentary social statistics and is willing to make a sizable commitment of time. Such an audience is technical in the sense of being drawn from a community of people with special training. *Tally's Corner* is a book for many seasons and many kinds of readers The more dramatic language of ordinary readers implies that *Tally's Corner* draws on a wider community than does *The American Occupational Structure.*

Narrative: The Intellectual Structure

Though these books differ in the kind of audience each presupposes, they are alike in one substantial element of form. Both are narratives. They proceed sequentially through a beginning, middle, and end. The earlier parts of each book are routes toward an end, a conclusion. I mean by "structure" something closer to the sociologist's understanding of parts and wholes and their relationship to each other. I do not mean "structure" in the sense of an underlying, latent paradigm as in French structuralism. It is the relation of chapters and parts to each other and to the whole that is here considered. These books are arguments, not random collections of material. The beginning chapters would make no sense at the end and vice versa. The middle chapters, although conceivably interchangeable within that section, cannot stand alone or be exchanged with the beginning or the conclusion. In a sense (which will be qualified later), the ending is the aim of each book (Kermode 1966; Ricoeur 1984).

Even at the level of content there is great similarity. *The American Occupational Structure* begins with a chapter that discusses, in order, stratification theory and mobility research, methods of data collection, and the organization of the book. *Tally's Corner* begins with a chapter less explicit about its parts but also divided into three very similar sections. The first discusses the problem of the poverty cycle and the then current crisis in black families. It proceeds to discuss methods of study and closes with a description of Tally's corner and the men who make up the group under study. Both books end with a chapter summarizing what they have found and drawing conclusions for wider issues.

In the discussion of their materials, and in the opening parts of chapter 2 of *Tally's Corner,* both books present a body of materials to be explained by the remainder of the work. In the introductory chapter of *Tally's Corner,* Liebow writes that his study is "an attempt to meet the need for recording and interpreting lower-class life of ordinary people, on their grounds and on their terms" (10). But it is not a hit-or-miss attempt. It is guided by the policy concerns for the cycle of poverty continuing across generations among urban American blacks. *Tally's Corner* is an effort to use its data to explain that cycle.

The American Occupational Structure is also couched in the logic of explanation. In the first paragraph of the book Blau and Duncan announce that their objective is to conduct a systematic analysis of the

occupational structure and through that arrive at the major foundation of the stratification system. "By analyzing the patterns of these
occupational movements, the conditions that affect them, and some of
their consequences, we attempt to explain part of the dynamics of the
stratification system in the United States."

The parts of each book are consistent with these objectives. Having
stated their intentions, the authors discuss the methods used and then
proceed to describe and analyze the data. Chapter 1 is introductory. In
Blau and Duncan this is followed by two chapters that state the findings that characterize the occupational structure. Following this are
two chapters detailing the method that will be used in explaining that
structure and a third, which is a transition. The method is used to
present the model of the mobility process and, toward the end of the
chapter, is detailed in a presentation of data on the role of education
in that process. Then follow six more data chapters on such matters as
inequality of opportunity, especially the role of race, geographical and
social mobility, kinship, marriage, and differential fertility. This is the
logic of independent variables and their use in explaining the dependent variables—the present occupational position of the respondents
and the mobility patterns they displayed. The book ends with a concluding chapter, which serves as capstone and goal of the analysis.

In *Tally's Corner* there is a similar middle of discrete topics—jobs,
marriage, lovers, children, friends. The conclusion is also playing back
of the data on substantive questions. The greater space given to
method in *The American Occupational Structure* than in *Tally's Corner* is significant and will be discussed below.

Framing Devices:
The Suspension of Disbelief

In presenting their studies as something other than literature, social
scientists distinguish a product of imagination from a product of fact.
It is the facticity of their data that must be established if readers are
to be compelled to accept the conclusions of authors. If authors could,
at the very beginning of their work, know that readers will trust the
veracity and acumen of authors, the recourse to the agency, to method,
would be unnecessary.

That is not the case. Instead, the character of argument requires a
rhetoric directed at hostile, skeptical, and doubtful readers. The studies examined here, in differing ways and to different degrees, imply
readers who say, "I'm from Missouri. Don't tell me; show me."

While this is the case, and is indeed the basis of rhetoric, there are limits to the recalcitrance of readers. There are assumptions that must be made if the show is to go on at all. Samuel Taylor Coleridge pointed out that the audience at a drama must engage in "a willing suspension of disbelief" if the audience is to treat the actions of actors on a stage in a particular time and space as those of others elsewhere. It is the art of the brilliant soprano playing Madame Butterfly that enables a fat and fortyish Italian lady to convince her U.S. audience that she is, for a short time and space, a geisha in her early twenties in the Japan of the 1860s. The audience has accepted the frame of the opera.

Until quite recently, and still conventionally, paintings have had frames to tell viewers where the painting begins and where it ends. The frame is an attempt to lead viewers, and in this case readers, toward the kinds of matters worth attention and away from those that will distract. It helps to define what is content and what is not.

In both the documents being analyzed here, the frames are antecedent to the plot and narrative. the narrative structure of the books implies further that the material, the data, are fit sources for the orderliness with which they will be described and analyzed; that they truly represent fact and not imagination. Yet each work is only a representation of its study. It is not the actual set of events. As Hayden White has written about narrative in general: "Every narrative, however seemingly 'full', is constructed on the basis of a set of events which *might have been included but were left out* . . . in which continuity rather than discontinuity governs the articulation of the discourse" (White 1981, 10).

The American Occupational Structure

What is the unique character of *The American Occupational Structure?* What does it do that other mobility studies have not done? The authors tell the reader that the study is unique in the kind and amount of data used. The size of the sample (twenty thousand of the twenty-five thousand surveyed) permits kinds of analyses not possible previously. Most important, it enables the authors to investigate the conditions associated with mobility. Past studies had been directed almost exclusively toward the amount of mobility but not the conditions that might explain it. Such studies had also investigated how mobility patterns were affected by various factors—race, education, social origins. The authors reformulated this problem by decomposing the concept of occupational mobility into its constituent elements: social or career origins and occupational destinations. But instead of asking what effect one variable has on mobility—race, for example—they "ask what influence it exerts on occupational achievements and how it modifies the effects of social origins on those achievements" (9).

The substantive questions about upward mobility in U.S. society are not unique to this study, as the authors recognize. To what extent is the occupational structure characterized by mobility between and within generations? What conditions favor and deter mobility? It is the amount of data and the techniques of analysis that permit new answers to these questions.

In creating a narrative of fact sociologists are characteristically searching for generalizations beyond the sheer description of material collected. They meet the problem of extracting the universal from the particular. Readers must cope with the problem that few studies are able to obtain clear and unambiguous data on which to base conclusions. Authors must also cope with the limits, or "impurity," of data so that readers will utilize the data in the ways authors intend, as if the data were purer than it can be. How to deal with the limitations of data is a common problem for writers.

One facet of the frame lies in the relation between concept and data. In the first paragraph of chapter 1, Blau and Duncan tell the readers that theirs is a study based on "a considerable amount of empirical data" from a representative sample of over twenty thousand *men* between the ages of twenty to sixty-four. The reader learns that the data are from a national survey planned by the authors and conducted in March 1962 as an adjunct to the monthly Current Population Survey conducted by the U.S. Bureau of the Census. The survey was titled "Occupational Changes in a Generation."

At the very outset the audience is asked to believe that *the* American occupational structure can be discussed without including women and households. They are asked to share a meaning about "the American occupational structure" that excludes women and treats the meaning of mobility in individual rather than family terms. (I shall discuss this later in commenting on the concept of mobility as a shared element between audience and author.)

A second aspect of frame is in the adequacy of data. In chapter 1, Blau and Duncan admit several deficiencies in the data. Census Bureau procedures and policies led to a cumbersome time lag between planning and approval of plans, which made it difficult to make changes between the pretest and the final survey. Census policy made them unable to gain data on attitudes. Was the sample adequate? Here the authors go outside the frame and the painting. They refer the reader to a census report on the sample. The sample was approximately twenty-five thousand, but only about twenty thousand returned a usable questionnaire. The sample excluded the institutional population, including men in the military, thus reducing the universe represented to about 85 percent. In two appendices the authors deal with this problem of missing data, including nonresponses to particular questions They do so by a pattern of assumptions and a use of decennial census data that lead to different conclusions about the limited credibility of the data obtained in response to questions about the respondent (male) and his father. In the case of father's occupation they are less sure than in the case of father's education. In both, however, there are disclaimers about the "purity" of the data obtained.

To give a specific example and its use, take the case of the accuracy of respondents' data about the occupation of the father when respondents were sixteen. The authors matched the pretest sample with the data on the father at approximately son's age—sixteen—in the raw decennial census returns. In chapter 1 they report that of the 123 matched cases, 30 percent showed a discrepancy between respondents' designation of their father's occupation and what the census material showed about the father at that time. The appendix indicates that of the 570 in the pretest sample, a match was possible in 123 cases. Another way of reporting that result in the text might have been that of the 570 pretest sample, the accuracy of designating the father's occupation could be assured in 15 percent of the cases. Even in census post-interview studies (p. 15), the authors point out that occupation is not consistent in 17–22 percent of the cases. (Notice that I have refrained from using a modifying term such as "only" or "at least.")

The problem is a common one in social research. The data are seldom as good as the model of scientific methods would demand. But do deficiencies vitiate the ending? How can readers be convinced that the study is acceptable? The authors must prepare readers for what will lie inside the frame by argument that leads readers to check their doubts for the purposes at hand. They must suspend their disbelief in the inadequacy of the data.

(The admission of difficulties in the data is itself a show of credibility, establishing the veracity of the authors and their commitment to reveal data. If they are willing to admit flaws in their data, then they should be believable and trusted to be honest about other matters.)

The basic argument is, in part, given in the series of reasoned estimates and simulated data such as that discussed above. In part that process is developed in appendices, which require a further dilution of the audience, excluding those who lack the training to understand or who are willing to accept the data on the strength of the authors' word. Even with the efforts to correct for missing data, inaccuracies, and limited reliability, the data depart from the model of adequacy. Blau and Duncan argue that while there are sources of error, the data are no

worse than government census data in particular and survey research
in general. These are conventionally accepted within the profession
and so, too, they are a warrant for accepting the adequacy of the present data.

"The conclusion, however, is not that the OCG data on socioeconomic
background are free of error but merely that they may be almost as
reliable as CPS [Current Population Survey of the U.S. Census] data
on current occupational status . . . it must be conceded that very little
was done to estimate the effect of such error on conclusions and inferences. In that respect, unfortunately, our investigation is all too typical of the current standards of social research" (16).

In placing some of the methods for dealing with these problems into
appendices, Blau and Duncan further limit the audiences to whom
they speak. Within the text and in the beginning, however, they qualify the "purity" of the data. All this lies outside the frame. When they
begin to report the study, such qualifications are not constantly alluded to, although they are not ignored. It is left to the reader to make
the necessary discounts and limitations. As we might imagine, a style
of writing that constantly reminded readers of the limits on the data
would become even more cumbersome and boring. They lie outside the
frame and not in it. It is the reader who must apply a discount, who
must willingly suspend disbelief.

Tally's Corner

In one sense the production of a frame is a set of instructions to readers about how to read the work. In *Tally's Corner,* both the foreword
and the first part of chapter 1 provide the policy direction that orients
the author. An argument is made for the usefulness of studying black
cornermen. Like *The American Occupational Structure,* the comparison with other studies of black lower-class life is made. Past studies of
black lower-class life and poverty have largely focused on women and
children. The black male as an element in understanding poverty had
seldom been studied.

The other consideration that will make the study worthwhile is the
extent to which the incidence of poverty is much greater among blacks
than among whites. Blau and Duncan assume the reader's agreement
with their assessment of the importance of studying occupational mobility. Liebow does not take his reader's agreement for granted. Having convinced the reader, he can now go ahead.

At the outset, Liebow, like Blau and Duncan, must face the issue of
the validity of his study in a self-conscious manner. In his *English
Pastoral Poetry* William Empson points to the use of the Fool in *King*

Lear as a device often used by playwrights, a comic foil to the tragic character of Lear, an internal critic. Such devices, writes Empson, serve to prevent the audience from dismissing the "argument" of the play by lampooning it before the audience can do so (Empson 1938; Gusfield 1963). They rid playgoers of their disposition to offset the seriousness with the comic and leave the main plot acceptable. The playwright must confront and diminish the unwillingness to suspend belief before readers do so.

Where Blau and Duncan go to great lengths to establish the worthwhile quality of their data, Liebow treats the matter in several pages and one appendix. The bulk of Liebow's material is drawn from observations of his participation with two dozen black men who "hang out" on a corner in Washington, D.C. The study of these men is defended in several ways. One is as a correction to the emphasis on women and children in earlier studies, as we have seen. Another is the belief expressed by the author, and others, that interview and questionnaire methods have either excluded lower-lower class black men or have not resulted in valid information. What has been learned from these may be a false picture. His study, says Liebow, will correct this by recording and interpreting lower-class life "on their grounds and on their terms" (10).

The method of participant observation also raises problems for readers. If the focus of the study is on national problems of poverty, why devote a book to some twenty particular men chosen for ease of study? How can you make any general assertions from so special a study? Liebow utilizes a ploy of diminution, of claiming not to attempt to convince readers of the certainty of his data and his analyses: "The present attempt, then, is not aimed directly at developing generalizations about lower-class life" but in examining one minute segment, "to attempt to make sense of what was seen and heard, and to offer this explanation to others" (16).

Liebow asserts that he deliberately did not develop a research design and hypothesis prior to working in the field. His analyses are therefore post facto. In a footnote quoting Robert Merton's criticism of participant observation, Liebow counters Merton's criticism that conclusions drawn from this data "remain at the level of *plausibility* (low evidential value) rather than leading to 'compelling evidence' (a high degree of confirmation)" *(Social Theory and Social Structure,* 93–95, quoted in *Tally's Corner,* 12). Liebow counters by saying that the timing of the hypothesis is unimportant. Whether hypotheses are developed before or after the data are collected is immaterial. Their validity rests on their future replication. But like Blau and Duncan's recourse to the limits of conventional procedures, "given the present state of the art, we can ill afford to look 'merely plausible' explanations of human behavior in the mouth" (12, n.6).

Such a position disarms the critic, who may then decide that the study is not worth reading or no longer look for signs that the author has any point of view to which he or she will try to compel the reader's assent. Liebow, like Blau and Duncan, is aware that his conclusion belies giving us "just the facts." He does, however, as I will show later, want the particulars—the observation—to illuminate the universal, the general problem of black ghetto poverty. He does make it necessary to suspend our disbelief in the adequacy of his data for the questions of the study.

There is a further issue arising in *Tally's Corner* from the method of participant observation, one largely dealt with by Liebow in an appendix on fieldwork. Are his accounts of the actions of the men on the street corner accurate? How could an obviously well-educated person (male judging by the name) achieve the necessary rapport with lower-class, poorly educated men? The reader does not know until told that Liebow is white, a major piece of information in a field study of blacks. Liebow's account of his "fitness" is less an argument than a biography. His father owned a grocery store in a black area of Washington and he grew up in a black neighborhood.

Where *The American Occupational Structure* had recourse to method, to agency, in establishing the grounds for belief, *Tally's Corner* uses agent, the character, and experience and competence of the author. There is necessarily a different kind of presence in each of these books. Blau and Duncan remain in the shadows and aviod a presence. It is the data applied by method that is the action of *The American Occupational Structure*. The authors are behind the curtains, puppet masters perhaps, but invisible to those who view their presentation.

In *Tally's Corner* the agent, Elliot Liebow, is constantly present. Belief in his ability to get the data and to report it honestly is essential to his presentation. The responsibility of the author for selection and conclusions is more evident in *Tally's Corner* than in *The American Occupational Structure*. Like their data, Blau and Duncan are unobtrusive. Like his data, Liebow is a participant.

It is necessary, then, for each of these authors to establish the community of readers and the objects to which they will attend. In order to proceed readers must grant the author trust in his accounts and accept the value of the study as worth their attention. To achieve this the author needs to persuade readers to place themselves in the necessary audience, to accept the conventions of judgement, and to suspend doubt and distrust—to share the author's belief in the value of his study. Without such frames, anyone and everyone is a possible reader and the foundations of the community must be reestablished on every page. The willingness to disbelieve and the compulsion to accept and be persuaded depend on the community that readers share (Fish 1980). This is a major point in this chapter and will be elaborated on throughout.

Plot and Story: Assuming the Community of Readers

I begin this section with a distinction between plot and story. By "plot" I mean a general scheme the text utilizes to provide meaning and significance to its parts. It is an abstract statement, as in "Boy meets girl; boy loses girl; boy wins girl." This simple and trite narrative is not about any particular boy or particular girl. Stories are concrete; they are particular people doing particular things. The plot of *Hamlet* is its narrative structure and is repeated in other dramas. The story is unique to Hamlet.

Social science is mostly a procedure for emplotment. Even Erving Goffman, perhaps the most eminent of sociological storytellers, titled his major book *"The" Presentation of the Self in Everyday Life* (quotation marks mine). By no means are sociologists adverse to storytelling, but narrativity in the structure of the studies analyzed here makes the relation of plot to story a matter of importance.

Paramount to my discussion of the rhetorical element in social research is the notion that how material is presented (the form) has a close relationship to what is presented (the content). An analysis of these two books must necessarily be attentive to the form as a matter of impact on what is presented to the reader. In one sense these studies are narratives about narratives. The authors depict the behavior of their subjects in the light of a sequence of events, but that sequence is more than a listing of events, as a chronology might be (White 1981; Plumb 1971). It has direction and theme to it. "Emplotment invites us to recognize a traditional class of configurations" (Ricoeur 1984, 164). In both studies the concept of an occupational career is the central model or metaphor that integrates and gives point to the material presented. These books have the career as their plot.

The American Occupational Structure

The data that Blau and Duncan use as the major material under scrutiny consist of five variables from each respondent *(R)*. These are the occupation of R's father when R was sixteen; the highest grade of school R's father completed, the first full-time job of R, the educational attainment of R, and the present job of R. These are perceived as a sequence in which some variables follow others through time. In what is often seen as the major contribution of *The American Occupational Structure* this is referred to through the metaphor of a "path." Thus, first job cannot occur after present job, and son's educational attainment cannot occur before father's occupation. The model of a career is imagined in the metaphorical concept of a path and multiple regression coefficients established between the five variables with the concept of path as the metaphor for careers. (I cannot explain these concepts within the confines of this chapter. Nontechnicians, please hang on. This chapter does not depend on this bit of technical training.)

The use of plot enables the authors to talk about "the American stratification system" and mobility. It enables them to use existing data on men as if the plots of groups represented the totality of stratification and occupational status (income plus education), as if it represented the way in which each unique case can be perceived. As a metaphor or model it must necessarily ignore two major categories: women and households. Although they do recognize and use in their data single parents or guardians other than fathers, they do not gather material on women in the labor force, the institutionalized population, or the military. Nor do they consider the contributions of women and other family members, including extended family, to the respondent's position in the stratification system. Even by 1960 many households achieved middle-class income positions through the occurrence of joint earners.

I have already discussed several qualifications to the "purity" of the data used in *The American Occupational Structure*. The authors are conscious of these infirmities and, from time to time, call them to the attention of the reader. The analysis of data is, however, in the main conducted with an assumed data base in which the "reality" is an abstract and aggregated one. Liebow concentrates on one group of about twenty men. Blau and Duncan talk about twenty thousand. Such a number cannot be observed by "hanging around," nor talked about as specific and particular persons. To talk about them is to create a set of abstractions in which the particularities are dismissed and the aggregated similarities are the matters of attention.

The issue is recognized by the authors. In discussing the basic model of mobility as a path in which educationalal level attained is prior to the respondent's first job, they realize that this is not always so. In many cases (exactly how many is not known) the entry-level job may occur before completion of education, and/or the first job was only "temporary" and not the beginning of career. This they see as a flaw in their planning of the study: "We are inclined to conclude that their reports were realistic enough" (166). Their error, they say, lay in the meaning the authors gave to those reports as referring to the same entry-level status.

Blau and Duncan are aware that this uncovers a still more fundamental issue in the means of aggregating the twenty thousand cases, in giving a homogeneous meaning to the responses. They echo Hayden White's description of the problem of historical narrative: "The fundamental difficulty here is conceptual. If we insist on any uniform sequence of the events involved in accomplishing the transition to independent adult status, we do violence to reality. . . . As soon as we aggregate individual data for analytical purposes we are forced into the use of simplifying assumptions" (*The American Occupational Structure*, 166–167).

The authors then decide to adopt the assumption that "first job" has the same significance for all the respondents in its temporal relation to educational attainment and later work experience. Without such an assumption, the measures of association would be impossible since the meanings of the variables would then be diverse. They write, "If this assumption is not strictly correct we doubt that it could be improved by substituting any other *single* measure of initial occupational status" (107).

Tally's Corner

In an interesting manner Liebow makes use of the same plot of the "normal" career of attempted occupational mobility to make his data understandable. Liebow begins the "Men and Jobs" chapter with a graphic description of a white truck driver who stops at the street corner and asks the cornermen if they want work. They shake their heads and say no. Here is no plot but a story—a unique occurrence happening to particular people. Liebow, however, sets himself the task of explaining this story through a more general account of the role of jobs in the life of the street-corner men.

The story that Liebow has described makes sense, in his account, by comparison with a "normal" account of careers and the role of jobs in careers. On the corner "getting a job, keeping a job, and doing well at it is clearly of low priority" (34). Explaining why this is so is the substance of much of *Tally's Corner*. It makes sense to do so only if the reader is already convinced that the street-corner men are not like most others; that in U.S. society the desire for turning jobs into careers, for social mobility, is the norm, and the absence of a career is something to be explained. If fires were normal occurrences, the happening of a fire would not be news.

Again, the attribution of the absence of career and mobility motivation in the cornermen will remain at the level of "story," of a concrete, particular set of people whom the author has known, unless it can be generalized to more than the cornermen. In his foreword, the sociologist Hylan Lewis points out that this is a study of "losers" and does not describe those who have become "winners" and succeeded at legitimate careers or have taken illegitimate careers as successful paths to mobility.

Achieving Reality: The Art of Facticity

In their study of a biochemical laboratory the sociologists Latour and Woolgar (1979) paid great attention to the processes by which the laboratory's findings achieved an "out-thereness" quality when reported in publication. The rhetoric of scientific presentation must minimize the role of the writer in constructing the reality of "fact." Social scientists stand above the flux of interests and conflicts because what they know cannot be denied. It does not rest on sentiment or self-interest but on what is truly "out there."

Both *The American Occupational Structure* and *Tally's Corner* wrestle with this problem, from different standpoints and with different mechanisms of coping, but cope they must. Put in the concept of the analysis of fiction, each author claims to show and not to tell (Booth 1961). But as Booth also points out, in literary works it becomes impossible to do one without the other. In this and the following section I will amplify this judgment in these nonliterary works.

Tally's Corner: The Art of Showing

I have already mentioned the problem of the personal relation to material that participant-observers face. They rest much of the claim to believability on readers' willingness to trust the veracity and observational skills of the author. Two questions are posed, the first of which we will analyze in this section; the second is reserved for later. The first question bears on the veracity or accuracy of what has been observed and reported. The second bears on the significance or mean-ing of those reports as they relate to the framework or structure of the book and on its conclusions.

By no means is Liebow content to show only what he has heard and seen. He wants to explain it and to advocate that explanation as an aid in understanding something more general—the problem of black poverty. As he points out in the very beginning of the book, one often-discussed aspect of that problem has been the absence of the father and/or husband from the family in the black lower class. In chapter 4, "Husbands and Wives," Liebow examines this problem using his obser-vations. The writing consists of descriptive statements, analytic state-ments, and "protocols" (the notes and quotations used by Liebow—the primary material).

Chapter 4 begins with a descriptive statement about Liebow's sub-jects: "A few of the streetcorner men expect to get married sooner or later. A few are married. Most of the men have tried marriage and found it wanting."

Why should the reader believe Liebow? Has he reported "fact"? Since we know, from the appendix, that he spent a year observing the corner, at various times of the day and night, what we are given is a selection. There is no survey of the neighborhood. How can we trust his report?

Much of this chapter consists of statements like the one above, in which the reader is told something about the cornermen and that something is analyzed. He tells a number of stories about specific mar-riages or consensual unions. These become the basis, the evidence, for the analytic statements. In one part of the chapter, Liebow maintains that cornermen clearly distinguish between the demand rights of mar-riage and the privileges of consensual unions. He then tells a story, concretizing the analytic statement.

> [This] can be seen in the conflict between Stanton and Bernice. Shortly after they began living together, Stanton was arrested and jailed for thirty days. Upon his release, he went to their apartment where he discovered Bernice with another man. Over the next several weeks, Stanton refused to look for work. It *was understood* that he was making Bernice "pay." . . . Both men and women said this was a "terrible" thing for Stanton to do, that maybe Bernice hadn't done the "right" thing but she had a right to do what she did because they weren't married. (106; italics mine)

We recognize that these statements paraphrasing what Liebow heard are not the verbatim report of what was said or the contexts in which it was said, that they are the end product of a process. Why should we believe that this is a credible interpretation? What Liebow does, as most fieldwork reports do, is utilize his protocols from time to time. (I am doing the same thing when I quote from Liebow or from Blau and Duncan.) Consider the following use of protocol in the same chapter. Here Liebow is quoting from what he claims is a common justification for marital breakup used by the cornermen he observed: the theory of sexual infidelity as a manly flaw: "Men are just dogs! We shouldn't call ourselves human, we're just dog, dogs, dogs! They call me a dog, 'cause that's what I am, but so is everybody else—hopping around from woman to woman, just like a dog" (121).

This protocol, like most used in *Tally's Corner,* is indented as a quotation and single-spaced. It is, in some respect, "outside" the text. The shift in language and style further gives it a reality that separates it from the paraphrased statements of the author. It has the ring of reality, although we do not know to what remarks it was a response or the difference between what was said and what was recorded in Liebow's notes. As an illustration, however, readers can use it to check their own interpretation of the statement against the use Liebow makes of it. Agreement with the interpretation of the protocol heightens the trust of readers in the other statements Liebow makes.

The American Occupational Structure:
The Rhetorical Uses of Statistical Presentation

The use of numerical forms and visual devices—such as charts, tables, and graphs, and in this case path-coefficient models—serves additional functions beyond the analytical mechanism. The numerical form has a precision and a definiteness that verbalized measures lack. It enables comparison between classes. Thus, a table (p. 154, Table 4.5) is presented showing the percentage differences between men of different mobility scores both in the observed data and on the hypothesis that father's occupational status and respondent's occupational status are statistically independent within categories of education. The mobility score measures the distance "traveled" between the father's occupation and the son's on an interval scale on which every occupation has a status score. Thus, movement upward from 26 to 96 is a long distance, although the authors point out that the distributions (long or short) are arbitrary. What is not arbitrary, they assert, is that, *on the average,* respondents' own occupational status is higher than that of their father.

This is a typical pattern in quantitative studies carefully done and carefully explicated. Given the assumptions that had to be made, however, readers might be expected to view the operations with some skepticism. How can the data be accepted as a summarization of a factual world?

The use of numbers is itself a device that demonstrates that the results are a product of labor and care. To refer to observations of 24.9 percent and 15.5 percent grants a definiteness to the data. It converts "maybes" into "certainlys."

So, too, does the use of visual devices. Here the analogy to Liebow's use of protocols is apparent. Tables and other visual material are "outside" the text. They can then be referred to as the source of commentary in text. A frequent usage is as follows in reference to the same table: "Comparing the observed with the expected A distribution, *we see* that there is considerably more relative stability in actual fact than the hypothesis of perfect mobility predicts" (154); italics mine). The table has become the data. "The chances of upward mobility are directly related to education, *as Figure 4.5 shows"* (italics mine).

Another way in which the data become "real" is through the continuous use of the closed world that has been built. As we shall see, Blau and Duncan fluctuate between couching their statements in measurements terms or making assertions about the experiences of the entire aggregate. Thus, compare the statement about measurement—"The proportion of men who experience some upward mobility increases steadily with education" (157)—with the statement about persons:" it is the social composition of men on this educational level that accounts for their downward mobility" (161). Each group very seldom, if ever, yields uniform results. Even if sons on the average have higher occupational status than their fathers, many have lower occupational status. The disposition to treat the data as uniform by ignoring the qualifications is ever present and, as we will show, throws onto readers the burden of moving from plot to story.

Style and Its Deviation: Looking through Different Glasses

In a brilliant analysis of the rhetoric of news on Israeli radio, Itzhak Roeh describes a useful device for examining the use of words and word patterns in these two studies (Roeh 1982). Roeh finds that in the straight news broadcast, where most items describe official and elite acts and statements, the typical form of the sentence is assertive. Subject, verb, and object follow in that order; for example, "The leader of the Left in Lebanon says that Lebanon is approaching a civil war."

Here an event is described without limitations. In the news magazine that follows the news broadcast, sentences are more likely to begin with subordinate clauses; for example, "In the western parts of the town of Tiberias the police have fixed check posts." Here the event is limited to a specific place.

Roeh's examination of these differences leads him to conclude that the first form, what I call assertive style, conveys respect and objectivity. The latter style permits greater creativity and implies a less "factual," more tentative existence. Roeh uses the metaphor of glass to convey these differences. The form of language that asserts fact without becoming reflexive is called *transparent*. The more subjective style is called *opaque*.

I have already made a number of references to how patterns of language use in these two works affect their status as factual accounts. Here I will analyze the language of these two studies to see whether "facticity" is, or is not, established.

Style as Cadence: The Function of Dullness

I have already remarked on the dull quality of the language in *The American Occupational Structure*. Sentences are long and the language quite formal. The style is marked by a deliberate lack of style. There is a seeming lack of concern for unique, unconventional, or surprising use of language. The very conventionality of the language is like the male suit of clothes. Its very uniformity conveys the stereotype that makes trust in the wearer believable (Fraser 1981, 227–234). It presents the message "I don't spend time and thought on fashionable appearance." There is an even cadence and rhythm to the sentences that detracts from attention to the language. (As my colleague Bennett Berger has expressed it, the most desirable state of things appears to be one without words, if that were possible.) Much of this is accomplished through lengthy sentences with long subordinate clauses; for example: "The importance of the type of community in which a man was brought up for his occupational success can only mean that more urbanized environments prepare youngsters better for high-status occupations" (263). A succession of sentences like this, not atypical in *The American Occupational Structure,* has something of the effect of continuous monotonic drumming.

Tally's Corner offers a sharp contrast to this style. The use of ordinary language makes for images that are concrete and distinct: "Few married men, however, do in fact support their families over sustained periods of time. Money is chronically in short supply and chronically a source of dissension in the home" (131). The repetition of the word *chronically* in the second sentence gives a rhythmic change and a "surprise" that may make a reader conscious of the language. The use of verbatim and vernacular passages from the speech of the cornermen contributes as well to unexpected language. *Tally's Corner* has a literary "feel" to it. In contrast, *The American Occupational Structure* seems to guard its monotonic style as a means of shoring up the sense of a real rather than an imagined set of "facts." The style seems to say that this is hard material to get and to analyze, and therefore the accounts are more reliable.

Here style and access are not unrelated. *Tally's Corner* holds the interest of the reader and does not exclude those uninitiated into sociology. By the same token, it is an easy read. It demands much less of the reader's attention and scrutiny than does *The American Occupational Structure*. The very boredom that *The American Occupational Structure* may induce shuts out lesser-trained and interested readers. In turn, the dull quality of the language requires readers to pay close attention to what is a careful and complex argument. The danger of one is the safety of the other. Liebow's readers may be more likely to follow the sequence from start to finish, but do so casually. Readers of *The American Occupational Structure* may be inclined to skip around in it, but do so while paying close attention.

Shifts in Style

Each of these studies is reported in several different "languages." A major distinction in *The American Occupational Structure* is between verbal and visual material. I have already mentioned the significance of the use of visual forms. In discussing the verbal materials I shall examine some distinctions between sentence forms and their possible effects.

Tally's Corner utilizes three distinct forms. I have already described and discussed the distinction between the ordinary language of the author and the vernacular talk of the street-corner men and women. Here I will concentrate on the distinction in *Tally's Corner* between the author's language in describing and analyzing his "people" and the language used when he discusses "social science." In problems of style Liebow and Blau and Duncan each face the central problem to which I have alluded throughout this chapter: the argumentative and thus rhetorical character of the study.

Within the text of *Tally's Corner* Liebow varies between describing and analyzing. Even when analyzing, however, Liebow sticks close to ordinary language: "The streetcorner is, among other things, a sanctuary for those who can no longer endure the experience or prospect of failure" (214). Much of the discussion of implications of the study for theories of lower-lower-class behavior and Liebow's response to other sociologists is contained in footnotes. In *The American Occupational Structure* most of this is found in the text.

In first teaching *Tally's Corner* in a methods course, I was surprised to find that much of the argument addressed to sociologists rather than laypeople was found in the footnotes. Here the language is less likely to be "ordinary." In the following quotation from a footnote Liebow discusses his qualifications to another theory, with which he expresses much agreement: "The first is that the stretched or alternative value systems are not the same order of values, either phenomenologically or operationally, as the parent or general system of values: They are derivative, subsidiary in nature, thinner and less weighty, less completely internalized, and seem to be value images reflected by forced or adaptive behavior rather than real values with a positive determining influence on behavior of choice" (213).

This bifurcation of text and footnotes seems a device that separates the audiences or readers. It keeps the style of *Tally's Corner* clear, and in the same study it also proves Liebow's credibility as a social scientist by showing that he can make the proper "noises." It has more significance than a union card display, however (as will be discussed below).

Despite the general rejection of self-consciousness about their use of language, Blau and Duncan evidence at least two important shifts in language in addition to the verbal-visual dimension. Both are forms of what I call the assertive-qualified dimension. They are analogous to Roeh's distinction between the transparent and the opaque.

Roeh's usage is pertinent to this chapter in two ways. In *The American Occupational Structure* there are at least two kinds of statements: those that summarize, examine, or describe the collected data and those that present interpretations derived from the examinations, descriptions, and summations of the data. This is a distinction based on content. Within these differences there are also matters of form. Assertions can be made in qualified as well as assertive forms, and interpretations can be made in similar fashion.

Blau and Duncan do more in *The American Occupational Structure* than report how they did their study and what they found. A great many paragraphs contain interpretations of data in which the authors shift into dramatic language. This is language that imputes motives, purposes, emotions, and other concrete elements to agents, to persons. Thus, the final sentence in the chapter on analysis of the role of education: "The relative deprivation of social status implicit in downward mobility is suffered most often by men in the intermediate educational brackets, and their exposure to this greater risk of deprivation *may well* make them a potentially explosive force in periods of economic crisis" (161; italics mine).

The use of the qualifying term "may well" is a means of putting the reader on guard that this sentence does not have the same evidentiary value as others. From the same section here is a more assertive statement describing the data: "Downward mobility, however, does not exhibit a corresponding linear association with education" (157). This is technical language. The downward mobility is nobody's particular mobility and is not a product of any human act, but is rather an abstract concept.

In general, and more impressionistically, there appears to be a pattern to these usages. In some chapters, the assertive statements are contained within paragraphs that have discussed the method involved in reaching the assertion and that qualify the assertive strength of the statement. In others there appears to be a greater use of short assertive sentences to introduce the paragraph. The concluding chapter is especially given to this latter effect. Some chapters engage in more shifts from technical to dramatic language than do others.

The following are instances of what I refer to as assertive and qualified statements. Both are taken from lead sentences in paragraphs but from different chapters:

Assertive: "Upwardly mobile couples tend to have fewer children than others with the same social origins." (414, from the conclusion)

Qualified: "In sum, although the additive model cannot be accepted without reservation, it comes very close to predicting all the effects produced by a simple classification of couples as mobile or nonmobile." (379 from the chapter on differential fertility)

It is difficult to know how to explain such seeming patterns. They appear to be related to the different authors. Substantive chapters and sections, as well as those on method, seem more qualified in their assertions and less likely to shift into dramatic language than do those specifically devoted to advancing a theory (as in the conclusion). Nevertheless the distinction also seems to hold for substantive chapters written by the theorist, Blau, and those written by the methodologist, Duncan. To what extent these reflect general differences in style between the qualified assertions of methodologists and the assertive style of theorists, or between Otis Duncan and Peter Blau, is well beyond the scope this chapter.

Two aspects of style are, however, common throughout *The American Occupational Structure*. First, the general use of social-science language in the verbal text is consistent. Unlike *Tally's Corner*, there is no shift from social science to informal language, although there are shifts from statistical analysis to social science language. Second, to varying degrees there is a general use of dramatic language when the authors move beyond data to concretize and give added significance to their material.

Polemical Nexus and the Altered Audience: Creating Moral Significance

It will be useful to raise a further question about these books: what do they appear to ask readers to do? Are they to be the same persons with the same beliefs and desires as before? Is there a praxis, a practical implication, of these studies? If there is, and I believe there is, how do the authors try to accomplish it?

Both *The American Occupational Structure* and *Tally's Corner* are important works in their fields. Blau and Duncan's book has had an important effect on the development of method-path analysis. Yet if a method did not lead to worthwhile substantive significance it would be an empty agency. Both books produced substantive findings of importance. In this section I examine the two studies as ways of compelling belief in their significance. Another way of putting this question is to ask: what are the authors trying to convince readers is both true and important in their study? What difference should it make that things are as the authors have found them?

The Polemical Nexus

In *Tally's Corner* Elliot Liebow does not go to much length to convince readers that the U.S. black has experienced much discrimination and that such patterns of racial relations ought not to exist. And in *The American occupational Structure* Blau and Duncan do not attempt to argue the general virtue of achievement as a worthy tenet of social stratification: "In a liberal democratic society *we* think of the more basic principle as being that of achievement. Some ascriptive features of the system may be regarded as vestiges of an earlier epoch, to be extirpated as rapidly as possible" (161; italics mine).

Insofar as readers are seen as antithetical and hostile to the ideas being presented the work has a polemical quality. It seeks to convert those who are initially in disagreement with the "message" of the work. But Blau and Duncan, as well as Liebow, also assume some knowledge and belief shared by the community of their readers, which makes the selection and analysis of materials sensible and significant.

The polemic, however, is not against the symbolic hostile reader. It is also addressed to a specific other—to social science works that are contradicted by the present work. It is here that the direction and relevance of a book is made clear to its readers. Hayden White again: "Every historical narrative has as its latent or manifest purpose the desire to *moralize* the events of which it treats" (White 1981, 14).

In *Tally's Corner* the polemic is directed against a then current mode of explaining black poverty. That explanation is found both in popular thought and in the writings of other social scientists. It is sometimes called the "culture of poverty," sometimes the class-values approach. In the story of the truck driver and the reluctance of the cornermen to work, Liebow writes as if he could read the mind of the truck driver who has been able to recruit only two or three men after twenty to fifty contacts: "To him, it is clear that the others simply do not choose to work . . . these men wouldn't take a job if it was handed to them on a platter" (30).

Both in the chapter "Men and Jobs" and in the concluding chapter Liebow refers to social scientists who explain black poverty as, in part, a result of cultural characteristics. Improving the work productivity of lower-class blacks is a problem of improving their motivation to achieve higher goals, of changing "work habits and motivation" (quoted from Allison Davis, "The Motivation of the Underprivileged Worker," 90, in Liebow, 30).

Put in Burkean terms, the key dramatistic concept in this account is that of the agent. With a theory that emphasizes the limited ambitions of the agent, the act of rejecting work is understandable. It fits the reader's assumed understanding of how "such people" would act differently from you and me. Liebow's rhetoric assumes a different dramatistic concept in his explanation of the identical action. As is true of most sociological studies, his emphasis is on the scene as providing the motivation for the act. Analyzing the stories that he relates through paraphrase and protocol leads Liebow to see the action of the cornermen as appropriate behavior given the skills they possess, their limited education, and the character of the menial jobs available to them.

Consider the issue of "deferred gratification" or "present-time" orientation, which had been accepted by many sociologists as a distinction between middle- and lower-class people. One of Liebow's "stories" illustrates his thesis. Tally has asked him to hold eighty dollars of his pay. When Tally retrieves the money, Liebow asks why Tally doesn't put his money in a bank, since there are many close by. Tally responds:

"No, man . . . you don't understand. They closed at two o'clock and they closed Saturday and Sunday. Suppose I get into trouble and I got to make it [leave]. Me get out of town and everything I got layin' up there in that bank? No good" (69).

It is not that the cornermen and the reader have different future orientations. They have different futures.

I emphasize this part of *Tally's Corner* because it is important to the rhetoric of fieldwork and, as we will see, to Blau and Duncan as well. In *Rhetoric in Sociology*, Ricca Edmondson (1984) suggests that field studies utilize one or both of two enthymemes (an enthymeme is a truncated syllogism in which one of the premises is understood but unstated): the ordinary man and/or the rational man. Liebow's usage in the analysis of the cornermen and their work life is of this character. He is saying to his readers: "You and the cornermen are no different in your values and goals. If you were faced by their situation you would behave in the same manner." The scene explains the act once you, the reader, understand the scene. There is a vicious cycle of poverty, but it is not a result of historical continuities or cultural values. Sons behave like fathers because they face the same situations. Once readers perceive the scene they can truly understand the "fitness" of the act in that scene.

The same appeal to a background knowledge of the reader appears in Liebow's account of marriage among the cornermen. Liebow uses his stories of the cornermen to demonstrate the contradictions between their account of why their marriages break up—the theory of manly flaws—and what is "truly" at work. The first theory, echoed in many social science writings, is that lower-lower-class males do not value monogamy. Not so, writes Liebow. They give many indications of placing a high value on marriage and stable families. The problem, and the ubiquitous marital breakups, are a result of the cornerman's inability to play the role of breadwinner in a fashion adequate to him and to "normal" U.S. standards. When these phenomena are viewed against the scene, the life situation of the cornermen, then "both 'serial monogamy' an cultural distinctiveness tend to disappear. In their place is the same pattern of monogamous marriage found elsewhere in *our* society but one that is characterized by failure" (220; italics mine).

The appeal is again to the background knowledge of the reader in conjunction with the material presented about the cornermen. The reader must agree with Liebow in his description of conventional U.S. marriage patterns and with his understanding of the cornermen. The generalizability of fieldwork, in this instance as elsewhere, lies in this reconstruction of the logic of action of those studied. Edmondson is, I believe, correct about the rhetoric of field studies within the sociological paradigm. In sociology the scene-act ratio is dominant; the act—behavior—has been shown to be "appropriate" to the scene (Burke 1945, chap. 1). With anthropologists and psychologists it may well differ. Almost by definition, cultures differ and individuals differ. The appeal to the "ordinary person" or the "rational person" may not be as much in use in those disciplines as in sociology, where it is paramount.

The American Occupational Structure and Its Social Significance

Blau and Duncan make no case for the direct relevance of their study to matters of public policy. Nor are they as explicit in the early parts of the book about versions of social stratification with which they disagree. The posture of authorial absence would not permit any indication that the authors knew ahead of time what versions of U.S. stratification were being contradicted by their book. At the outset, in chapter 1, the authors present their targets of revision in methodological terms. What they will do that others have not done is relate variables to one another. They are less interested in the association between father's occupation and son's than in the influence of one variable on another and the co-joint influence of the two on son's contemporary occupational status. Thus father's origin has an influence, but it has that influence, in part, by influencing the kind and amount of education that in turn has an influence on son's occupational status.

This methodological polemic against single-variable associations leads, however, to conclusions of a substantive nature. These are foreshadowed by remarks in chapter 1 about a previous study by Lipset and Bendix (1959). The reader is told that the Lipset and Bendix study is the most extensive secondary study of social mobility in several industrial societies and, on the final page of that chapter, that in the conclusion the authors will suggest reformulations of the theories presented in the prior study. Indeed that study and its generalizations will emerge as a major foil against which *The American Occupational Structure* is to be seen.

Perhaps the central problem of mobility and stratification studies among sociologists in the late 1950s and early 1960s was that of the extent of opportunity for social mobility in the United States. Was the United States an open society in which people could overcome the detriments of social origins and climb to higher places on the stratification ladder? Lipset and Bendix (1959), using secondary analysis of survey data, conclude that mobility in the United States, though considerable, was no greater than in other industrial societies. Further, they support the conception of a "vicious circle" of poverty such that occupational and social status tend to be self-perpetuating. In describing that concept Blau and Duncan use the Lipset and Bendix study as the best statement of the theory (199–200). Their quarrel with it rests on two conclusions, which they derive from their data and analysis: (1) a considerable amount of occupational mobility does occur in the United States, and (2) while father's status is significant to son's, its effect is largely that of influencing the degree of education achieved by the son. However (and this is explicitly stated as a major conclusion of the study): "Far from serving in the main as a factor perpetuating initial status, education serves primarily to induce variation in occupational status that is independent of initial status" (201).

The exception to their conclusion, however, is the case of the U.S. black. Here Blau and Duncan agree with Liebow that the "vicious circle" theory of poverty applies. They find its source in racial discrimination.

The Scene-Act Ratio

At bottom, Liebow, Blau, and Duncan are sociologists or social anthropologists. Their basic paradigm is that of scene. The relatively high levels of mobility in U.S. society are not, as Blau and Duncan find it, a matter of the capacities of the individuals who overcome their initial social origins. It is, instead, the influence of an institutional structure—the school—and its cultural principles that create the opportunity structure making mobility possible. In concluding the book, the authors make the leap from a set of measured findings to conclusions about U.S. society and its stratification system. Explicitly labeling their conclusions "speculations," they see the role of education in supporting high mobility rates as evidence of a fluid rather than a rigid class structure. The causes of the United States' high rate of occupational mobility lie in the universalistic principles of "our industrialized society" (431). The weakening of kin and communal ties and internal migration, in conjunction with education, all contradict the particularistic and ascriptive barriers to mobility. The act, mobility, is congruent with the scene. The existence of the scene is itself reflected in the action of occupational mobility.

Significance and the Normative "We"

It does not take a great amount of imagination to recognize the political significance of *The American Occupational Structure*. From one standpoint the logic of the book might have been followed had the authors not written a conclusion but were content with a summary of findings. The findings alone, however, do not instruct readers as to where these findings might lead. The facts do not speak for themselves. They do not instruct readers what to do or to feel about the facts shown. A summary of findings lacks moral significance.

Blau and Duncan are explicit in their appeal to a set of standards by which the findings are to be judged. At various times they find it necessary to provide the reader with some vantage point, some stance from which to give importance to their study by linking it to something known and supposedly accepted by the reader. In the beginning of chapter 5, perhaps the major chapter describing the concepts and methods of the study, the authors distinguish between ascriptive and achievement systems, as "pure" types. They write: "In a liberal democratic society *we* think of the more basic principle as being that of achievement" (163). As in Liebow, the interpretations involve an appeal to "what everyone knows," to the normative "we."

In this respect, the absence of women and households in the sample of persons studied, conventional as it was for sociology in the early 1960s, implies a readership that assumes the insignificance of women, either as members of society or as significant to the occupational work force. Their absence, under either "father's occupation" or "respondents," was not deemed a matter important enough to be extensively justified. Here the audience and the authors seem to have shared a particular version of mobility. It is doubtful that a U.S. sociologist doing a similar study today could make such an assumption about the concepts of "occupational structure" or "social mobility."

The Two Genres

To some extent there is a dialectic of genres in the two books we have looked at. The concrete, particular, and dramatic character of *Tally's Corner* does not prevent its opposite from occurring. Both in the footnotes and in the text where Liebow must describe the general situation of blacks and of the lower lower class (an abstract term itself) he must assume the aggregative, abstract "society" that Blau and Duncan study. Where the authors of *The American Occupational Structure* are limited by their data, they also express a need to convey a more concrete and particular account, even if speculative.

Yet it would be grossly misleading to say that each becomes the other. The styles, methods, and authorial presence of Liebow are not those of Blau and Duncan. The dramatistic genre of Liebow makes different demands on its readers than does the technical genre of Blau and Duncan. Both ask readers to follow them in sequence, not to read the conclusion before the introduction or the section on methods after the substantive chapters. Each throws onto readers the burden of the background knowledge necessary to make sense of the materials. Each throws onto readers the burden of discount. Blau and Duncan ask readers to ignore, for the extent of the study, the limitations that the collected data impose on facticity. Liebow, despite the disclaimer of provability, develops an argument couched in terms reflecting a factually existent world encompassing far more than Tally's corner. In this sense the books do become each other. Liebow begins in doubt, uncertainty, and the plausible but ends with definiteness and certainty. Blau and Duncan begin with certainty and provability and end in plausibility.

Nevertheless, the differences between the two studies, possibly the two genres, lie in what the reading experience seems to be for their readers. In reading Blau and Duncan the readers are the equal of the writers. Once admitted into the fratority of admissible readers, they are in the same place as the authors. The data the writers have gathered are presented to the readers. The questions skeptical readers would ask are asked by the authors, and the agency—the methodology—governs both writers and audience. Readers must come to the same conclusion as do the authors because readers, like the authors, are rational beings who are exposed to the same data and, in part, are members of the same cognitive community as the authors.

The methodology of *The American Occupational Structure* is like the scaffolding of a building: it is essential to erect the structure, but once erected it may be dispensed with. The conclusions are the end product, and all else, including the analysis, are only stations on the way to the end of the line. Once readers, have become convinced of the validity or invalidity of the study, their task is done and the means used to reach the end become irrelevant, no longer needed.

What does remain, over and above the findings and conclusions, is the image of stratification conveyed by the metaphor of the "path." Such imagery, akin to the concreteness of story, exercises the imagination of readers. The picture of the factory system in Marx, of the bureaucracy in Weber, of the folk community in Toennies—these have been a major source of the power of sociologists in intellectual life (Nisbet 1976). The image of the path provides a standard of "career" to the life cycle that contrasts with the shortened image of the respondent stepping into the shoes of the father.

Yet the organization of *The American Occupational Structure* is, in its emphasis on plot, not oriented toward change through the process of reading. Not so with *Tally's Corner*. Here the audience cannot readily separate the means from the ends of the study. A bald resumé of *Hamlet,* in a page or so, would sound like many other plots. Reading an abstract or summary of *Hamlet* is not the same as reading *Hamlet.* Reading a summary of Veblen is a poor substitute for reading Veblen. The empathic response of putting oneself in the "role of the other" is elicited by the concreteness of the stories. It is through these that readers can *appreciate* the reasonableness and ordinariness of the cornermen's attitudes.

Creating Meaning and Changing Facts

Another way of stating the differences between these two genres is in recognizing what seems to occur in the process of reading each of them. Blau and Duncan are intent on proving the accuracy of a state of fact. The meaning of social mobility is taken for granted as something shared with their readers, as I have pointed out in discussing the absence of women and households. The general framework of perception and understanding is assumed. Thus the absence of women in the sample is not something that has to be defended. The use of the experimental report as model can proceed. The behaviors being reported on—occupations, stratification, mobility—have meanings that are assumed as fixed.

Liebow's task, or function, is quite different. He takes behavior that has been given a common meaning and attempts to change readers' perception of it, to create a new perspective within which the meaning of the action is changed. The orientation to career and to marriage is now to be seen as no different from that of the reader. What is different is the scene within which it acts.

What Liebow can accomplish is a change in the reader's evaluation and understanding of behavior. The end product is an appreciation of the behavior of the cornermen by understanding why they act as they do. Blau and Duncan cannot provide new meanings, do not instruct the reader on new meanings, although the concept of path is a new metaphor. What they can do is compel an alteration in what is believed within the structure of already existent meanings. Liebow cannot support an aggregative sense about his twenty people that can apply to a large population. What he can do is render an existent meaning of behavior that readers hold as no longer the only, or even the most plausible, meaning available.

The problem of sampling is a crucial one for Blau and Duncan because they are claiming to describe aggregative facts about central tendencies. They assume readers who share their interpretation of the meanings of events and actions—the status value of an occupation, for example. Given the problem of their study, it could not be done with a sample of twenty men.

Liebow's study is not vitiated by the small size and particularity of his subjects. His object is the interpretation of behavior, the creation of meaning. Having shown that the cornermen are not to be understood by conventional interpretations, he has cast doubt on generalizations based on large samples that assume the conventional interpretations to be true.

Writing social science appears to depend on an assumed community of fact and meaning. But reading is more than the outcome of already given frameworks of understanding. It can, and does, lead to shifts and ruptures with what has gone before (Leenhardt 1980). New facts are assimilated, new meanings emerge. The discovery of general facts and the interpretation of specific meanings are not necessarily accomplished in the same manner, nor do they persaude the reader in the same way.

MARJORIE L. DeVAULT
Women Write Sociology
Rhetorical Strategies

A RENEWED INTEREST in rhetoric has accompanied the recent "discovery" that language is used to persuade in every field of cultural and scientific production. The line of theorizing associated with this discovery emphasizes the crafted nature of scientific and social scientific analyses and the constitution of their claims of objectivity. As this volume demonstrates, rhetorical analysis is being applied in a variety of relatively new ways. One aspect of this project should involve asking if gender matters—or better, asking *how* it matters, since twenty years of renewed feminist scholarship tell us that it virtually always does. I will suggest, as well, that an analysis of rhetoric as gendered process will illuminate the social construction of "women's place" within intellectual communities.

Since the rebirth of feminism in the late 1960s, women in virtually every discipline have begun to search out the history of women's contributions. This fact in itself has significance for an investigation of rhetorical process, since it suggests the importance of a gendered tradition for those who would do intellectual work. These women have sought a rhetorical tradition that models distinctively female voices (as other nonwhite-male writers and thinkers have sought traditions in their voices). These investigators, though not all sociologists, have learned to do a kind of archeological investigation that has taught them much about the sociology of communities of knowledge. Several general processes can be seen in the various inquiries (for example, Chicago 1975 on artists; Rossiter 1982 on scientists; Showalter 1977 on novelists; Deegan 1981, 1988; and Reinharz 1988 on sociologists). First, there is evidence that at least some women practitioners seem to produce work "outside" or marginal to (that is, different from) the predominant male forms of their times—in other words, there is evidence of the development over time, with some continuity, of "female" traditions. (There is evidence as well that similar processes produce traditions of black thought, and distinctively black feminist thought, see, e.g., Collins 1986.) Second, there is evidence of systematic segregation: women—no matter what the content of their work—have been channeled into particular spaces within disciplines, which, over time, have been defined as the subareas appropriate for women. These areas have simultaneously been defined as those that are least prestigious—the simplest and least "interesting" subfields. Finally, there is evidence of a process whereby the gap between men's and women's concerns and relevances interacts with gender segregation to systematically influence judgments of scientific and aesthetic quality and importance. Hence, women practitioners do not develop the reputation necessary for active and continuing participation in their fields, and disappear from the historical record more quickly, and for different reasons, than male counterparts (Spender 1982; Tuchman and Fortin 1984; Tuchman 1989). These processes shape the construction of disciplinary canons. Too often, men have presented accounts of male experience as accounts that are gender-neutral. Texts about women's experiences—when they existed—have been read as minor revisions, works that merely add small pieces to the overall picture.

Rhetorical processes—like all social interactions—are deeply gendered. Speakers and listeners produce and respond to statements on the basis of deep but usually unnoticed understandings of gender. In general, women's right to speak (or write) authoritatively is attenuated and circumscribed. For a woman to do scholarly work means speaking in arenas not normally conceded to female speakers. When women are trained as sociologists, for example, they are trained to think and speak in the manner of the disciplinary tradition. They learn that, if they are to be heard, their texts must enter a discourse whose contours reflect male perceptions and concerns. The readers whose judgments are influential—the teachers, editors, reviewers, and colleagues who will incorporate and perhaps extend their work—have, in the past at least, mostly been men.

Women have opportunities to view the world from standpoints that are distinctively female. Of course, individual women in sociology do not all take up distinctive women's concerns and issues. Some attempt to position themselves as knowers outside of gender. But others—more and more as a community of feminist scholars has emerged—have embraced the position of marginality and have sought to give it fuller expression. These writers who address distinctive women's concerns face special problems of audience. They write as sociologists, building upon the insights of a sociological tradition and intending that their texts should become part of that tradition. Many of them, however, also intend that the inclusion of women's voices should transform the discipline. In order to enter the discourse, they must show how feminist concerns are instances of established sociological concerns, producing texts that fit into a sociological tradition. But if their texts fit too well they may subvert their own transformative project. These observations suggest several questions: To what extent is it possible to examine women's experiences in terms consistent with the established discourse of sociology? Through what rhetorical means do researchers who write about women "translate" so as to facilitate the entry of texts into a male-dominated discourse? How do the rhetorical conventions of social science influence readings of research reported by women?

The rhetorical analyses now under way in the social sciences typically adopt a method whereby recognized classics are examined in order to reveal elements of presentation and to specify how the language and style of the research report convey meaning. These studies examine rhetoric when it works smoothly and well; they bring to light the craft (presumably only partly conscious) that makes these works convincing and powerful. Indeed, it is hard to imagine another way to proceed, since rhetorically unsuccessful works are likely to disappear. But what makes a classic? In using terms such as *successful* or *unsuccessful* we take up a standpoint within an intellectual circle created and maintained by male scientists writing to and judged by their male colleagues. One might also ask on whose terms these works have been successful. With what kinds of readers have they succeeded? And perhaps most troubling, what can be said about works that might have spoken to those who have had no voices in the discourse? Presumably many of the documents we would like to examine have been lost or destroyed. And much of women's social theorizing has perhaps gone on elsewhere—in novels and poetry, or kitchen-table conversation, for example. Any search for a feminist tradition in sociology must begin cautiously, with skepticism toward the "data" that are available, but with confidence that suspicion arms us to understand more than is evident to more sanguine investigators.

For Example

In recent years, a community of active feminist scholars has begun to influence the conduct and reporting of sociology. Dale Spender (1982) suggests that this activity is not so unusual as we might think—that women have for many years produced distinctively feminist thought, and that women's writing has often been suppressed, sometimes in vicious, personal ways and sometimes through the routine practices of the intellectual world. I am concerned with routine practice and its implications for contemporary feminist research. In the discussion that follows, I will examine two recent books by sociologists who have written about women's experiences: *Men and Women of the Corporation* by Rosabeth Moss Kanter, and *The Mirror Dance* by Susan Krieger. Both are recent books (Kanter's was published in 1977, Krieger's in 1983), written by feminists whose concerns have been shaped by the women's movement and feminist scholarship. Both are case studies of groups, and both aim to illuminate continuing sociological concerns through the case-study method. Kanter, in *Men and Women of the Corporation,* examines the work lives of male and female employees (including executive wives) in a large firm. She is concerned with the relationship between organizational structure and behavior: she argues that in any organization, opportunity, power, and group composition shape the way individuals respond to their work situations. Krieger, in *The Mirror Dance,* examines the lives of women who participate in a loosely structured, primarily lesbian women's community in a midwestern town. She is concerned with the relationship between community and identity: she argues that in any community, similarity provides a basis for community but also makes it difficult for individuals to maintain their individual identities. Both studies are based on extensive involvement in the settings they describe, including interviewing and participant observation.

In spite of these similarities, my discussion will focus on differences in these authors' approaches to topic and method. While both authors frame their data in terms of continuing traditions of investigation, Kanter's topic is more amenable to placement in a predominantly male tradition. She does a thoroughgoing translation that makes "the women's issue" a special case of more general organizational concerns, and her rhetorical strategy draws on the social significance of the corporation, a traditionally male arena, to highlight the significance of her research. Krieger, concerned with the experiences of women in a relatively closed and largely invisible community, works with a topic that cannot be attached so easily to established traditions, and her presentation emphasizes the particularity of the group she studied. Although both studies are based on fieldwork, they are written with different assumptions about method as well. Kanter adopts the voice of authoritative sociology—a sociology of variables and theory that provides a single interpretation for the reader. Krieger aims to explore a new method for the presentation of field data, and she adopts an unconventional mode of presentation—one that emphasizes voice and pattern, and requires a kind of reading unfamiliar in sociology.

Kanter's book is widely known and read—well on its way to becoming a sociological "classic"—while Krieger's is less widely circulated and known. One temptation in this analysis will be to read Kanter's as the "successful" effort at placing women's concerns on the disciplinary agenda, but I want to resist this temptation and urge my readers to do so as well. My intent is not evaluative: I have learned much from both authors, and my aim is to provide a reading of these texts that will highlight possibilities and problems in sociological writing about women's lives. It is necessary to say, too, that there are many varieties of feminist research, and I do not mean to suggest that I have covered the field (see Reinharz forthcoming). I have chosen to discuss texts I know and admire, which I bring together here because they have provoked my thinking about writing sociology.

Constructions of Topic

Krieger's introduction to *The Mirror Dance* begins with a simple statement: "This book is about individual identity in a women's community." With this sentence, she has done two things: she has made a claim to speak about the general issue, "individual identity," but she has also revealed that she will discuss a women's community, and by the end of the first paragraph she specifies that this community is "composed primarily of lesbians." In the paragraphs that follow, she develops the idea of "loss of self," a problem in the women's community that seems related to its considerable intimacy and its separateness—to the point of stigmatization—from the rest of the town. Only after several pages of description quite specific to the women's community (and therefore built around the pronoun *she*) does Krieger return to a more general formulation of the issue of identity: "Now all social groups—communities, organizations, families—confront their members with this kind of conflict. In all groups there is a tension between the individual's desire to be part of a whole and the desire to be different"(xv). It is clear that Krieger believes the experiences of these lesbian women will be relevant to others; however, her attention is focused on the particular experiences of those she studied.

In the first chapter, where she sets the scene, Krieger repeats the rhetorical move that makes the community she will describe seem a special one, hidden from everyday view. She inverts the typical case-study introduction by beginning with a portrait of the ordinary and "representative" community, then moving on to a small, atypical part of that community. The chapter begins with four paragraphs that describe the town in terms that make it a kind of town the reader can imagine: "It was a medium-sized midwestern town. . . . It was a town in the middle of America. . . . It was a town where people had families. . . . It was a gray place beneath a gray sky" (3-4). The description gradually builds a picture of the very ordinary town. But with the fifth paragraph the reader learns that none of this is to be Krieger's topic. The topic will be something else that happens in this town, something that is not much seen, but that Krieger begins to show. Significantly, Krieger moves in this fifth paragraph from description of a place to a different kind of account that tells about things happening: "Once a month on a Friday night, a group of women would gather upstairs in a church not far from the center of town and meet and talk about what it was like to live here and to feel different—to feel part of a separate community" (4). The separateness of this "separate community" is highlighted by this shift in language, seven paragraphs of moving process that describe how people got to this community and what they did once there.

Krieger's introductory material emphasizes separateness and particularity. This is an ordinary town, and the problems to be discussed are similar to other general problems of identity, but this book will focus on specific identity problems, the specific problems that seem likely to arise in lesbian communities. The effects of such an introduction will probably depend on the reader: lesbians, members of a group not often heard in and for itself, are placed at the center of the text and know immediately that this text—unlike most—is about people who share their experiences; readers who are not lesbians are placed in something of an outsider's position, perhaps unsure about the extent to which the problems to be discussed will be similar to their own.

Kanter's introduction to *Men and Women of the Corporation* begins differently, with epigraphs from Karl Marx, Adam Smith, and Peter Drucker. With her own first words, Kanter reinforces the authority of these theorists: "The most distinguished advocate and the most distinguished critic of modern capitalism were in agreement on one essential point: the job makes the person." In several paragraphs that describe how she will examine this process, Kanter draws on the mystique of commerce and the weightiness of the modern corporation to emphasize the significance of her topic and the particular firm she studied: "If jobs 'create' people, then the corporation is the quintessential contemporary people-producer. . . . Indsco is a good place to visit, not only because it is among the biggest and most powerful of the multinationals that dominate American industry but also because it is socially conscious" (3). Kanter signals clearly her intent to deal with a site that is not only known to most readers but an important place, known because it is a significant location for the exercise of power.

Kanter's descriptive strategy in this introductory section is in one sense the opposite of Krieger's: she begins with the most generally applicable statement of her problem and only gradually develops its distinctive outlines for women. As she describes the modern corporation's work force she maintains a carefully gender-neutral language, even as she indicates that men and women are unevenly distributed among work categories. It is not until the eighteenth paragraph that she tells the reader that "the women's issue also appears as an important subtheme in this book" (8). Even in this paragraph, she is careful to maintain a basis for considering women's and men's experiences in similar ways: it is important, she argues, to consider the "roles, positions and constraints affecting women in the public arena, *as well as* the men who have traditionally peopled organizational research." And she adds, "The fate of women is inextricably bound up with organizational structure and processes *in the same way* that men's life-at-work is shaped by them" (8-9, italics mine). These italicized phrases, joining women's fates with men's, have two kinds of effects. One is to point toward Kanter's argument (which she sets out explicitly in her preface) against theories that posit "special" female characteristics. The other, I think, is to provide for those readers who are not women a path toward interpreting "the women's issue" as a problem anyone might have.

In Kanter's first scene-setting chapters, she continues to emphasize the relevance of her topic to all kinds of "ordinary people." In the first chapter, for example, she begins: "Every day a large proportion of all Americans don their figurative white collars and go to work in offices, where they take their stations in the administrative machines that run large organizations" (15). And she concludes the second chapter, a description of the corporation, by commenting that this particular firm is "neither a good nor a bad example . . . just ordinary people, reflecting the dilemmas created for them by the way they make their living" (43). What Kanter does very skillfully with such framing is to include readers of all kinds in the scope of her discussion.

Kanter is even more explicit about such bases for comparison and connection in the final chapters, which summarize the implications of her study. "Feminists and men in dead-end jobs," she suggests, "both have a stake in seeing that organizations change" (264). And in her final sentence, which urges efforts at reform in spite of imperfect knowledge, she extends the scope of her argument even further by explaining, "It is the people caught in such situations—and the people who cannot even find a job—women and men alike, that make me unwilling to wait" (287).

When Krieger summarizes in her concluding chapter, she argues, like Kanter, that the experiences of women she has written about are relevant to others as well: "[The women] speak of experiences particular to lesbians. At the same time, they inform us about problems we all face. Like the women of this study in relation to their group, we are all to some extent outsiders in the communities to which we belong. Yet we need our communities to take us in when we are uncomfortable and ambivalent as much as we need them to welcome us when we seem to fit in, when we merge and conform" (169). Here Krieger provides explicit instructions for readers who may be searching for a basis for comparing the dilemmas of these lesbian women to more typical dilemmas in the wider community. But once she has provided such instructions, she returns to the efforts of these particular women to build a community, and ends her book with a statement that honors those particular efforts: "There is perhaps no more worthy endeavor in social life than the struggle to build communities that might be truly accepting of their members. This study has recorded that in a midwestern town, in their own way, a small group of women attempted to create such a community" (169).

Both Kanter and Krieger present their case studies as researches that illuminate issues extending beyond the groups they studied. This kind of presentation is central to any piece of sociological writing, which must aim at attaching the text to a body of scholarship. But the differences I have discussed point to different possibilities for positioning texts that deal with women's experience. By making "the women's issue" an instance of the issues of organizational power and mobility that have long preoccupied men and male theorists, Kanter produces a text accessible to male as well as female readers, a text whose relevance to the concerns of men is clear. Throughout the text, she provides instructions for applying her findings to men's situations as well as women's, and her language facilitates such application. In Krieger's *Mirror Dance,* this kind of framing is much less prominent. Ultimately, her desire to speak about general issues of identity and community is overshadowed by another purpose: to provide a portrait of a particular community not often depicted sympathetically, from the "inside." She makes a text that points toward application to more general issues, but does so subtly, leaving the details of such application to the reader.

To make a feminist issue an instance of some traditionally male concern, as Kanter does, is effective in some ways, risky in others. It probably eases the entrance of a text into the discourse of a discipline still largely built on an agenda shaped by men. But it may also tend to submerge particularities of female experience—the particularity so necessary to Krieger's kind of text, and to the feminist project of making previously neglected experience more visible. Krieger's strategy

has characteristic strengths and risks as well. It provides a richly tex-
tured view of the lives of those she studied. But it may also tend to
construct a topic that can be dismissed by readers not already interested in this community.

Some feminist issues are undoubtedly more amenable than others
to placement on a traditional disciplinary agenda. The problems of
women in managerial positions that Kanter deals with, for example,
have emerged as more and more middle-class women have entered the
paid labor force and have begun to share the experiences of men. They
are problems of women (and some men) in a male world. By contrast,
the problems of identity described by Krieger are problems that *might*
emerge in any community, but that in fact are much discussed—that
emerge as "problems"—in lesbian communities more often and more
urgently than in most other communities. One can imagine other predominantly female experiences that might be even more difficult to
study in terms of conceptual frameworks shaped by male concerns. It
is possible, but probably misleading, for example, to study housework
as a form of work like paid labor, rape as merely another kind of vic-
timization, or pregnancy and childbirth as purely medical experiences.
Thus, even if some feminist concerns can be framed quite effectively
as instances of established topics, others will require a different sort
of rhetorical treatment.

Method and Interpretation

Both Kanter and Krieger work with case-study methods that
emerge from an established sociological tradition. Both speak about
personal involvements in the settings they have studied, and both describe some of the personal interests that have shaped their researches. Both provide methodological appendices setting out the
details of method that serve as warrant for their claims. Both reveal
as well some of the false starts and troubles of their investigations.
While they work with similar materials, however, Kanter and Krieger
use the building blocks of the case-study method to construct very different texts. Case studies have traditionally occupied a somewhat am-
biguous position relative to quantitative and interpretive branches of
the discipline: case studies can be pointed, theoretically, in either direction. The two books I am concerned with represent the opposing
impulses of case-study research. Kanter uses her field observations to
build theory, producing a text that controls interpretation, while
Krieger experiments with a method that displays patterns of voices,
and leaves much interpretive work to her readers. In this sense, the
texts represent two approaches to feminist research as well: Kanter

takes up feminist concerns within a well-established, authoritative methodological tradition, while Krieger works in the style of a developing critical tradition (associated strongly, though not exclusively, with feminism).

Krieger's text is avowedly "unusual," "clearly an experiment." She is present as author only in the introduction, where she develops a statement about the problems of merger and separation, in a first chapter where she describes the setting, and in the postscript, where she provides a brief summary. The body of the text is made up entirely of her respondents' accounts of community life and events. Krieger guides the reader into her text: as she ends the description of the setting, she begins to introduce the voices that will constitute the text: "The community seemed to offer a promise: 'Here are women who can understand me, touch me the way I want to be touched,' Melissa felt. At the same time it provided an experience which was disconcerting: 'In the process of all that happened, all that mutual discovery of pleasure within our community, I think I lost a sense of my own development separate from other people' " (6). In this paragraph Krieger uses quotation marks to present the voices of her respondents as evidence, framed by her own authorial voice. But with the next sentence, which begins the first substantive chapter, she leaves out the quotation marks, which would separate her own voice from those of others: "She saw several different lesbian communities in town, said Ruth, though she understood what people meant when they said 'the community' " (7). With this sentence, Krieger has invented a convention, inviting the reader to listen in and to experience the very merger and separation she means to examine.

Krieger's text proceeds by way of this convention. A chapter titled "The Web of Talk," for example, begins: "There was this hotline that went around all the time, that kept the community together, felt Shelah. People were always talking about each other. It was not necessarily malicious, said Chip, but it was what traditionally was known as gossip. Things just went like wildfire, Leah observed" (25). Some accounts are longer, providing stories about individuals and their relationships. Each chapter collects accounts about particular issues, events, or activities. The reader begins to recognize names and to connect individuals. The material that makes up this text is clearly talk, and the reader with sociological training sees that much if not all of it must have been produced in response to the kinds of questions Krieger has reported she asked in interviews. In spite of the absence of authorial voice, this material is talk that has been edited, sorted, collected, and combined in a variety of ways. Krieger argues in the introduction that her text's "analysis emerges through its ordering" (xvi). She indicates that the text is "composed of an interplay of voices that echo, again and again, themes of self and community, sameness and difference, merger and separation, loss and change" (xvii). The voices she presents "analyze and comment upon one another and guide the reader to an appreciation of the conflicts surrounding identity in the community" (xvii).

Kanter's text follows more conventional prescriptions for sociological writing. She includes examples and talk, but she subordinates these to her own voice, telling the reader in abstract language how to understand each piece of evidence. The core chapters of her book are organized around key processes that become the variables in her theoretical model: opportunity, power, and numbers. She comments in a concluding chapter that although she has discussed responses to particular situations in a specific organization, her intention has been to find "overarching dimensions of the person-organization relationship" (245), and her rhetorical move is always to use the specific as an element in more general description. Kanter's concluding chapters, then, in a section of the book titled "Understanding and Action," represent her arrival at a coherent theoretical statement. Her introduction to this section suggests that the reader should appreciate the distance between observation and theory, and the analytical work through which she has imposed order on unruly realities:

> As I pulled together and looked for meaning in information from varied sources (objectified survey questions, official company forms, formal interviews, group meetings, and idle comments made in passing in casual conversations), I identified three variables as central explanatory dimensions: the structure of opportunity, the structure of power, and the proportional distribution of people of different kinds (the social composition of peer clusters). These variables contain the roots of an integrated structural model of human behavior in organizations, one that builds on but enlarges other frameworks, one that can point out dilemmas and guide change efforts. (245–246)

She encourages the reader, too, to understand the particular bits of information presented in the book in terms of these three major variables and no others. She goes on to list general hypotheses related to each variable that can be derived from her study, and then to comment in some detail on how her observations complement and extend several influential schools of thought on organizational processes. In many ways, Kanter interprets more completely for her reader than Krieger does in *The Mirror Dance*. While Krieger allows the voices of her respondents to simply "comment upon one another," Kanter's own authoritative voice is the controlling one in her text.

Krieger's text also leads to a conclusion, but a conclusion of a somewhat different sort. After two sections dealing with the dilemmas and conflicts of insiders in the community, a third section considers contacts with "the outside world" and circles back through respondents' comments to a sense of the integrity of the community and the protection and privacy it provides. Krieger, however, is a more cautious interpreter than Kanter. Her summary indicates the tone of her presentation: "As the previous chapters indicate, the web of personal entanglements in which identity is formed in this lesbian community, or in any community, is exceedingly complex. *The Mirror Dance* has attempted not to simplify that complexity, as social science ordinarily does, but rather to present it in something like its original form by depicting the community through the voices of its members" (169).

Krieger's text is both permissive and demanding; it allows readers to participate in constructing its meaning, and therefore requires careful attention and a kind of active reading. In her introduction, Krieger calls for a specific approach to reading: the text, she says, provides one interpretation but is also "open to other interpretations. It invites the reader to join, to take part, to overhear the gossip of women in one particular subcommunity . . . to muddle through their difficulties with them" (xvii). Where Kanter boasts of movement from the confusion of raw data to orderly theory, Krieger embraces the complexity of "gossip"; where Kanter speaks authoritatively, Krieger invites the reader to "muddle" along. Most readers of this chapter will probably have learned from professional training and the wider culture to read these descriptions evaluatively: speaking with authority is admirable, "muddling" a bit *outré*. Krieger practices a mode of presentation that may be unusual, but is disciplined nonetheless. Her account is "not intended to be objective; nor is it arbitrary." Instead of a set of hypotheses, she presents a "structured representation of a particular problem . . . in a particular setting" (xviii).

Krieger's text represents one approach to a method self-consciously different from conventional sociological representations. It can be seen as part of a developing tradition of fieldwork that emphasizes the representation of individual "voice." While this tradition is not exclusively feminist, the emphasis on voice has been central to much writing about women. Many feminist researchers aim at providing speech for women who have been left out of discourses, assuming the validity of each woman's experience and then subjecting it to analysis as women did in early feminist consciousness-raising groups. Learning from the tradition of oral history, and increasingly from experiments in anthropological writing, researchers in this tradition are cautious about defining the experiences of those they study, and search for unobtrusive ways to represent different realities. Often, they draw techniques from other disciplines, as Krieger draws from her understanding of fictional representation. *The Mirror Dance,* an experiment within this budding tradition, is interesting for its form as well as its substance. But like any text, it calls for a reader prepared to understand the aims and assumptions of its tradition.

The rhetorical strategies of these two authors call for very different kinds of reading. Kanter, in *Men and Women of the Corporation,* tells her reader explicitly how to interpret the evidence she presents and what to conclude from it. She draws out the implications of her findings in relation to other theoretical frames. She makes suggestions for action. The text is designed to lead to a single conclusion. This kind of presentation, conventional for social scientists, calls for a skeptical reader, one who either finds a basis on which to differ with Kanter's analysis or is compelled to accept it. The active work of reading, in this model, is critical work, aimed at possible flaws in the analysis. Krieger's text is quite different. Though it is "built on" her interpretation of her interviews, it is "open to other interpretations." It presents complexity without telling the reader how to sort through it. It refrains from spelling out theoretical implications. This kind of text calls for a devoted reader who will work at appreciating the patterns Krieger has displayed in the text. In this model, processes such as comparison, synthesis, and extension are central to the activity of reading. Most sociologists are taught to do "critical" rather than "devoted" reading. A text such as *The Mirror Dance* seems awkward and difficult at first. It does not supply an explicit argument, easily transported into a reader's own texts. Its innovative strategy brings with it the risks of dismissal by readers unwilling to read in a new way.

Writers and Audiences

Feminist texts have developed with the emergence of a feminist audience. That audience overlaps with a larger sociological community. Authors with feminist aims must position their texts with respect to these two audiences. Some aim more clearly toward sociological legitimacy, some toward a specifically or exclusively feminist readership. Many attempt to speak to both circles, on the reasonable assumption that feminists and other sociologists have much to learn from one another. Both of the issues I have considered in this chapter concern relations between rhetoric and audience. The question of topic is a question about who will be interested in a text. Writers construct topics with audiences in mind; feminist writers must make decisions about their overlapping but different constituencies. The question of method and how it is portrayed is a question of authority and its sources. Some feminists wish not to monopolize authority but to share interpretive power with their readers. They must experiment with new forms, for which audiences are only beginning to develop.

Judgment resides with the audiences for texts. Writers with dual allegiances, who write for two kinds of audiences, are often judged wanting by one or the other. Dominant groups, of course, have the power to make judgments stick. There is evidence, for example, that women (Showalter 1977) and black novelists (McDowell 1986) who are part of distinctive traditions have been considered inferior in relation to dominant traditions of their times. Their distinctive forms and languages are too often seen only in terms of more widely accepted literary conventions. Rhetorical studies of scientific texts reveal that evaluative processes in these apparently objective disciplines also depend on the form and style of texts. And in sociology, as in literature, distinctively feminist traditions may be suppressed through routine evaluative practices. *Men and Women of the Corporation* is easily recognized as an important work, and on its way to becoming a sociological "classic." The fate of *The Mirror Dance* is less certain, though my hope is that sociologists will make room for such texts. An audience for both feminist and experimental texts in sociology does seem to be developing. My aim has been to highlight the importance of innovative texts and to urge that as we continue to experiment with feminist writing, we attend as well to the interpretive and evaluative processes that surround and support new texts.

ALBERT HUNTER
Setting the Scene, Sampling, and Synecdoche

The Question

WE HAVE ALL READ, skimmed, or noted in passing descriptions of settings in a research report. Such descriptions are usually found near the beginning of a report sandwiched between an initial statement of the problem and the analysis that follows. They also often include a description of the research methods used in the study of the setting. These seemingly necessary, routinized, and too often boring genuflections to scientific canons are, however, substantively significant symbolic rituals of social science. In this chapter I will look at these "commonplaces" for both their scientific substance and their symbolic significance. As suggested by John Donne's epigram at the beginning of this book, these mere descriptions are very important both for understanding and for believing the research. The questions I address center on the symbolic role these descriptions play in scientific discourse. More simply, I ask, "Why do we continue to write and to read them?" Answering this question from a rhetorical perspective allows us to combine the scientific and symbolic perspective, and to further explore the relationship between understanding and believing.

The "data"—the texts I will use as grounded examples—come from my interest in community research, and I have selected a few well-known community case studies as exemplars. The analysis could be extended as well to other examples and to other types of case studies—of organizations, small groups, social movements, and the like—and also to other types of research reports in which such descriptions are found. A more complete empirical analysis might profitably explore the different degrees and types of such "descriptions" normally provided in different styles or methods of research—that is, field versus survey or experimental research. For the moment, however, we will focus on the qualitative case study based on field research.

The first questions posed in the analysis of these "introductions" emphasizes a dramaturgial metaphor of "setting the scene." Specifically, I look at how author-analysts describe the scene, and most important for subsequent credibility, how they position themselves in it, their point of view. Rhetorically we are concerned with how they position themselves in the tripartite social relationships existing among themselves and the subjects and the readers of the research. The second set of questions look at how these introductory descriptions are used to locate the given case under study relative to a larger universe of similar cases. Here we address issues of validity and credibility that deal with sampling and the generalizability of the research. Two often-used strategies are comparing the case to an archetype, or positioning the case in a population matrix of similar cases. The third set of questions explore how introductory descriptions are used to make generalizations or inferences not to a population of like units or similar cases, but to a larger whole of which the case is a part. This linkage across scales or levels of analysis is both metaphorical and functional, and I label this synecdoche.

Setting the Scene

Setting the scene of a case study is like presenting in words the first impression one gets when entering a theater, what one senses in that momentary pause of actors posed on the stage as the curtain rises and before the action begins. One has come to see a play, actors in action, and one is first confronted with a static physical stage. One senses that things have not yet started, not until the first actor appears moving and talking on the stage. But the stage itself is full of meaning and significance. It is a physical embodiment, a residue of others' actions—playwright, stage designer, carpenters, and painters, among others (Becker 1982). These actions communicate conventionalized meanings, such as indoor or outdoor, historical period, or a season of the year. The conventionalized meanings or preconceptions place the action in a shared symbolic space, but only to the degree that they are in fact shared by artist and audience. And though the physical stage is to some degree conventionally understandable, the full significance and meaning of a given door, window, or prop may only become apparent as the action unfolds and gives it meaning. Such conventions, in short, fix, locate, or delimit in time and space the action that will follow; and reflexively, the setting gives meaning to the action just as the action gives meaning to the setting. The more contemporary use of "minimalist" or "abstract" stage settings communicates a spatial and temporal "anywhereness" and "timelessness" that is a major claim of universalism or generalizability for the action that ensues. The metaphor of the drama is, of course, explicitly and widely used in sociological theory (Goffman 1959). For example, Becker et al. (1961) write of students' socialization in medical school: "As in other dramas learning the lines is not enough" (4); and Kanter's (1977) title for Part 1 of her study is simply "The Players and the Stage" (13).

Just as conventions or assumed mutual knowledge are utilized in setting the stage of a play in order for the audience to be able to make sense of the author's intentions and the actors' actions, so scene setting in social science research is based on a set of assumptions about the relationships among author, actors, and audience. In social science research reports these identities are more appropriately labeled researcher, subjects, and professional colleagues; while in rhetorical analysis of fictional writing they would be author, character, and reader (Booth 1961). In social science the type and the amount of description given a setting are related to the different types of social relationships that are involved in different types of research methods. The description of the research methods themselves may be thought of as an explication of the nature of these tripartite social relationships. In short, the discussion of methods involves fixing clearly the social relationships that exist among the three, while the research report itself is an extended expression of the rhetorical relationships existing among them. The description of the setting is a statement of how the researcher came to view and know the setting and how the reader should view it. It is here that the metaphor of a traveler or stranger is often invoked to communicate an outsider's first impressions:

A stranger unfamiliar with the ways of Middletown, dropped down into the city, as was the field staff in January, 1924, would be a lonely person. (Lynd 1929, 21)

Yankee City is situated on a harbor at the mouth of a larger river in New England. The pilot of an airplane looking down some 10,000 feet might see the harbor as the dark hand of a giant with its five fingers reaching for the sea. (Warner 1963, 1)

To the average Bostonian, the West End was one of the three slum areas that surrounded the city's central business district. . . . He rarely entered the West End and usually glimpsed it only from the highways or elevated train lines that enveloped it. (Gans 1982, 3)

I came to Buffalo Creek a stranger, by which I mean not only that I was unacquainted with the people and their ways but also that I was a truly strange person from every point of view that made sense in their world. (Erikson 1976, 16)

Most descriptions of settings begin with the most boring of details, which while reading (if one does so at all) one is likely to mumble and nod passively while rapidly turning the pages. In community studies such things as geography, climate, and size are usually followed by a list of census variables. This is especially likely when the community is small and assumed to be little known, or when it is referred to by a pseudonym (Middletown, Springdale, Regional City, or Oneville, Two- ville, Threeville). The use of a pseudonym, most often for ethical rea- sons (confidentiality), is a device that immediately places the author and reader in a distanced relationship where the reader must accept not just the validity of the analysis, but in scientific cannons must accept that the case does in fact exist. (Remember the infamous "Re- port from Iron Mountain.") The pseudonymous case also thwarts the scientific canon of direct replication of the research. This distancing from the reader is simultaneously expressing the author's close rela- tionship to the subjects and a concern with their welfare. If a case is named and presumably widely known, few authors give excessive de- tail (either contemporary or historical)—for example, case studies in New York City, Chicago, or San Francisco. Therefore, the amount of the description given is inversely related to the assumed prior knowl- edge shared between author and reader.

After presenting an "outsider's" view, or first impressions, research- ers then usually describe how they got to know the scene, or better, get behind these superficial scenes. That is, the researcher presents a description of methods that focuses in large part upon the social rela- tionships of the researcher to the subjects under study. At this point the researcher is often simultaneously doing three things: presenting a description of the nature and amount of social contact with subjects, establishing the degree of empathy to the subjects (positive or nega- tive), and establishing the "voice" that will be used in presenting the report. To be believed, and not just understood, the researcher at- tempts to communicate simultaneously an objective distance to the subjects (read alternatively, a closer tie to professional colleagues) and a social and emotional closeness to the subjects that convinces the reader one really did get behind the scenes.

In establishing "voice," researchers, like modern "scientific" novel- ists (Booth 1961), often attempt to remain as "transparent" as possible. This is especially the case in the analysis proper, where one is likely to find a wide use of the passive voice. But in prefaces and appendices used in setting the scene of the research itself (not just setting the scene of the research site), researchers usually make themselves quite visible as personal actors on the scene. An example that is pictorial

rather than rhetorical is the photograph in *The Urban Villagers* of
Herbert Gans sitting around a dinner table with an Italian family.

> I lived in the West End from October, 1957, to May, 1958 . . . I wanted
> to know what what a slum was like, and how it felt to live in one.   (Gans
> 1982, xiii)
>
> In early 1973 I was approached by the law firm Arnold and Porter
> and was asked whether I might suggest the name of a sociologist who
> could spend some time in West Virginia and survey the situation at
> first hand. We decided that I should make a brief visit to Buffalo
> Creek myself. . . . I came back from that visit so awed and depressed
> by what I had seen that I volunteered my own services to the firm . . .
> I mention all of this because I benefitted from a courtesy that comes
> naturally to the mountains but not in the flatter terrains where I have
> lived most of my life. I would like to convey somehow that the gift of
> being treated with a degree of trust I had not yet earned meant a
> great deal to me personally and contributed enormously to this
> study.   (Erikson 1976, 10–11)

Expressions of trust, acceptance, and empathy in the case study are
all indicators or claims for the validity of observations. Becker even
suggests that the criterion of "deviance" practiced by participants may
be used as a convincing indicator of getting behind the scenes: "Students readily accepted our explanation that we were there to gather
material for a book on medical education. The best evidence that our
presence did not noticeably alter their behavior lies in the fact that
they were willing to engage in behavior the faculty disapproved of
while in our presence" (Becker et al. 1961, 26).

Though presenting oneself as an empathetic participant in order to
heighten the reader's belief in the researcher's understanding of the
setting, the researcher also tries to communicate a transparency to the
reader, to act as a neutral conduit or linkage between the subjects and
the readers. For example, Erikson writes for several paragraphs about
the use of first-person "words" from subjects gained from legal deposi-
tions and his own interviews:

> Much of what follows is theoretical of course since that is part of what
> a sociologist can contribute to human understanding, but I have tried
> to let the theory fall between the natural segments of the story rather
> than making it the main theme. . . . the report itself relies heavily on
> words spoken by the survivors of the Buffalo Creek disaster. . . . For
> the record, then: the words represented in this book as having been
> spoken (or occasionally written) by the people of Buffalo Creek are
> reproduced here in their original form . . . [and after thinking about
> "tidying up the grammar" he decides not to]. The language spoken on

Buffalo Creek is marvelously expressive and often quite beautiful. (Erikson 1976, 13, 15)

Chapter 2 is a tour through Indsco: Its offices and people, ranks and grades, history and culture, activities and rewards. Here the people begin to speak for themselves, as they do through the rest of the book. (Kanter 1977, 5)

In some ways my book is an instance of what David Riesman and Nathan Glazer have called the continuing conversation between the upper and the lower levels of our culture. . . . Thus, although I came to the West End from the upper level, I have tried to describe the way of life of lower level people as they might describe it themselves if they were sociologists. In a sense, then, I am reporting to the upper level for them. (Gans 1982, xiv)

Another critical positioning of the researcher in the rhetorical and scientific scene is the question of defining the audience for the research. Multiple rather than singular positionings are often involved, as there are often multiple audiences, though usually a dominant audience and positioning is apparent—namely, fellow sociologists. Most prefaces, introductions, and especially acknowledgments clearly indicate that the subjects themselves are also one of the audiences. Subjects may simultaneously be readers, reading about themselves, and most authors are, apparently, fully aware of this. (See William Foote Whyte's 1955 Appendix on Doc's and Chick's reactions to reading *Street Corner Society*.) This primary contact is perhaps one of the key ingredients in giving a humanistic tone to so many case studies, and also explains why other methods, such as survey research, with the long chain of social relationships and numerous data transformations interposed between researchers and subjects, take on a tone of more "scientific" distance and objectivity.

Some researchers also state directly or indirectly that they are writing in part to an audience that is broader than a narrow circle of fellow social scientists. Gans (1982) states directly: "I have tried to write this book as much for for the planners, caretakers, other policy makers, and the general public who influence them, as for my colleagues and for students of sociology. . . . Conversely, I have suppressed—somewhat—the desire to contribute to the theoretical discussions and arguments that go on inside sociology but that are of little interest to the nonsociological reader" (xiv).

Similarly, Erikson (1976) throughout his book indirectly defines a broader audience by positioning himself as an interpreter between fellow social scientists and this broader audience: "Now sociologists have given a good deal of elaborate thought to what the term 'community' does (or should) mean" (129). "It was once fashionable in the social sciences generally to compare human communities to living organisms" (193). And he further distances himself from fellow sociologsts by suggesting that the research was at once oriented to both narrower and broader nonsociological purposes: "I was not in a position to set the pace of this research because I had to be ready at a time of someone else's choosing to testify in a court action involving tens of millions of dollars . . . the event I was trying to understand seemed so much larger than the professional lens through which I was looking, and the traditional methods of sociology do not really equip one to study discrete moments in the flow of human experience" (12).

There are of course many other social and rhetorical relationships that could be analyzed in the model I have outlined. One of the more complex might be, for example, those involved in a case study of the sociology of science, where the affinities and ties between researcher as author, subject, reader, and colleague might be hopelessly intertwined. Limited as the above examples are, I hope they have indicated ways in which researchers set a scene in large part by positioning themselves in rhetorical and social relationships with subjects and readers. These positionings are critical in communicating to the reader not only an *understanding* of the analysis (a usual claim for the presence of such descriptions) but also the *credibility* of the analysis, why the reader should believe it is true. The next question to which we turn asks how the setting itself is positioned within a broader social and, especially, scientific context. For the case study, these questions center around the "typicality" of the case being studied, and the claims of generalizability that researchers may make for their analysis and conclusions. If the foregoing questions may be boiled down to the simple question of "What's what?" the following questions begin to address the simple but significant question: "So what?"

Sampling

Rarely do social scientists study a particular setting as an end unto itself. Rather, the scientific objective is to study the specific case in order to make some broader generalizations that will contribute to abstract theoretical knowledge about a broader class of phenomena. Two questions become particularly sensitive in the case study: how does this particular setting exemplify a more general class of phenomena? And related but different: to what degree is the particular setting representative of a larger population of similar units (communities, organizations, and the like)? The answers to these questions are also a traditional part of the scene setting in research reports. There are two primary ways that sociologists attempt to convince the reader that the specific case under study is essentially and empirically "representative." The first is the use of the archetype, a comparative point of reference that is an abstract, idealized essence of the phenomena (an "ideal type"). The second involves the use of an empirical matrix of population parameters in which the specific case may be located to give the reader an idea of where it "fits."

The Archetype: The Case Compared to an Ideal Type

In describing the setting the author is trying to establish a common ground with the reader; to say, in effect, this community is like others you have known and/or read about, or alternatively to suggest how it differs from those commonly assumed known communities. This seeking of a "commonplace" occurs at two levels, one disciplinarily in terms of the prevailing theory and research (hence the use of numerous citations to prior research) and the other is to the reader's more personal experience of similar settings. A still prevailing commonplace within community case studies assumes the form of an archetype, specifically, comparison to an idealized rural village. This is true at both the professional and personal levels. The prevalence of this archetype over several centuries in Western social thought is clearly in evidence in earlier community case studies such as Harvey Zorbaugh's *Gold Coast and the Slum* (1929), through Herbert Gans's *Urban Villagers* (1982), and Kai Erikson's *Everything in Its Path* (1976). Note that this archetype of community is applied in both urban and rural settings, and that it is even alluded to in survey studies of communal ties and urban networks such as those by Fischer (1982) and Wellman (1979). More recently historians have challenged the validity of this archetype (Bender 1978; Laslett 1965), but questioning the archetype's empirical validity misses its rhetorical value as a frame or commonplace defining a domain of research activity, including a set of shared concepts, questions, and hypotheses.

Some writers, such as George Hillery (1968), have attempted to codify the variables or dimensions of the "communal" archetype much as Max Weber did for "bureaucracy." This has given rise to definitional debates of "community" that the more empirically oriented find of questionable utility (see Hunter 1974 and 1976 for examples). The rhetorical value of the archetype, however, lies not in its historical veractiy nor in its conceptual precision, but in its discursive utility. As I have suggested elsewhere, one of its uses is to provide "a common

whetstone on which to sharpen the cutting edge of competing ideas."
The superseding use of the archetype is to provide an assumed common
understanding, the simple idea that people are talking about the same
"thing" without which discourse of any kind would be impossible. Numerous examples of the use of this archetype for comparative purposes
exist in the literature, and few differ from the early and succinct statement by Zorbaugh (1929): "The community, represented by the town
or peasant village where everyone knows everyone else clear down to
the ground, is gone" (16).

Placing It on the Map and in the Matrix

Earlier I suggested that the description of the setting may be used
to familiarize the reader with the specific case both academically in
relation to the professional literature and through an appeal to the
more personal experience of the reader. Both of these techniques are
comparative; the first refers to "known" studies, whereas the second
refers to widely assumed "known" places. Though placing the case on
the map is seemingly done simply to let the reader know what it is
like (described but unanalyzed), it is also done for the purpose of generalizing from the case. The unique case is seldom studied for the case
itself, but for the knowledge it will shed on a set of similar cases. This
larger set of cases, the population of cases, is, however, variably defined. It may be defined narrowly and in the extreme limited to the
unique setting under study (rare), or more broadly to include at the
other extreme universal aspects of human existence (much less rare).
Though one of these positionings, narrow or broad, may be clearly
claimed as the operating perspective of the author, slippage often occurs in either broadening or narrowing this initial positioning as one
proceeds through the analysis. For example, Erikson initially makes
a consciously narrow claim and an insightful reversal of the logic of
generalization: "The problem is that sociologists usually select the
scenes they study because those scenes shed light on some more general propositions in which they were interested beforehand. That is,
the particular case is selected in the hope that it will inform and give
support to a larger generalization. My assignment on Buffalo Creek,
however, was to sift through the store of available sociological knowledge to see what light it might shed on a single human event, and this,
clearly, reverses the normal order of social science research" (12). And
in the concluding chapter of the book he again consciously and almost
apologetically (to whom? the residents of Buffalo Creek?) broadens this
claim: "The second reason for studying an event like this, however, is

to consider the way it contributes to our understanding of the anatomy of disasters in general. . . . The second conclusion will reflect on the nature of disasters in general" (246–247).

In short, it is difficult for analysts not to claim the most they can get away with for the importance (read generalizability) of their study, and on the other hand when contradictions are anticipated or exist with other research, to retreat to a narrower specification of the limits and uniqueness of their case.

The matrix in which the case is placed is usually not a fully elaborated n-dimensional matrix, but a partial construction from a more selective and finite set of dimensions or variables. Also, rarely is the matrix actually displayed as such (for an exception, see Hunter and Fritz 1985), but it is usually not too difficult for a reader to construct one post hoc. The use of prior literature is usually most important in constructing this matrix. It is used first to define the variables or dimensions that are considered worthy of attention (of propositional and theoretical significance), and though by definition these will not be variable in the single case, the analysis will, as is often claimed, "shed light" on those propositions by giving the results that exist for one more value of the variable represented by the case under study. The second use of the literature is to fix the case comparatively with other cases, to show how it is similar to or different from them. And finally, the matrix may be constructed by referring to the population parameters of the universe to which generalizations will be made, and placing the given case within this matrix. I suspect (hypothesize) this more likely occurs when the analyst is making an argument for the case being "typical" or "average" in a statistical sense. Note, for example, the following "place settings" by Robert and Helen Lynd in *Middletown* and Becker et al. in *Boys in White:*

Middletown
A typical city, strictly speaking, does not exist, but the city studied was selected as having many features common to a wide group of communities. (3)

Boys in White
The curricula of medical schools are similar in length and content. (50)

All medical schools live in symbiosis with a general hospital and outpatient clinics. (50)

Medical   schools   are   nowadays   nearly   all   affiliated   with universities. . . . Like most, however, its [University of Kansas Medical School] autonomy is rather great. (50)

We have, thus far, noted some of the dimensions along which medical

schools vary. There are certain basic relationships that are common
to all schools. The intensity of the the problems arising from them
vary, but the problems themselves are to be found everywhere. We
believe that the kinds of behavior, the conflicts, the understandings
and misunderstandings we have observed in our school, are among
those to be found everywhere. (51)

We write in the conviction that the way in which these young men
develop their perspectives on the present and future is, in its essentials, like that in which other medical students develop theirs. (51)

In setting the scene the archetype and the matrix both come into
play. For one way of thinking of the archetype is as the idealized cell
within the crosscutting axes of an n-dimensional matrix. The archetype, however, seems to speak to a more abstract, universal, and timeless philosophical "essence," while the "typicality" of a case defined by
a matrix of empirically presented variables seems to speak to a more
scientifically defined empirical and variable "real world" ("essence"
versus "in its essentials").

The above refer to the use of "archetype" or "typical" place setting
as a means to convince the reader that the setting under study is therefore generalizable to other similar settings. Some cases are selected,
however, by much the same means, for directly opposite ends, namely,
to highlight the atypicality of the case—in short, deviant case analysis. Here, as well, the archetype and the data matrix are used, but to
show that the case under study is at some extreme from the idealized
cell of the archetype.

In *The Urban Villagers* note how Gans simultaneously expresses
both the atypicality and the typicality of his deviant case—that it is a
typical deviant case:

I wanted to study the way of life of a low-income population because
planners and caretakers act on the assumptiom that this way of life
is simply a deviant form of the dominant American middle-class
one. (xiv)

To the average Bostonian [not an Urban Villager], the West End was
one of the three slum areas that surrounded the city's central business
district (3)

In most American cities there are two major types of low-rent neigh-
borhoods: the areas of first or second settlement for urban migrants;
and the areas that attract the criminal, the mentally ill. . . . The former kind of area, typically, is one in which European immigrants—
and more recently Negro and Puerto Rican ones—try to adapt their
nonurban institutions and cultures to the urban milieu. Thus it may
be called an *urban village*. . . . In sociological terminology, these are
ideal types, and no existing neighborhood is a pure example of either. (4)

Setting the scene is also often a temporal act of placing the case in history. In such accounts the reader is, in a sense, let in on the construction of the scene, how it has been built over time to become the setting now observed. This is especially likely when the analysis itself is dynamically oriented to some aspect of social change and with some eye to predicting the future course of that change. The Lynds (1929), again, express it most succinctly: "It is a commonplace to say that an outstanding characteristic of the ways of living of any people at any given time is that they are in process of change. . . . In the face of such a situation it would be a serious defect to omit this developmental aspect from a study of contemporary life" (5). Similarly, Erikson (1976) leads into the entire Part 2 of his three-part study with the place-setting metaphor of a "map": "In this case, we need to locate the people of Buffalo Creek in the larger sweep of history and on the wider social and cultural map, and that process begins with a look at Appalachia" (48).

The process of setting the scene therefore involves much more than "mere description" of the setting and the research. It amounts to placing the setting of the research in a physical, temporal, theoretical, and empirical context. In doing this authors make claims and attempt to convince readers as to the representativeness and generalizability of the analysis that will follow. Authors draw upon shared knowledge, both "lay" and "professional," between themselves and readers. Such "positioning" is especially critical in the case study, where a "commonplace" criticism has always been the generalizability of the analysis. Though the analysis itself may, of course, be critiqued and evaluated as to its internal validity, the answer to the broader question of "So what?"—the external validity—relies much more upon this critical rhetorical and scientific positioning of the case under study (the sample) with the set of similar but unstudied cases (the population). In the next section we turn to a slightly different question, the use of the case study to generalize to larger wholes of which it is a part—the issue of synecdoche.

Synecdoche

Up to this point I have looked at scene setting as an attempt to address the issue of generalization of case studies by using a sampling perspective, asking to what degree one can generalize from this particular case to a larger set of similar cases. Synecdoche, the use of a part to stand for a whole, raises a slightly different issue, namely, the degree to which understanding the structure and processes of a smaller unit may shed light on a larger unit of which it is a part. Synecdoche is a type of metaphor used to understand some larger social unit by likening it to a smaller unit with which everyone is familiar. The "family" probably serves as one of the more common archetypes for such metaphorical comparison (for example, the family of nations).

Synecdoche, however, communicates more than a metaphorical comparison of a well-known smaller unit to a less well-understood larger unit, for it also suggests that the smaller unit is not just "like" but a faithful reproduction or reflection of the larger unit. Therefore, by studying the smaller unit one may understand the larger unit because critical components of the larger unit are reproduced or reflected in the smaller. In this sense the smaller unit is a "socioculus," not just "like" but a "smaller-scale version of" the larger unit. In this light I suggest that the Lynds studied Middletown not simply to understand life in similar towns but, rather, as cultural anthropologists they wanted to make more general statements about U.S. society and culture as a whole. For example, their opening sentence in chapter 1 states a clearly limited objective: "The aim of the field investigation recorded in the following pages was to study synchronously the interwoven trends that are the life of a small American city" (Lynd 1929, 3). However, by the opening sentence of the third paragraph on the same page they are suggesting a slightly broader objective: "Two major difficulties present themselves at the outset of such a total-situation study of a contemporary civilization." And in stating one of the criteria used as to why "Middletown" (Muncie, Indiana) itself was selected, they again allude to a purpose that is broader than simply understanding other similar communities: "that the city be as representative as possible of contemporary American life" (7). And the opening sentence of their conclusion repeats the same refrain: "A number of people, after hearing of the field investigation recorded in the preceding pages, have demanded, 'Well, what are your conclusions? Is American life growing better or worse?' " (496). In short, the Lynds are attempting to understand something about "life" or "civilization" in the United States by studying one small part of it . . . a single community.

Moving to a different domain, a similar assertion is made by Kanter (1977) in her study of a large U.S. corporation: "In short, many details of life and behavior inside Indsco reflect the culture, language, and style of mainstream American industry three-quarters of the way through the century" (7).

In synecdoche the ability to make assertions about the whole by studying a single part is not based only on the idea of metaphorical reflection but also on the idea that critical linkages exist between the two levels. These critical linkages are often reported in setting the scene of case studies because the linkages often contain the central propositions of the analysis. For example, in their historical introduction to *Middletown*, the Lynds describe its "industrial revolution" in the 1880s as a broader-based regional phenomenon: "Such modest ventures in manufacturing as the community exhibited were the tentative responses of small local capital to the thing that was happening to the whole Middle West" (13). And also a nationally linked phenomenon: "When the earlier boom was renewed in '91 it was engineered by the Eastern land syndicate and carried forward by the local boosters' association" (16). Of course the major national linkage attempted by the Lynds was their restudy, *Middletown in Transition* (1937), which explicitly looked at the effect of the national and worldwide depression of the thirties on the local life of Middletown.

Synecdochal reflections are not limited to assertions of structural parallels between the smaller unit and the whole—that is, mere "mirror images." Often the difference in "scale" itself is seen to be so great as to make such comparisons as different as that between appleseeds and a tree, or the proverbial tree and the forest. The dynamic relationships among parts, or "processes," however, are often asserted to be similar, since the processes of the whole are seen in some sense to be aggregations of the processes in the smaller unit (emergent processes); or conversely, the processes occurring in the whole are seen to be carried out within the smaller units (manifest processes). Whether these processes are viewed from the bottom up or the top down often depends on theoretical predilections and of how one merges one's data to one's theory.

To make the linkages of synecdoche between the part and the whole requires a model or theory of how they are interrelated, since the whole is alluded to, whereas the part is investigated. It is not unlike the paleontologist's need for theories of anatomy and physiology in order to reconstruct an entire animal from a fragment of a fossilized femur. In this sense the use of synecdoche in a case study is a claim that the case is not simply a *reflection* of the whole but a *functioning* part of the whole.

This part-whole relationship has been a central concern in the sociological study of community and is expressed in the continuing concern with the erosion, loss, or eclipse of community *(gemeinschaft)* by the more modern, larger-scale social organization of modern society *(gesellschaft)*. Case studies of specific local communities have often focused on the nature and the specific mechanisms of penetration into the local community of larger, external institutions (see Vidich and Bensman's 1960 study *Small Town In Mass Society*).

Another way of thinking of this linkage is the currently popular perspective of treating specific social units as "open systems." In recent years open-system models have been applied to the study of a number of substantive areas in addition to community—formal organizations, social movements, the family. These models suggest that issues and processes characteristic of the larger society penetrate into and are reproduced in the smaller-scale case. Alternatively, the larger units and processes emanate from and are made up of the aggregate interplay of these smaller units. The study of the smaller-scale single case, therefore, can shed light on these functional relationships to the larger society. Erikson (1976), for example, takes great pains to show how Buffalo Creek not only reflects but is directly linked to larger social and cultural units. Take, for example, his discussion of the rise of the modern welfare state:

> When we talked previously about the modern mountaineer, that numbed and dispirited creature shuffling off to welfare offices of one kind or another, we were talking about somebody who already suffers the effects of shock. And this revised portrait is not exclusive to Appalachia. It could serve as a reasonable likeness of people anywhere who seem to have lost out in the contest for status and a proportionate share of the land's wealth, so it should be no surprise if we sometimes catch fleeting glimpses in the portrait of the kinds of people who live in sharecroppers' cabins, on Indian reservations, in black ghettos, on skid rows, in immigrant quarters, or wherever it is that the victims make their homes. (132)

Similarly, Kanter (1977) throughout her book is concerned with the penetration and interlinkage of women's roles in the larger society to the internal structure and functioning of Indsco: "The women's issue also appears as an important sub-theme in this book. Why is the women's issue joined with examination of the effects of organization structure? ... First, no study of human behavior can any longer be considered complete that ignores the special roles, positions, and constraints affecting women in the public arena. ... At the same time the fate of women [in the larger society] is inextricably bound up with organizational structure and processes in the same way that men's life-at-work is shaped by them" (8–9).

And as a final example, Gans (1982) writes about the total destruction of the West End Italian "slum" by institutions of the larger society. After leveling the community, which seemed "strange" or "deviant," these institutions then erected a new community more in their own image: "The area I studied no longer exists. Declared a slum in 1953, it was torn down under the federal renewal program between 1958 and 1960, and its residents dispersed all over the metropolitan area. At this writing (January, 1962), the first residents of the new West End—a luxury apartment house complex—are just beginning to move in" (xiii).

In the case study the unique peculiarities of the given setting can always be noted, but these peculiarities are often portrayed as but slight variations on a more general theme. Yes, local conditions make every case unique, but the *same* structures and processes from the larger society (welfare), linked to and interacting with the locally unique, simultaneously produce slight variations of these parts within the same whole (the black ghetto, the Indian reservation, or an Appalachian hollow). This is generalization not by sampling but by synecdoche.

Fractal Geometry and Social Synecdoche

This model of synecdoche bears a striking resemblance (metaphorical or real?) to recent developments in mathematics, the geometric study of fractals and the Mandelbrot set (Mandelbrot 1983). Specifically, these complex geometric structures ("complex" in the lay and in the mathematical sense of comprising real and imaginary "complex numbers") are forms generated by the same processes (equations) being repeatedly applied to different scales of analysis. Applying the same process repeatedly at different scales results in a "cascade" (a term taken from initial studies of whorls within whorls generated in fluid turbulence). The geometric forms that develop at the different scales are generically like one another in appearance, a result called "scaling." The forms, in effect, reproduce themselves at different scales through a series of iterations of the same equation, but still show some "local" variations. As Mandelbrot defines it, "When each piece of a shape is geometrically similar to the whole, both the shape and the cascade that generate it are called *self-similar*" (34). Furthermore, depending on how one sets up the parameters of the generating equation (the cascade), these different forms may all be interconnected through the different scales of analysis or "observation." That is, the resulting shapes are directly linked parts of the same whole even though each "snapshot" at a given scale may at first appear to be a distinct, discrete, or closed structure. The small and the large, the micro and the macro, are functionally and physically interconnected.

Fractal geometry has been applied directly to the study of numerous physical natural phenomena ranging form the Brownian motion of small particles to the analysis of noise and error in communication channels, to the shapes of coastlines and snowflakes. What were previously considered deviant, irregular, and amorphous shapes in nature, at least compared to the ideal geometric shapes of Euclidian geometry such as circles, triangles and squares, are in fact seen to be the rule rather than the exception. As Mandelbrot observes, "Clouds are not spheres, mountains are not cones, coastlines are not circles, and bark is not smooth, nor does lightning travel in a straight line" (1). From these observations Mandelbrot developed his new geometry of nature to describe the "irregular and fragmented patterns" in the natural world that lay around us. The resulting geometry is not a simple mechanical modeling of "ideal types" where deviations in the data are simply taken as error that can be ignored. Pattern and irregularity are no longer antonyms. Again, Mandelbrot asserts that "the most useful fractals involves *chance* and both their regularities and their irregularities are statistical. Also, the shapes described here tend to be *scaling*, implying that the degree of their irregularity and/or fragmentation is identical at all scales" (1).

Now, these exciting mathematical developments may appear to be merely another hasty "metaphorical borrowing" when applied to social phenomena. Mandelbrot himself, however, has performed such an application in the analysis of price changes on stock and commodity exchanges (334–340). Specifically, he studied cotton markets at different time periods and different scales from daily to monthly data points. As he concludes, "One starts with the distribution of *daily* price changes over a period of five years of middling price variability. And one finds that if this distribution is extrapolated to *monthly* price changes, its graph goes right through the data from various recessions, depression, etc. It accounts for all the most extreme events of nearly a century in the history of an essential and most volatile commodity" (339).

The parallels between fractal geometry and the rhetorical use of synecdoche in setting the scene of social science research is no more metaphor than the use of any mathematical or statistical technique in the analysis of social data. Fractals and synecdoche are parallel developments that can aid us in moving from the often bland assertion that a given study and its setting should be "seen in context" to more directly studying the exact nature and operation of how it is the case and its context are connected. The need to link micro to macroanalyses within the social sciences may require an equally innovative language and creative borrowing of whatever metaphors we can find.

Conclusion

The scientific parallel to the everyday assertion that "the facts speak for themselves" is the idea that the quality of the analysis is what convinces the reader of the validity of the research. In this essay I have suggested, however, that the question of credibility is rhetorically established early on in the research report in the routine and ritualized "setting of the scene." Here author-researchers establish their positions with respect to the scene, the subjects, and the reader. Second, the setting itself must be convincingly positioned with respect to a wider class of natural phenomena in order for the research results to be believed as applying not only to the case in point but to a wider class of phenomena—in a word, generalized. The use of theoretical "archetypes" and empirical sampling frames or "matrices" are scene-setting techniques used to convince the reader of the strategic position of the particular case within a population of like phenomena. Finally, researchers reporting on a single case are also often involved in generalizing findings from the particular case to larger wholes of which it is a part—in short, synecdoche. Here direct linkages from parts to wholes, not mere reflections, are needed to establish the credibility of results and to legitimate the significance of the research beyond the case in point. I have likened this last type of analysis to recent developments in the fractal geometry of Mandelbrot sets, wherein the same processes or functions are iterated at different scales. The patterns observed at the different scales are functionally interconnected, show local variations, and yet are similar in their general form. I suggest that analysis and argument by synecdoche is, in short, an important tool for linking micro and macroanalyses and is analogous to a fractal geometry of society.

Above all, in this analysis, specific and limited though it may be, I have attempted to show by example the power of the rhetorical perspective in the general area of the sociology of knowledge. Such a perspective can provide a valuable corrective to a naive positivistic empiricism by bringing to the fore the fact that the scientific process and scientific products are socially constructed. But it goes beyond this simple but powerful assertion by providing a specific framework for critiquing, analyzing, and understanding the symbolic techniques by which scientists make their claims to truth. Such a perspective can contribute to a more careful and precise execution of empirical research, and also to a humble tempering of our limited claims to truth. As we have seen, the seemingly simple process by which we describe the research setting involves in fact a complicated set of assumptions and assertions about the social and symbolic world or research. Setting the scene has significant implications, therefore, for the credibility of theoretical generalizations we may wish to make for facts we claim to have found about a particular case in point.

LAWRENCE T. McGILL

Doing Science by the Numbers

The Role of Tables and Other Representational Conventions in Scientific Journal Articles

PEOPLE tend to think that what makes something scientific is the systematic and logical way information is gathered about some empirical phenomenon. But science equally involves the act of communicating this information to others. In order to communicate with another scientist, a scientific writer must adhere to the use of particular representational formats, highly specified schemes for conveying what has been observed. Put another way, a written text can't be taken by a reader to be scientific until it has conformed to the forms of science. This chapter illustrates how certain representational formats, such as statistical tables, come to be taken by readers as scientific, and how the use of standardized representational formats enables social scientists to develop specific strategies for reading scientific articles.

Issues in the Construction of Scientific Representations

Becker (1985) suggests that the transformation of privately held ideas (both scientific and nonscientific) into publicly available representations of those ideas involves four steps: selecting, translating, arranging, and ultimately interpreting those ideas. In scientific communities, the overarching consideration behind each of these representational issues is control over professional turf. Access to scientific circles is restricted, and knowing how to present oneself as a scientist, using standardized scientific representations, is a prerequisite for entry. One is constrained to adhere to certain norms for translating one's findings into the language of the profession. The world of possible vehicles for expression is limited strictly to those vessels that will hold water with other scientists.

One's identity as a scientist is inextricably bound up with one's ability to manipulate the forms of science and to appear in forums understood to be scientific (this is the *translation* step in Becker's model of representation construction). To use such forms and forums is to solidify one's claim to membership in the scientific community. To use other forms and forums may call into question one's label as a "scientist."

Numerical tables, in particular, turn out to be very useful vehicles for conveying information in a "scientific" fashion. Quite simply, this is because the key results of most scientific investigations are numbers. The appearance of numerical tables in a journal article conveys to the scientific reader a sense of proximity to the data collected by the author of the article. In accordance with the scientific norm of communism (Merton 1973), such a strategy appears to place the data gathered by one scientist into the hands of the entire community of scientists. In effect, the presence of tables reassures the reader that the author's conclusions are not simply made up—that the reader could replicate the analysis and come up with the same results. As one student remarked in an interview for this study, "When I see a table or graph in an article, it's like a white lab coat!"

Gusfield (1976) also points out that scientific reports are written so as to emphasize the centrality and determinative influence of method and to deemphasize the influence of the human agents who collected, organized, analyzed, and presented the data for other scientists to see. What better way to convey an impression of letting the data speak for themselves than by presenting them, lined up and ready for inspection, in tabular form.

As it turns out, though, most readers find it unnecessary to read the tables in order to be persuaded that the conclusions being advocated did in fact follow from the data. This is because most readers have, by and large, already accepted the implicit agreement struck between scientific author and scientific reader: "If you show me your data, I'll believe you're doing science." Displaying one's data in a table appears to hand control over interpretation of the data to the reader, a very generous rhetorical strategy. Whether the conclusions actually *do* follow from the data is a question many readers fail to pursue.

In general, when a scientific article conforms to standard representational formats, its mere appearance begins to communicate the message that the study was conducted "scientifically." When everything in an article appears as it should—that is, it appears in a prestigious journal, it bows to the appropriate literature, it describes the methods used to gather the data, it has tables, and so forth—readers may assume that everything is "business as usual" and simply go about getting whatever information they want from the article, without conscious concern for the rigor with which the research was conducted. That is, readers tend to *assume* scientific rigor as long as everything is presented the way it should be.

Much of what takes place at the stage of *selection* (the first step in Becker's model of representing information) also attempts to communicate the message that the author has conducted the study "scientifically." For example, if an article doesn't include references to the literature or if it omits a description of how the data were collected, it isn't likely to be taken as scientific.

Scientists concerned with publication in professional journals are also unlikely to take licenses with the proper *arrangement* of their findings (the third step in Becker's model). Since the scientific norm of universalism holds that the same evaluative yardstick must be held up to everyone claiming to be a scientist, it behooves authors to make it as easy as possible for readers to see that they have touched all the proper scientific bases. Readers tacitly judge the credentials of a study (as demonstrated later in this chapter) by the presence of sections dealing with methods, results, background literature, and so forth. If such sections do not appear where they are supposed to appear, readers must work harder to assure themselves that someone's study is in fact scientific. The harder readers must work, the less likely they are to read the study, and the more likely they are to suspect that someone is trying to put something over on them.

The scientific author must also anticipate how the audience will *interpret* the information presented in the article (the final step in Becker's model). The author must first assume that the audience will possess requisite literacy in the areas needed to decode the representation. Readers of scientific journal articles are assumed to be able to comprehend reasonably clear prose; to be able to extract information from tables, graphs, and charts; and to possess a graduate-level understanding of certain concepts central to the field of study. In general, the reader is assumed to be a person with essentially the same qualifications, competencies, and interests as the author.

While it may be reasonable to assume that one is writing for other scientists like oneself, the audience usually is not homogeneous, and interpretation is a process over which an author has only very limited control. But putting things into a scientific format does lead to the adoption of certain types of reading strategies among social scientists, as the rest of this chapter illustrates.

Toward a Model of Journal Reading:
An Empirical Study

To gather information on how social scientists read journal articles, I conducted interviews with ten graduate students and seven professors in the social sciences. The students were enrolled at the time in classes in which journal articles made up a part of their assigned reading. I asked them to comment in detail on how they read specific articles assigned in class. I asked the professors to tell me about how they read and use the information in social science journals in their work, and to comment on the strategies they use to write articles for publication in scientific journals.

Readers' "Normal Expectations" concerning Journal Articles

One of the most important factors affecting the reading of journal articles and tables is the standardized formatting of articles and tables. The Census Bureau's *Manual of Tabular Presentation,* for example, observes that "the role of style [that is, the use of a standard format] as an aid to the understanding of the data is frequently overlooked. By promoting uniformity in the treatment of many details, it builds up an attitude of 'normal expectation' on the part of the reader" (Jenkinson 1949).

In other words, standardizing the format of tables makes them less trouble for readers to interpret. Myers (1950) explains how tables are arranged so as to satisfy the needs of two basic types of readers:

> There are two kinds of readers: the one who runs and the one who stops and digs. The table must be suited to the needs of each. The table must be simple and clear cut; if it contains only data which will interest the reader at the moment, the reader is much more likely to read and remember than if the table contains seemingly extraneous material. The title must tell exactly what the data are, not how the reader ought to interpret them. The facts in the body of the table must be arranged in a logical order for the point being discussed. The most important facts should appear first, because they are more likely to be remembered clearly and also because the running reader may not get to the end of the table. (6)

Because tables are organized hierarchically, partial consumption of the table is encouraged, enabling different types of readers to get different things out of the same table (Gilmore 1984). In other words, readers can read for different levels of information in the table, ranging at one extreme from simply acknowledging that a table is in fact there on a certain page when it is referred to in the text, to performing elaborate statistical calculations on a series of numbers embedded deep within the rows and columns of the table. In between lie such activities as reading the descriptive title of a table, looking at row and column headings, checking for p or r values, or making quick comparisons of numbers within and across columns or rows.

As the statements of both professors and graduate students make clear, the standard division of journal articles into abstract, introduction, methods, results, discussion, conclusion, references, and tables also encourages partial consumption of the entire article. The bottom line is that when representations of information are standardized, readers can develop standard ways of reading them, including standard shortcuts as well.

The standardization of scientific journal articles affects the reading of scientific articles in at least three ways: (1) it minimizes the time and effort readers must spend in reading articles; (2) it enhances readers' ability to discern whether an article is relevant to their interests; and (3) it allows readers to discriminate among articles according to their level of statistical knowledge and according to their ideological position concerning so-called qualitative and quantitative representations of information. I will talk about each of these in turn.

Minimization of Time and Effort

A common attitude taken by both professors and students is: "I try to get through articles as fast as I can." Virtually all of the strategies they use in reading journal articles aim at paring down the amount of information to be taken in.

The professors said they first do a great deal of "flipping" back and forth through journal articles, looking for clues in the articles as to whether closer attention is warranted. Some readers look at the first few pages of each article fairly carefully, and then quickly leaf through the rest of the article to see if anything catches their eye. If an abstract appears on the first page of an article, it will usually receive careful consideration. Occasionally, a reader comes across a journal that does not provide abstracts. This shortcoming is enough to provoke a sense of "irritation" in at least one professor.

One of the statisticians in the sample goes straight to the book review section of the statistical journals he reads because "they're the easiest things to read" in the whole journal. He also carefully peruses the comments sections that typically follow each article, not (as I first thought) for purposes of formulating a critical point of view from which to read the article, but simply to figure out what the article is about!

"What goes into this journal is really pretty arcane stuff! I'm just try-ing to get a handle on what the article will be about, what body of literature it relates to, and so on." In other words, it becomes more efficient to read what others (who have presumably already slogged through the article) say about it than to read the article itself.

Since readers are usually in a hurry to get the reading behind them, section headings are greatly appreciated.

> I pay a lot of attention to the typographical design of an article, the headings, subheadings, and so forth, using the information in them to determine what I'm going to read. The reader's decision is about what to read, where to start. I use the headings to decide this. . . . Assuming I get past the abstract, I decide whether I'm interested in the method-ology or the conclusions. Of course, I've already got a pretty good idea of what's in the conclusions from the abstract. So, I'll usually go to the discussion, and from there decide whether to spend time with the methods or not. These are all decision points: the abstract, the discus-sion, and so forth.

The students also focused on specific sections of articles so as to max-imize reading efficiency. Most students read abstracts and introduc-tions and pay close attention to discussion sections. Their motives for going through articles this way are different from those of professors, however. As one student suggested, this strategy is instrumental in getting by in classes: "I read the discussion first and then just glance at the statistics; the professor wants us to get the conclusions not the statistics."

The methods and results sections tend to get neglected by students. As one student explained: "The methods and results section is always difficult to read because it is written in a style that indicates it was written because it *had* to be."

In addition, virtually all of the students skimmed over the tables without focusing on them. One student said that, at best, he might read the description of a table and then look at it "globally" to see if it tended to matched up with the description.

The explanations students give about why they read (or don't read) tables further illustrate the importance of saving time. For example, those who tended to be familiar with the kind of tables used in the article said they skimmed the table quickly because of that familiar-ity. Those who were relatively unfamiliar with the kind of table being used said they skimmed the table quickly because they felt that the return on an investment of their time in reading the table would be low.

In other words, the students' orientation toward reading these articles is that they must "get through" them in order to meet the requirements of their classes. These students take pains to avoid the dross, that material extraneous to "the point" the article is trying to get across. Statistical tables, descriptions of methodology, and results are thought of as canned procedures appearing in virtually every research article (that is, these are the sections that read as though they were "written because they *had* to be"). Their purposes are known and understood, and students pay attention to them only if given a good reason to. This brings us to the second aspect of how articles are read: the use to which an article is to be put by the reader.

Anticipated Use of Articles

One student gave an example of a good reason for reading the tables closely when he explained: "Unless I'm reporting on an article, I scan quickly over tables. I would never catch a mistake!" It turns out that the only student who dwelt on the tables for any length of time, making a serious attempt to interpret them, was in fact responsible for preparing an oral presentation of the same article to his class. He further indicated that he thought the article itself was poor, and that he probably never would have read either the text or the tables had he simply come across the article on his own.

Similar results hold for the professors. One professor explained that he reads the conclusions of articles first because it is the surest way of checking out whether or not the article will be relevant to his current projects. "If it provides additional evidence [for my own arguments], or if it dramatically contradicts something I believe, then I'll continue to [read]. If it doesn't do either of those things, I probably don't get any further."

Numeracy and Attitudes toward Quantitative Representations

Beyond considerations of time and effort, whether readers are quantiphiles or quantiphobes may affect the way they read journal articles. Both the graduate students and the professors interviewed in the study can be divided into subgroups that tend to be either qualitatively or quantitatively oriented in their styles of research. But no one in these groups indicated that they avoid reading articles that are quantitatively oriented.

Only one student and one professor claimed to lack the knowledge necessary to adequately interpret the numbers in tables. The professor, who admitted to having never used a table in any of his own writings, laughingly suggested, "I thought that being a philosopher was supposed to make me exempt from these detail things!" The rest of the participants, though tending to fall into either qualitative or quantitative camps, were all numerate. In other words, any avoidance of tables in journal articles by these readers cannot simply be attributed to lack of knowledgeability.

Among the graduate students, all but one agreed that "the use of quantitative techniques adds to the precision of scientific work." In addition, all of them disagreed that "in the field I'm going into, the use of quantitative techniques is not important." Not surprisingly, then, all but two felt that the tables in the articles I examined with them were integral to the article and irreplaceable.

Two students, though, felt that the tables were largely unnecessary. One said that the tables were "silly" unless you wanted to replicate the data, but she did say that the tables helped to organize the data for the reader. The other student said that the tables were "distracting."

The professors were asked to speak at length about the place of tables in scientific articles, and of the relationship between qualitative and quantitative representations of information. Four of the professors are basically qualitative in their orientation (that is, they mostly read journal articles without tables in them), whereas three are self-described statisticians (who mostly read articles that include tables).

Not surprisingly, the qualitatively oriented professors take the dimmest views of quantitative approaches to research and data presentation. Two of these professors are educational psychologists who feel that quantitative work is inordinately valued in their field.

> In the psychology department, I think there's a certain madness that seizes psychologists: the worship of quantitative representations. Things like: you *have* to include tables in your dissertation. There's an implied equivalence between the scientific and the tabular. . . . Concerning quantitative pieces, I think too often we impute value to data sets that they just don't possess. The data don't interpret themselves; there's no intrinsic interpretation to be gotten straight from the numbers. We always impose a valuation of some kind of our own upon the data.

The other educational psychologist, in response to the question "Does quantification add to the precision or value of scientific work?" replied, "The use of quantitative techniques makes for precision, yes, and triviality. I think there's actually a kind of pseudo-precision we can talk about. Quantification oversimplifies; it loses sight of much that is important."

The other two qualitatively oriented professors are music educators. In glancing through some of the music education journals one of them reads regularly, I found them liberally laced with tables, graphs, and diagrams. I remarked to him, "In looking through these, one really can't help but be hit in the face by all the graphs and tables, and so forth." He replied, "Yeah, but it's really kind of dangerous, I think. Some of these people, I think, just stick in numbers and feel that makes something research."

The other music educator also takes the position that the field of educational psychology, and music education research in particular,

> has to get out of this scientistic mode of "numbers as equivalent to knowing." . . . I resist the mindless, scientistic, sheer number-crunching that goes on in so much of research. You know, putting in tests of significance as if they were really meaningful. Numbers by themselves are *not* meaningful. . . . The field [of music education research] is really pretty much dominated by statisticians; the studies that come out are largely correlation studies between different variables. You know, these are all people who believe that scientific work *consists of* statistical work.
>
> Statistical work is precise for what it does, but it's also imprecise for what it doesn't do. It would be meaningless in most cases to go out and collect statistical data on qualitative, subjective, or normative matters. Statistics are a very crude tool for this sort of thing. Each type of research does what it does. Each adds a dimension to our understanding of things.

Like the position taken at the end of this quote, the more quantitatively oriented professors tend to take a more equivocal position on the two types of research. They tend to emphasize the interdependence and inseparability of qualitative and quantitative research issues. I asked one of them, "What proportion of the material you read is qualitative and what proportion is quantitative, or is that a fair kind of distinction to make?" His reply:

> I agree with you that that's not really a fair distinction. All the quantitative stuff I deal with is generated because qualitative story lines are developed. Subjective judgments are always made in advance of quantitative data collection. And the qualitative stuff I read has implicit in it some sort of quantitative measure, although this is rarely admitted. For example, you could have a report that says "most women in this program went through in less than six weeks; a more or less typical woman in the program experiences such and such." As soon as you mention the word "typical," that means something to me as a statistician. It means a modal type or a stereotype. That can be quantified.

The second of the statisticians states the case for quantification even more strongly. I asked him, "Would you say that quantification adds to the precision or value of scientific work?"

It's essential. How can you describe anything empirically without quantification? How can you describe that you went about the process of investigating your phenomenon in a sound way without quantification? Quantification is necessary to describe what you've done so others can understand what you've done. You can *generalize* without quantification. But even in qualitative work, you can't avoid the use of numbers.

[To the question "Can you give me an example?":] Well, like in sample survey organizations, you have to say that you completed interviews in x percent of the cases, for example. . . . It's very hard to make a good argument without numbers. The alternatives are either anecdotes or gross generalities, which you have to hope that your audience just won't penetrate!

The third statistician claims that the distinction made between qualitative and quantitative types of work is "a straw man, an unfortunate dichotomy."

Now, I'll give you an example of why I say that. Look at *Boys in White* [Becker et al. 1961], certainly something that's highly respected as an exemplar of good qualitative work. But you and I both know that it's full of quantitative concerns—it's full of counts of this and that kind of behavior. What makes that book worth reading is that its conclusions and interpretations are grounded in solid data. Now, I can disagree with the quality of the data, the way it was measured, the characteristics of the design, the sharpness of the hypotheses, and so on, but at least the data were there, so that I could see where the interpretations were coming from. . . . The most far-reaching philosophical works, I would say, transcend this dichotomy. What this dichotomy does is to restrict the people who use this distinction to being pretty sophomoric about what research is.

Four Types of Scientific Journal Readers

As a result of this range of ideological stances concerning the quantitative representation of information, there seem to be at least four types of journal readers in the social sciences (further differentiating the two types, "runners" and "diggers," mentioned above), each with their own distinct approaches to the reading of tables. These types of readers might be labeled as follows: the theory person, the nonnumerate reader, the interest-driven statistician, and the statistical purist.

Theory persons are more interested in theory than in the data used to generate theory. Tables are largely ignored in their quests for new theoretical insights. One professor says:

[Since theory is] typically what I am most interested in, I might go to the introduction [of an article] to find [some] theoretical information [about the piece]. I may well pay attention to charts or tables, but it's pretty clear to me that I don't until I've decided that I'm satisfied with what I've read in the introduction and methodology sections. I depend upon a table when I want to know more descriptive information about the data.

I do stop with the text sometimes. Often it will really amount to setting the article aside until later, when there's a better time to consider the information in the tables. If I think the article is significant, I'll make a card for it and put it into a folder for my next manuscript. And then when I get around to working on that project, I'll pull the folder and look at the article further.

Nonnumerate readers were never trained to use, interpret, or think in terms of numbers. Considering himself a "philosopher," the professor I interviewed who most closely fits this type simply ignores numerical presentations, as in and of themselves irrelevant to his concerns. As he puts it, "The tables just don't register."

Interest-driven statisticians tend to "get around" to the tables, if so doing seems to promise some sort of payoff from the energy invested in reading them. One of these professors points out that "since the *Journal of the American Statistical Association* is heavily refereed by good people, I don't usually do as much probing of the tables there. . . . Reading tables requires effort. If the author has done his work, then it's not so bad. Otherwise, the reader has to work." Likewise, since his field (statistics) requires the creation and presentation of formulas, whether or not he reads the formulas also "depends on how hard I have to work! And it depends on my level of interest. Also, how good the notation is—the author's skill in presenting his ideas."

This professor also says that, on occasion, he may actually get out pencil and paper in order to work through the tables, but this tends to be less for the purpose of critique than to "get a better understanding of the argument, of the problem. What this does is get you involved in the process of thinking about the problem, independently of being told about it [through the text]."

There's a variation on the role of interest-driven statistician that is worth noting. One of the more qualitatively oriented professors, who happens to be competent in the use of quantitative methods as well, actually finds himself giving more time to the tables in articles than to the text. Because his field (music education) is struggling to become more research-based (and is beginning to generate lots of number-oriented studies), he finds that scrutinizing the tables in an article tends to be a good way of judging whether the time it will take to read the article is likely to be time well spent. "You can get a feeling for the

sophistication of the research from the way a table is set up, so sometimes I'll just be able to tell from looking at the tables whether I should
bother with the article at all."

Finally, *statistical purists* tend to be almost antagonistically critical
of articles from the outset, placing a primary emphasis in their reading
on methodological considerations. The professor in this study who ex-
emplified this type was of the view that everything is derived from
"the data." After scanning the table of contents and reading the abstract, he plunges immediately into the tables. His general philosophy
toward the reading of journal articles is illustrated by the following
excerpt from my interview with him:

> First thing, I leaf through to see where the table are. [He flips through
> an article at hand, to illustrate what he's talking about. Surprised:]
> There aren't any! Now, I'm not going to say that you can't write a
> discursive article, but you must have data bases for them. And just
> because I say you have to have data bases doesn't mean that you have
> to have a controlled study, so that causality can be inferred. But I
> shouldn't be left to *guess* at the basis of the statements being made in
> the article.

Another example from the same professor:

> Now, when I read these things [journals], I actually do sit down and
> go through them, looking at them like this. [He opens to a page, scans
> it for a few seconds, looks at the adjacent page in the same way, turns
> the page.] Now, look at this. [He points to a particular table, after
> examining it for about ten seconds.] Without reading this, I know
> these people don't know a good goddamn about the healthy use of sta-
> tistics. This table number 4, looking at experiments 1 through 9 and
> comparing chi-squared measures—this is clearly an incorrect use of
> statistics. . . . Now, I'm not particularly interested in the subject of
> [this article], but I might just file this away in a special folder I keep
> for inappropriately used statistics!
> [He continues, looking at a different article.] On the other hand,
> [this article] is something I would be interested in. How interesting!
> They've worked out something on the homogeneity of variance here;
> for years, I was the only one who ever worked these out; so I'll look to
> see how they did it. [At this point, he read aloud to me a paragraph
> describing the derivation of the measure of homogeneity of variance.]
> Now, to the unschooled, this might sound pretty good. But there is
> actually a lot of bullshit filler in this.

Conclusion

In this chapter I have tried to show two things. First, I have tried to
illustrate the dialectical nature of the relationship between the way

people read scientific articles and the way scientific information is typically represented. In short, when representations of information are standardized, readers can develop standard ways of reading them, including standard shortcuts as well.

Second, I have attempted to show that the tables (and other representational conventions) in scientific articles serve at least two functions for readers. The manifest function of tables is, of course, to serve as organized presentations of data that allow a reader to follow an argument in the data to its "inevitable" conclusion. Tables (and other conventions), however, also serve a latent but equally important function, in that they communicate the simple, yet very powerful, message to the reader that one is in the presence of Science.

JAMES BENNETT

Merton's "Social Structure and Anomie"

Suggestions for Rhetorical Analysis

SOCIOLOGY and rhetoric are two entirely separate things if sociology is conceived as establishing facts, and rhetoric ("mere rhetoric") is viewed as a way to affect, even deceive, an audience regardless of facts.

But sociology and rhetoric are essentially the same thing if rhetoric is the study of the beliefs and values held by audiences, the better to persuade them. In that sense, the handbooks produced by rhetoricians after Aristotle wrote the first around 330 B.C. were a forerunner of sociology, just as some media researchers today practice a form of sociology.[1] Or sociology and rhetoric may seem the same if rhetoric is "mere rhetoric" and sociology is viewed as a jargon-filled way for sociologists to speak only to one another, with no scientific basis.

Insofar as sociology and rhetoric are conceived as utterly separate or essentially equivalent, no issue arises about the relationship between them. A problem occurs when sociology and rhetoric, though distinct, nevertheless are thought to interrelate somehow. Our task might be to propose plausible definitions of the two and, by juxtaposing them, see if anything useful results.

The prospect of defining sociology is so formidable that, rather than attempt a *concept,* I offer instead an *example* of sociology. The example might come from classroom discussion, a conference presentation, or conversation. All these have explicitly rhetorical aspects in the processes of speakers and audiences, but analyzing transcripts and ethnographic material would be unwieldy on this elementary level. In any case, it would be difficult to distinguish rhetoric from "the presentation of self in everyday life," which would reduce rhetoric to an existing area of sociology and leave nothing unique for rhetoric to do. Sociology also exists in books and published articles. For purposes of this chapter, the representative of sociology (by synecdoche, one might say), will be Robert K. Merton's 1938 article "Social Structure and Anomie," in its original version. (Henceforth this article will be cited by a page number in parentheses.) So influential an article clearly "is" sociology, no matter what sociology is. If paradigms were political entities, Merton's article would be a kind of heuristic "constitution."[2]

That leaves open the question of what rhetoric is—a huge question. Plato often referred to rhetoric as an art of opinion or appearance, distinguishing it from dialectic, the art of discovering truth. Since Plato, rhetoric has been condemned in those terms by other idealists, such as Saint Augustine, a rhetoric teacher turned Christian. In the hierarchy of being, rhetoric is located in the middle: from above, it has been attacked by idealists, and from below by dialectical materialists, who oppose religion and capitalism as mere rhetoric or ideology. The subject matter of rhetoric is opinion and phenomena: the prestige of rhetoric rises and falls as research and thought transcend, dig beneath, or accept appearances. The major attack on rhetoric came in the sixteenth and seventeenth centuries, when new scientific systems, such as those of Peter Ramus and René Descartes, distinguished logic or scientific method—research into the nature of things—from rhetoric, the attractive presentation of unfounded opinion. That is the dominant meaning attached to rhetoric in the present, scientific epoch.

Nevertheless, while some were attacking rhetoric, others have insisted that it has a value and integrity of its own. Aristotle was the first to establish rhetoric as an area of systematic study, with its own kind of knowledge about persuasive things: authoritative traits of character, effective varieties of argument, emotions that affect one audience or another, and appropriate styles and sequences of presentation. More recently, Perelman and Olbrechts-Tyteca (1969) proposed a "New Rhetoric" to return to argumentation as an autonomous field of study. In other periods, rhetoric has expanded to include the entire educational regime of a society, as in ancient Rome; or it has revitalized a single field, such as philosophy in fifteenth-century Florence or literary criticism in eighteenth-century England.

Given this vast history, a single comprehensive definition of rhetoric is as unlikely as one of sociology. What has persisted in rhetoric through all these variations, however, is a concern with the interrelations among speakers, speeches, and audiences, even when a piece of writing would probably never be delivered to a live "audience." Therefore, as an exercise in rhetorical analysis, we will question an article for evidence *in the article* of its "speaker" or author and its intended audience, the reader. The speech or article can also be analyzed for the structure of its argument in relation to its goal of reaching the reader for which it was apparently intended.

Our specific question then becomes: *How much evidence can be obtained from a rhetorical analysis of an article and to what use can that evidence be put?* Given the empirical character of sociology, it would seem that data about an article should come from: (1) interviewing its author and those who read it at the time it was published and perhaps subsequently, especially those who were influenced by it—that is, *those who were persuaded* to do something as a result of reading it; and (2) content analysis of the text following the various specific interpretations that have been made of it, including later alterations by the author. I certainly do not propose that rhetorical analysis replace those empirical questions, a monograph on which could be a valuable piece of work. The question for *this* brief chapter is how much a kind of study that centers on the text itself might enrich other approaches. That makes of rhetoric a contributory means of understanding, rather than an art of deception in contrast to a method of truth.

The plausibility of a question about internal relations in an article is enhanced if we recall that Merton in "Social Structure and Anomie" focused on "certain phases of social structure" itself, rather than biological—that is, external—conditions of deviant behavior. That is the fundamental point of departure of Merton's article. Similarly, our standpoint is to examine the internal structure of the article rather than its empirical circumstances and referents. Merton's aim was to pose new problems for investigation, and that is also our aim. If Merton's success in opening up a new subject was due at least in part to features of the article itself, especially its argument, then we are justified in looking there.

(An article that is a rhetorical analysis of an article provides certain reflexive opportunities. Note how, in the preceding paragraph, I borrow from Merton's success to lend plausibility to this approach, thus attempting to increase my authority as a speaker. Of course, this works only insofar as the argument is perceived as sound.)

Do rhetorical strategies exist for asking new research questions? Sociologists more interested in shifting paradigms than in adding another piece to a current paradigm might pay close attention to the following discussion. (Note my selection of an ideal reader.) By "rhetorical" I mean the way an article is constructed, its internal character, not a series of advertisements or speaking engagements to call attention to one's publication, which are external to the text. This is not to say that social circumstances play no role in the success of speeches. As Merton says, "The problems mentioned outnumber those explicitly treated" (672).

The Argument

In making a rhetorical analysis of a piece of writing, should one begin with the author, the reader, or the argument? It makes sense to begin with whichever of these is dominant in a particular case. The others will fall into place around that center. In "Social Structure and Anomie," as in the typical scientific article, the argument dominates. The author conceals his personal qualities as much as possible (his personal qualities appear as impersonal qualities), and the intended reader is defined in large part by the argument: that is, as one who will grasp and extend the analysis proposed in the article.

How does rhetorical analysis of an argument differ from a summary or abstract of an article for scientific purposes? Scientific reading abstracts from a text the essential points that relate to data, hypotheses, and facts. It has little or no use for incidentals of presentation, except to remove those that might distract a reader or seem unprofessional. Rhetorical analysis, on the other hand, pays attention to anything that affects or might affect a reader: for example, the *sequence* in which points are made in a text. Sequence is important because it is the way an author leads a reader from the beginning of an article to its conclusion: that is, how an author *induces belief* in a reader. This assumes that a reader at the outset needs to be persuaded. That need is clearly present in the reader of a paper that aims at proposing a new categorial scheme of social analysis (that is, a new set of beliefs), as this one does.

The best way to specify an argument for rhetorical purposes is to make an outline of the text, trying to cover everything—each paragraph, if the article is well written—in a way that makes sense in terms of forward movement from one section to the next. To save space, I shall not include an outline (although that would have a certain visual value for the reader) but proceed to a description of the article.

The argument of "Social Structure and Anomie" is in five parts. The first two paragraphs are an introduction. Paragraphs 3 to 8 set forth relevant elements of social structure (ends-means). The third section, paragraphs 9 through 14, cover nonsocial structural factors that predispose toward deviate (I use Merton's word) behavior: the individual is given a role here. Paragraphs 15 through 18, the fourth section of the article, focus on social factors that are pressures toward deviation: class structure is introduced here. Paragraphs 19 and 20 might be organized with section 4, since they depend on that analysis, but they seem rather to belong with the final two paragraphs, as part of the conclusion. The author's concern is to propose a scheme of socio-logical analysis. He specifies the basic terms of the analysis in the first substantive section (section 2) and deepens the analysis in the final substantive section (section 4). From this perspective, the especially problematic section is the middle or third section: what is the author's position on nonsocial factors?

That nonsocial factors are a primary concern of the author is evident in the first sentence of the article: "There persists a notable tendency in sociological theory to attribute the malfunctioning of social struc-ture primarily to those of man's imperious biological drives which are not adequately restrained by social control" (672). This point of view, he says, begs a question about the nonbiological conditions that "in-duce deviations from prescribed patterns of conduct. In this paper, it will be suggested that certain phases of social structure" induce those deviations. In the second paragraph, he gives the aim of the paper: to outline a conceptual scheme "designed to provide a coherent, system-atic approach to the study of socio-cultural sources of deviate behavior" (672). The intended readers would seem to be individuals interested in identifying new research problems.

In a rhetorical analysis it is important to notice how an author be-gins and to pay special attention to any turns or shifts that he or she intends to make, since these reveal the job of persuasion to be done. In this article, the author is clearly not addressing biologists, who would not beg a question about nonbiological conditions of social deviation: they would not ask such a question. "There persists a notable tendency *in sociological theory*": it is sociologists he is addressing, if that is not already apparent from the journal in which the article appeared—a fact external to the text, however. The author is concerned that some sociologists are looking for pressures toward deviance in nonsocial con-ditions. Though these pressures are "biologically derived" and "rooted in original nature," footnote 2 refers to "biological and personality dif-ferences" in the same breath. Thus it appears that the opponent here is not so much biology (unless biology is taken "in the broad sense," as economics is later taken [676]) as it is psychology. From all this we can begin to form the hypothesis that the author's aim is to persuade sociologists to shift from psychologically oriented theories of deviance toward more purely social ones. Both footnotes 1 and 2, however, re-veal a concern not to discard psychology but to include it: personality differences "may be significantly involved in the *incidence* of deviate conduct" (672).

Section 2 of the article lays out the two "elements of social and cul-tural structure . . . important for our purposes" (672). These are cultur-ally defined goals and the means to reach them. Means are further

divided into institutionally approved ones and others that are technically efficient ways to reach goals regardless of institutional norms
(673). Having made these distinctions, the author is able to give a series of possible relations between means and ends. Types of malintegration include the seeking of ends with any means technically at
one's disposal and the seeking of means with no thought of the ends
they serve. Types of equilibrium include successes in processes and in
products. Having set up these possibilities, the author selects one for
study: the type of malintegration that stresses goals over means. He
then provides an example from competitive sports (675) and expands
the field of examples to include other cases (675–676).

From the viewpoint of persuasion, what is remarkable about this
section is the impression it gives of logical rigor, all the more needed
in a scientific article in which the reasoning depends on nothing more
than common sense. The overall form of the article so far corresponds
to a series of alternatives, branching off from the "placement" of the
analysis in social structure (in paragraph 1) and ending with the specific location for investigation: the ends-dominant alternative. By thus
breaking apart "elements" of the social structure, the author has tried
to persuade the reader that the terms defining that location are plausible.

One might expect that the author would now, in section 3, introduce
the notion of social class, but that is delayed until section 4. Section 3
begins: "Our analysis can scarcely stop at this juncture. We must turn
to other aspects of the social structure if we are to deal with the social
genesis of the varying rates and types of deviate behavior characteristic of different societies" (676). The aspect of social structure addressed
in this section is the role of individuals. The three ideal types of cultural patterning now become "alternative modes of adjustment or adaptation *by individuals*" (676). The types, expanded from three to five,
are presented in a table of categories, but type V is discarded in a footnote.

Adaptation IV is the only new category here, and indeed this is the
type that receives the most attention in this section: it concerns social
"aliens," such as "psychotics, psychoneurotics, chronic autists, pariahs,
outcasts, vagrants, vagabonds, tramps, chronic drunkards and drug
addicts" (677). Most of these are subjects of psychology, though this
article does not describe *specific* psychological processes. This series
also includes typical subjects of the more local community-based sociology of the Chicago School in the 1930s. The author appears to be trying
to integrate adherents of the Chicago School into his more
social-structural scheme. Footnote 13 provides evidence for this hypothesis: "Nels Anderson's description of the behavior and attitudes of

the bum, for example, can readily be recast in terms of our analytical scheme" (677).

The chart of categories puts the possibilities "before the eyes" of a reader, as Aristotle (1959, 359) says an orator should try to do (usually by metaphor and other devices of visualization). In the paragraph following the table, a distinction is made between role adjustments in specific situations, to which the categories actually refer, and personality *in toto*. Covering the latter would "introduce a complexity unmanageable within the confines of this paper" (676), though what this article does not do other articles can. Adaptation I (conformity) is briefly discussed, then adaptation IV is given a fuller treatment by designating examples of it and ways it is generated. The section ends by noting that the adaptations of innovation, ritualism, and rebellion can also result from inaccessibility of institutional means: "The result will be determined by the particular personality, and thus, the *particular* cultural background, involved" (678). Particularity of incidence has thus been integrated into this concept of social structure.

Section 4 begins: "Our major concern is with the illegitimacy adjustment" (678). If this is the case, why did the author include section 3, on the role of individual factors in the genesis of the adjustments? We return to the hypothesis we proposed above. Though the author's aim is to urge adoption of the study of social rather than individual sources of deviance, he appears to believe that he will not persuade the reader to adopt this analytic scheme if he simply ignores personal factors. Rather, he must show how the characteristics of individuals intersect with the social structure he is describing. That is, the author is reintroducing that "notable tendency" he mentioned in the article's first sentence—to attribute deviance to biological or psychological factors—and showing how it can be accounted for in his new scheme. A reader who was committed to individual factors might not find this new scheme credible if individual factors were totally ignored. *The integration of those factors into the argument is at the same time the integration of a reader associated with them into the new system of belief.*

It is not until paragraph 15 (678) that the author poses the specific question for investigation: "Which phases of our social structure predispose toward this mode of adjustment?" He begins by using an example (taken from a Chicago sociologist, though a rather maverick one, Joseph Lohman). In the next paragraph (679), the author finally introduces the class structure as a condition of deviance. Then he defines that structure by a pair of terms (whole-part), as he defined social structure generally (means-ends): "It is only when a system of cultural values extols, virtually above all else, certain *common* symbols of success *for the population at large* while its social structure rigorously restricts or completely eliminates access to approved modes of acquiring

these symbols *for a considerable part of the same population,* that anti-
social behavior ensues on a considerable scale" (680). Paragraph 18
(680–681) applies the analysis to the association of crime and poverty,
insisting that the "full configuration" of "poverty, limited opportunity
and a commonly shared system of success symbols" must be considered, not merely the class structure.

One could also view this article as a way to persuade sociologists to
introduce explicitly political considerations into sociological analysis.
It is remarkable that reference to social class comes so late in this
article. Would the author have held the attention of the "biologically"
oriented sociologists he mentioned at the outset if the had launched
into a political analysis of the class structure? Probably not. Had he
done so, he might have weakened his opposition to that "notable tendency" of "biological" attributions in sociological theory. This implies
a hierarchical structure—of reality and of persuasion: the social is
closer to the individual (integration of the two comes quite easily in
section 3), but once social structure has been established, both in the
logic of the case and in persuasion, the author can move on to a more
political concept.

A political manifesto would have been even less effective in persuading professional sociologists. And yet the argument gradually does
come around to pointing out a defect in the class structure in the
United States. The rhetorical point of this might be to preempt or at
least to integrate Marxists, in the same way we saw the author assimi-
lating psychologically oriented sociologists (their position in itself, as
a logical possibility, and as belief in a reader), though no evidence exists in the text for the former, as it does for the latter. The defect he
indicates, however, is not in the class structure alone but in that structure combined with common success symbols in the society as a whole,
and the author does not say which of these should be changed.

The final four paragraphs may be read as recommendations. In the
first of these paragraphs (681), the author speaks of "lack of cultural
coordination" between common ends and limited institutional means,
giving examples from international relations, such as the bombing of
civilian populations. That would seem to suggest a need for social
change! But the following paragraph argues for a "stable social structure," with "satisfactions deriving from competition itself" (682). No
explicit recommendation for social change is given, certainly none for
changing competition as a central social value. The specter of chaos if
the regulatory structure of society fails, however, seems to imply an
incentive for action.

But in the penultimate paragraph, brakes are firmly applied to any
thought of social action: "It should be apparent that the foregoing discussion is not pitched on a moralistic plane" (682). Debates over social

issues are put aside in favor of agreement on one general point: "Whatever the sentiments of the writer or reader concerning the ethical desirability of coordinating the means-and-goals phases of the social structure, one must agree that lack of such coordination leads to anomie" (682). The explicit recommendation of the article is for further research. The author says that this brief article is incomplete; he then offers a series of problems the article did not cover and ends by saying: "It is suggested that these and related problems may be profitably analyzed by this scheme." That rounds out the aim of the article announced in paragraph 2: "The many ramifications of the scheme cannot all be discussed; the problems mentioned outnumber those explicitly treated" (672).

The argument of this article may be characterized by its topology. By "topology" I mean the basic concepts or topics that structure the article. In the rhetorical tradition, the topics began as actual places (*topos* in Greek means place), such as a street, that could be visualized in association with an outline of key words. Orators could remember a speech (long before teleprompters) by taking an imaginary walk along the street and retrieving each key word as they passed the building associated with the word (see Yates 1966). The basic words themselves came to be called places, and those that were general notions, such as nature-nurture, science-art, ideal-real, were called commonplaces. These devices were thought to have considerable power not merely in helping orators *remember* and *deliver* speeches but, more important, in helping them *invent* arguments that would be effective in persuasion. Much rhetorical theory has been devoted to discussions of the topics. But when science attacked rhetoric as mere verbiage, the commonplaces became "commonplace," in the current pejorative sense.[3]

Merton's article is essentially a set of topics or commonplaces, in the good sense. (As such it is no less scientific. This is also a way new categories are introduced into the natural sciences.) The introduction makes a turn from *biological to social*. One might also detect an implicit turn in sociological analysis from a local community area, where the Chicago School had a notable tendency to locate their studies, to the whole social structure in general terms. This corresponds to the topic *part-whole*. In section 2, social structure is defined by use of the very old—one might even say commonplace—topic of *means-ends*. Section 3 further qualifies social structure by interrelating individuals with the structure: the topic *particular-general* is at work here. Class structure is introduced in section 4 by use of the topic *part-whole*. The conclusion turns on a distinction between ethical desirabilities and research possibilities, or the topic *thought-action*.

The topics work differently in the different sections. In both the introduction and the conclusion one term is *substituted* for the other: biological is "replaced" by social, as is action by further research. In the three substantive sections of the article, however, the strategy is just the opposite: the terms are *integrated*. Both in fact and in sociological analysis, social structure does not work if means and ends, individuals and structures, and parts and wholes are not coordinated. Operations on the terms—primarily separating and integrating—accomplish the work of this argument. The terms help define each other, and they work together: they are like ice tongs that in conjunction pick up social phenomena.[4] Furthermore, these operations provide the tension in the article, even its drama. Had the author been writing in the medieval period, he might have communicated to his audience most effectively by casting the terms as allegorical figures.

The strength of this reasoning for persuasion is that it is so "commonplace" that it is easily understood by a reader. The problem with it, however, is that the terms are in fact empty of specific empirical content. This article does not fill these "variables" with data. Later researchers did that. One can imagine Renaissance writers supporting their arguments with quotations from the classics. How does this author get authority for the empirical reality of his claims? Support for a few statements is given in footnotes by references to other publications, but these do not confirm the central thread of this new argument. Examples do. Examples, such as the one from competitive sports (675), not only put more abstract points vividly "before the eyes" of the reader, but also help persuade a reader of the possible reality of those points. Examples usually follow or exemplify the point, though the Lohman example (678) actually leads into the concept of class structure. (This has implications for a reading of the article as addressed to Chicago School–oriented readers.) Examples thus have at least three functions here: (1) they fill empty topics, (2) they exemplify statements constructed from the topics, and (3) they even assist in the discovery of a topic.

The Reader

Rhetorical analysis of arguments not only reveals a structure of reasoning, but also gives entré to the study of readers and authors. In the study of the argument, we came across evidence of the intended reader and concluded that the reader is not a biologist or psychologist but a sociologist. And yet the author's reference to that "notable tendency" toward "biology" in sociological theory implies that he is addressing sociologists who have that tendency and is trying to persuade them out of it. Further evidence for this hypothesis is that section 3 is devoted to showing how concerns with individuals can be brought into this scheme. Otherwise, that section would not seem to be needed in such a brief article, which could not possibly cover *all* other aspects of social structure. Why does it cover just *that* other one? The author's aim is not so much to refute the (non)sociological tendency as to include it, to show how it can be accommodated in this more purely sociological scheme. To have refuted or ignored it would have deprived him of the opportunity to integrate it—and them. Integration is very much on the mind of this author.

Integration of stray tendencies in readers need not concern authors who can assume an established conceptual scheme: that is, an existing pattern of belief in their readers. Had he been working in that context, the author of a sociological article would have been expected to provide data. But the aim of this article is to argue for the adoption of a new scheme. If he had made no effort to persuade, the author might have ended up talking to himself alone, like social scientists sometimes do who have a position they claim is radically new, but they set about "persuading with a hammer."

The major incentive the author gives to encourage adherence is the variety of research problems this scheme opens up. In the last paragraph he lists some of these as things his article *has not done*. Note that he does not deliver a sermon on the desirability of taking on these problems. The factual way the problems are presented only reinforces their attractiveness to readers who see themselves as scientists. The separation of research problems from social action also does this. One would expect the intended readers of this article—that is, the ones being addressed with an expectation that they will use the scheme—to be sociologists early in their careers who are looking for new research problems, and who may still be flexible enough to adopt a new set of categories. From external evidence, we know that the author himself was at such a stage of his career when he wrote this article. This description also fits certain graduate students who read this article in the postwar period (see Laub 1983).

This scheme is not *entirely* new, however. One of its strengths is that it provides continuity with existing tendencies in sociology (conflict between the generations of sociologists can be kept to a minimum), while developing a new, more sociological subject matter for sociology (the younger sociologist can find a unique niche). These are powerful persuasive appeals.

The Author

Since one of the main characteristics of scientific writing is its impersonality, one might not expect to find evidence of an author in a scientific article. Of course, the scientific stance does not help a rhetoric-analyst find such traits, unless it is precisely the scientific character that stands out so vividly: objectivity and impersonality are personal qualities. But since these qualities are, or try to be, uniform over all cases, they are too general to open up analyses of specific cases. Nevertheless, unique traits of character do stand out. As Wayne Booth (1961) has said, "The author's judgment is always present, always evident to anyone who knows how to look for it. The author can to some extent choose his disguises, he can never choose to disappear" (20). We have detected the intended reader. How can we spot the intended author? I set aside the author's institutional affiliation, Harvard University, given at the head of the article, as more or less external to the text for our purposes here.

One way to seek out the author is to regard features of the argument as qualities of the author, in the same way as the author of this article transforms types of groups, in section 2, into types of individual adaptation, in section 3. That is, the topics *argument-author* and *social-individual* are tropes: the means of structuring a movement from one "place" to another. One can imagine a mode of analysis that attempts to *unify* all phenomena into a single overarching form or formula. It is easy to see behind this a primary character trait of an author: a desire for unity. The scientific operation of *dividing* phenomena into their elements also translates into a trait or habit of an author. The argument of "Social Structure and Anomie" aims at *integrating* elements that it initially divides. Thus the most prominent character trait of this author is his desire to integrate basic elements.

For example, he starts by making abstract, almost philosophical, distinctions about social structure, then proceeds to specify the variety of ways the distinct terms interrelate and, by using examples, how these types connect with concrete empirical conditions. Even though he opposes sociological theories that account for deviance by the backgrounds and natures of individuals, nevertheless he attempts to integrate individual factors into his social-structural scheme. Even social action is assimilated in this article. At the end of the article, "ethical desirabilities" are shunned not only to avoid disagreements over action and turn attention toward research, but also because throughout the article the author had implied a need for action.

Aristotle (1959, 33) distinguished three types of speeches: forensic, in which a speaker seeks to persuade an audience that something or someone is wrong; epideictic, in which a speaker attempts to exhibit something, often his or her own skills or someone else's virtues, as in a funeral oration, or to demonstrate how something is done; and deliberative, in which a speaker recommends a course of action or a solution to a problem, often a political one. "Social Structure and Anomie" is a deliberative speech, but the course of action recommended is not "political," at least not in the usual sense. It is the "action" of professional sociologists in developing a unique and fruitful subject matter for their discipline.[5] Thus the author's deliberative character shines through, urging the adoption of his scheme. (*This* article, on the other hand, is epideictic: it aims to show readers phenomena they had not noticed.)

The author's urging is not without a sense of urgency. If a reader looks beyond the article's theoretical schematization to the social realities it abstractly describes, one sees appalling cracks in the social structure, threatening chaos. (After all, this was written in the United States in the 1930s, though in relation to our method that remark is cheating!) On occasion, the emotion that must accompany even a scientist's perception of such conditions is expressed in the form of italics. The first use of italics for emphasis in the article is an excellent example of a statement doing what it is saying: "Our primary aim lies in discovering how some social structures *exert a definite pressure* upon certain persons in the society to engage in nonconformist rather than conformist conduct" (672). The italics themselves exert a definite pressure, as insistent as a lecturer thumping on a table. Other instances, such as "must derive from sheer *participation*" (674), *activate* the subject for a reader. They give the argument emotional value, though fully integrated with the argument.

Not a page of this article goes by without italics, except the last page, which is a kind of cooling-off phase. On one occasion, there is the double emphasis of roman type within an italicized phrase: "when the channels of vertical mobility are closed or narrowed *in a society which places a high premium on economic affluence and social ascent for* all *its members*" (679–680).

The author's passion is directed mainly at the reform of sociology. But one can also detect compassion with the victims of anomie and a desire for a better social order, even if that has to take a detour through sociological analysis. In footnote 15 he says with sarcasm: "The ideology [of 'office-boy-to-president'] largely persists, however, possibly because it still performs a useful function for maintaining the *status quo*. For insofar as it is accepted by the 'masses,' it constitutes a useful sop for those who might rebel against the entire structure, were this consoling hope removed" (679).

We see an author with an interest, even a passion, in *integrating opposite things,* in order to expand and enrich sociology and, perhaps, to improve society. The helpful persona pulling the strings of this argument is well suited to getting the job of persuasion done. The article itself becomes a means of coordination or balance—a "contract"—between author and reader.

Stylistic Features

Rhetorical analysis looks at a piece of writing (or anything else) for its internal structure and for evidence of its author and intended reader. But any feature of a presentation, such as italics, is also fair game, because it can affect a reader. For example, Merton's verbal style is well suited to communicating with a scientific audience and to introducing new concepts to them: he makes an assertion, qualifies it, makes a distinction, interrelates the terms of the distinction in order to derive types, exemplifies the types, makes a further distinction, integrates it with the previous distinction, and qualifies that. He could continue but this is a brief article, so he concludes by pointing to further possibilities. The article gives a clear impression of logical divisions: each of the three main sections has six paragraphs each, though the final two paragraphs of the last section seem to belong with the conclusion. And yet continuity between the sections is sustained by concepts that almost have a personal feel to them: they seem to tell a story—a scientific one.

The language also develops a personal tone. In paragraph 1 he says: "In this paper, it will be suggested" (672). But in the next paragraph he says: "Our primary aim lies in discovering" (672). On occasion he slips back into the passive voice, but more often he uses "we" and "our," as he does throughout the paragraph that begins, "Our analysis can scarcely stop at this juncture" (676). He refers to "our competitive society" (677). That is, the author asserts his claim as a scientist at the outset of the article by using the passive voice, then shifts into a linguistic form that encourages *identification* of reader with author. He concludes the article by returning to the impersonal mode in a paragraph that beings, "This statement, being brief, is also incomplete," and ends, "It is suggested that these and related problems may be profitably analyzed by this scheme" (682).

Finally, what role do the footnotes play in this article? Of course, they provide citations, but only two of the twenty-one (14, 20) do only that. The primary role of seven footnotes (1, 2, 6, 11, 13, 18, 21) is to connect statements in the main text with aspects of psychological theory, further confirming our hypothesis that the author is endeavoring to assimilate the psychological position, or rather, psychological tendencies in sociologists. Six (3, 8, 10, 14, 16, 19) make connections with other aspects of social theory. Three (5, 15, 17) provide suggestions for further investigations. Two (4, 7) make incidental comments about ritualism, which is not a central concern of the article, and one (12) discards one type of possibility, adaptation v (rebellion). Footnote 9 has the almost playful function of giving a relevant etymology of the word *fortune*.

The footnotes do four things: (1) they integrate the argument with existing scholarship, which also adds to the author's scholarly bona fides; (2) they assist the argument in various ways, by making further integrations and suggestions; (3) they enable the author to comment on contemporary affairs, as he does in footnotes 3, 8, and 16; and (4) they enhance personal identification of a reader with the author, where the author speaks in a less formal voice, as in footnote 16: "a case in point is the increasing frequency of cartoons which observe in a tragi-comic vein that 'my old man says everybody can't be President. He says if ya can get three days a week steady on W.P.A. work ya ain't doin' so bad either' " (679–680). The relative absence of comments about idiosyncratic conditions in the United States in the 1930s and its theoretical orientation have contributed to the article's staying power.

Conclusion

It is unlikely that a social scientist would analyze a text in isolation from the text's *actual* empirical circumstances. What, then, is the value to social scientists of the type of analysis given above? One value is to enable the interpreter of a document to formulate research questions to pose to authors and readers, and hypotheses to try out on that larger field of evidence. Rhetorical skills can enrich one's preliminary reading and enable a researcher to see phenomena in a text that might have been overlooked in an exclusively "empirical" approach.

One of the foundations of modern science has been its rebellion against the text-based approach of earlier humanistic thought. Now it appears that science, which in this century even discovered that it has a history and a sociology, lost something by discarding an appreciation for texts. The integration of arts of rhetoric with methods of science may open up new possibilities for research in the twenty-first century. So little has been said in this brief chapter that much remains to be done.

Notes

1. In the *Phaedrus,* Plato (1961, 519) has Socrates remark that to attain the highest skill in the art of speech, one must have *knowledge* of one's audience. Thus true rhetoric is a *science*—of society. The *Rhetoric* of Aristotle, Plato's pupil, has been viewed as the scientific fulfillment of the *Phaedrus.* Kenneth Burke (1962, 580) has remarked: "The so-called 'commonplaces' or 'topics' in Aristotle's *Art of Rhetoric* (and the corresponding *loci communes* in Latin manuals) are a quick survey of 'opinion' in this sense," to be compared to the more laborious "survey" in modern social science.
2. For a rhetorical treatment of another article by Merton, see Bazerman 1981.
3. This paragraph abbreviates rather drastically about twenty-three hundred years of discussion of these terms, which have often been the content of "arts of invention." A comprehensive study of topics does not, however, exist. Since inventories of topics have attempted to cover how people actually think (utilitarian logic rather than symbolic logic), topics should have a role in artificial intelligence.
4. For an excellent study of topics in major transformations in social theory, see Davis 1971.
5. In the paradigm of the Chicago School of Sociology, life histories performed the same rhetorical function of legitimizing a new subject matter: "Human documents communicated to potential sociologists the kind of phenomena they should be dealing with," and to nonsociologists that sociology, the new kid on the block, *had* a subject matter (Bennett 1981, 149).

DAVID ZAREFSKY

How Rhetoric and Sociology Rediscovered Each Other

To UNDERSTAND how scholars in rhetoric and sociology have come increasingly to a concern with some common topics, one first must understand how rhetoric rediscovered itself. It is at once among the oldest and the newest of academic disciplines, and this paradox warrants explanation.

In classical times, rhetoric occupied a place of prominence in the intellectual realm. Responding to Plato's critique of rhetoric (which had been inspired by what he regarded as excesses of the Sophists), Aristotle defined rhetoric as the faculty of discovering, in the given case, the available means of persuasion.[1] This definition marked out an art ranging from the selection of evidence and arguments to the effectiveness of delivery. It made of rhetoric a practical art whose proper domain was decision making under conditions of uncertainty. About matters that are certain no one deliberates; but in the world of the contingent, the probabilistic, and the unknown, rhetoric is the method of choice. In particular, Aristotle regarded rhetoric as the means of deciding public questions—determining right action in the world of practical affairs. It was in this sense that he regarded rhetoric as the counterpart of dialectic (appropriate more to scientific questions) and an offshoot of both ethics and politics. The end of rhetoric was *phronesis,* practical wisdom.

The Romans elaborated and codified the Aristotelian system, largely as a means of pedagogy. Cicero, for example, schematized the "canons" of rhetoric as including invention (discovery of arguments and selection from among them), disposition (arrangement of materials in the argument), style, memory, and delivery. He also outlined the appropriate parts of the speech, from exordium to peroration. Quintilian went so far as to include the content of a speech under the domain of rhetoric, defined the ideal orator as "the good man skilled in speaking," and proposed a plan of education that would attain that ideal.

In the Middle Ages, with the church the dominant social agency, rhetoric became identified with a theory of effective preaching. The fourth book of Augustine's *On Christian Doctrine,* for example, is largely a restatement of Ciceronian principles in a theological context. The other major use of rhetoric during those years was as a theory of letter writing. Since the Roman texts were recovered sooner than the Greek, the early Renaissance was marked by renewed interest in the Ciceronian scheme.

Through all of these periods, although rhetoric's domain varied, it was seen, in Richard McKeon's (1971) terms, as an "architectonic productive art," that is, an art whose principles were drawn upon in creating other works. This is a far cry from the modern popular conceptions of rhetoric as bombast, emptiness, unnecessary adornment, guile, and—worst of all—freshman composition.

The decisive turns toward fragmentation of rhetoric came during the fifteenth to seventeenth centuries. First, in an attempt to clarify the relationship between rhetoric and logic, Peter Ramus essentially divided the canons, appropriating invention and disposition to philosophy and leaving rhetoric with style, memory, and delivery (Howell 1961, 146–172). The whole of rhetoric became identified with its least intellectual aspects. And those aspects were codified to the point of absurdity, whether in a listing of over two hundred figures and tropes or in the emergence of chironomia, the science of gesture. Books appeared with pictures of the gesture thought appropriate for expressing each of the emotions. A rhetoric so conceived was easy to derogate or even to dismiss, as many curricula have done from that day to this.

The other major development in these years was the disparagement of the contingent as a source of reliable knowledge. Descartes is the key figure here. His method of systematic doubt assured that rhetoric (or any of the human sciences) would reach conclusions inferior to those of a "closed system" such as formal logic or mathematics. The whole realm of practical affairs, therefore, was regarded as an unlikely source of knowledge claims, and public decision making was instead described as but the product of economic self-interest, class or racial prejudice, power, or some other reified construct thought to supersede the individual will.

In the eighteenth and nineteenth centuries, there were attempts to reformulate rhetoric in the manner of the classics, as an intellectual art with the depth and texture Aristotle implied. One thinks particularly of the British trio of George Campbell, Hugh Blair, and Richard Whately, and the American John Quincy Adams, who taught rhetoric for many years at Harvard and published lectures on rhetoric and oratory (Howell 1971, 577–612, 648–671; Ehninger 1962; Golden and Corbett 1968; Auer and Banninga 1963). But these moves had little immediate effect on either the academy or the public. By the late

nineteenth century, rhetoric had been relegated either to a minor sub-
specialty within English departments or to separate schools of elocu-
tion or expression, seen widely as finishing schools for young ladies
and often devoid of intellectual content. Meanwhile, the social sciences
evolved from moral philosophy and found stereotypes of the natural
sciences as their exemplars. They took as their goal the formulation of
lawlike statements about human behavior from which specific knowledge and predictions could be "deduced." In such an enterprise, rhetoric has no part to play; if anything, it is a mask that conceals true
motives.

The twentieth century, however, has seen significant change in the
conception of rhetoric, and the study of rhetoric today reveals a new
vitality and energy. In the most general terms, today's rhetorical
scholars, while not aping the classical sources, see their topics and concerns in the same holistic spirit that guided the classics. One might
almost say that the study of rhetoric has achieved a sort of "neoclassi-
cal synthesis." If anything, scholars have stretched the bounds *beyond*
those of the classics—examining private as well as public decisions,
considering acts and pictures as well as words among the available
means of persuasion. The capstone of this new energy and vitality,
perhaps, was the 1971 report of the National Developmental Conference on Rhetoric, which defined the term, in the broadest possible
sense, as the study of the ways in which symbols influence people
(Bitzer and Black 1971, 208, 220).

Three strands of contemporary rhetorical inquiry speak especially
to the rhetoric of research. First, rhetorical theory has been profoundly
influenced by the philosophy of dramatism, associated most closely
with Kenneth Burke.[2] Among the extensions of this general view are
sociological works such as Erving Goffman's (1959) emphasis on man
as actor and Hugh Duncan's (1962) *Communication and Social Order*.
Other manifestations within rhetoric include Ernest Bormann's (1972,
1985) theory that public discourse reflects fantasy themes that have
"chained out" from small groups and become a part of the culture, and
recent studies of narrative that imply that seemingly expository or argumentative texts also tell stories and that there is a narrative structure to much of human interaction (Mitchell 1981; Fisher 1984, 1987).
Broadly speaking, these works have in common an emphasis on producing discourse as a *social* exercise. The authority of a text resides
not simply in its content but in the whole social milieu in which it is
formed. Rhetorical scholars have employed this perspective in studies
of the rhetoric of social movements, finding in their discourse the symbolic enactment of purification rituals.[3] Dramatistic perspectives,

though, also have been applied to the structure of a single speech or other communicative act, using Burke's pentad in an attempt to explain an internal sense of movement within the text, and to biographical studies of individual speakers or writers.

From this perspective, research is seen as something more than what it obviously claims to be. It is also a rhetorical enterprise depending on such conventions as the impersonality of the author, the posture of objectivity, the use of precision and measurement to heighten the perceived competence of the researcher, and the use of the expository mode to suggest that one is setting forth uncontested facts and laws rather than making a claim on the reader's belief or action. Some commentaries on academic research have developed such themes—one thinks particularly of Richard Weaver's (1953) harsh treatment of social science rhetoric, Andrew Weigert's (1970) castigation of "The Immoral Rhetoric of Scientific Sociology," and Jeanine Czubaroff's (1973) essay on how gaining intellectual respectability is a rhetorical problem. Often such commentaries are polemical and go no further than the claim, in Herbert Simons's (1980) formulation, that scientists are "rhetors in disguise." The next step in rhetorical scholarship is to identify more clearly how this is so. In what ways does a scientific community serve as an *audience* whose expectations shape scientists' rhetorical choices? How do seemingly impartial scientists adopt a rhetorical *persona* (Campbell 1974)? How does (or should) a community test and warrant scientific claims? How does the recognition of science as a communal enterprise affect the authority of scientific claims?

A second strand of contemporary rhetorical scholarship is in the theory and practice of argumentation. For many years, argumentation remained a minor subfield within rhetoric, possibly because it was under the sway of what has been labeled "applied formalism" (Cox and Willard 1982, xiii–xvii). That is, formal deductive logic was taken as the model for all human reasoning, and nonformal modes were described as variations on, or imperfect attempts at, the analytic ideal. So, for example, the enthymeme (a rhetorical deduction) was described simply as a logical syllogism with one premise missing. Many of the common patterns of induction were dismissed as fallacies because the conclusion never followed from the premises with certainty. Argumentation itself was conceived as a normative study, concerned with how people *ought to* reason, and the norms were determined by reference to the analytic ideal.

The past quarter century has seen argumentation studies in a headlong retreat from "applied formalism." The two works most influential in this turn of events were Toulmin's *Uses of Argument* (1958) and Perelman and Olbrechts-Tyteca's *New Rhetoric* (1969), both originally published in 1958. From different starting points, both works reach the same conclusion: that the analytic syllogism does not adequately describe generally *accepted* patterns of reasoning in human affairs. The alternatives, therefore, are either to dismiss much of human activity as irrational or to abandon the analytic ideal. Both works choose the latter course and attempt, as a starting point, to describe how people actually do reason from data to conclusions. For Perelman and Olbrechts-Tyteca, the answer is found in an extensive discussion of techniques for strengthening or weakening a person's adherence to a thesis presented for assent. What is particularly noteworthy about their work is that they describe such seemingly nonlogical devices as figures of speech as actually having argumentative implications through influencing the audience's sense of choice, presence, or communion. For Toulmin, the answer was found in a layout of argument which recasts the syllogism's major premise as a warrant or license for an inference and, recognizing that the inference goes beyond the data, provides explicitly for rebuttals and qualifiers.

The danger with abandoning applied formalism, of course, is that it could be replaced by a vicious relativism, in which there would be no standards for the assessment of claims and all arguments would be equally valid. In such a system one would have no basis other than gut feeling or brute force to prefer one claim to another. To avert this calamity, both Toulmin and Perelman and Olbrechts-Tyteca offer a "middle range" standard between formalism and relativism. For the Belgians, the standard is their construct of the universal audience, which exists in the mind of the speaker and serves ultimately as the judge of contested claims: those arguments that would pass muster of the universal audience are to be considered valid. The universal audience is not addressed by partisans, propagandists, or salespeople, but is thought to be addressed by philosophers and scientists. This conception, then, leads us to think of the scientist (including the social scientist) as an advocate, and from that perspective one is led quickly into a consideration of how scientists argue—particularly if their methods and procedures are thought to be the best means to validity.

Toulmin took a somewhat different approach to this problem, finding the basis for valid argument to be field-specific. His idea was that each field generates, in the course of its practice, criteria for the assessment of claims. In *The Uses of Argument,* Toulmin (1958, 14) was vague about the meaning of a field, holding only that two arguments are in the same field if they are of the same logical type. In his later work, *Human Understanding* (1972), he has come much closer to equating fields with academic disciplines. He describes the evolution of disciplines toward compactness, that is, widespread agreement on purposes, methods, and fundamental principles. Atomic physics is Toulmin's clear example of a compact discipline. Sociology probably would be seen as a diffuse or would-be discipline and rhetoric, like most of the arts, as either undisciplined or undisciplinable.

Scholars influenced by Toulmin's program have proceeded in at least three directions. First, they have engaged in considerable dispute about the meaning of the term *field,* finding it to be defined by such varied criteria as logical or rhetorical form, subject matter, common purpose, or shared world view (Zarefsky 1982). Although this dispute continues, increasingly writers are lamenting that the terminological tangle is standing in the way of research. The need has been identified for more case studies of argument practice, in order that comparative studies might yield insight about the boundaries of a field. Journals within the field of rhetoric increasingly are offering such case studies.

Second, scholars influenced by Toulmin have attempted to describe, and perhaps evaluate, argument practice within individual fields, focusing especially on academic disciplines. In their recent text, for example, Rieke and Sillars (1984) treat argumentation in law, scholarship, religion, and business; Toulmin et al. (1985) include many of the same examples and also focus specifically on science and the arts. In one essay, I tried to examine how historians employed causal arguments, using the U.S. Civil War as a case study (Zarefsky 1980). What hampers some of these efforts is the rhetorical scholar's lack of thorough grounding in the field being analyzed; for this reason the cross-fertilization between scholars in rhetoric and other disciplines is essential. There are hopeful signs in this regard. The Iowa conference on "The Rhetoric of the Human Sciences" brought together such scholars, and the conference papers included one by an economist on the styles of argument employed in the conduct of economic research, another by an intellectual historian on rhetorical considerations in the historical narrative, and one by a political scientist lamenting the absence of sustained ideological argument in that field (Simons 1985; Lyne 1985; Nelson et al. 1987). Recognizing that the next step is to demonstrate the utility of a rhetorical perspective in actual cases, the project has encouraged the publication by the University of Wisconsin Press of a multivolume series of detailed individual studies on the general theme "The Rhetoric of the Human Sciences." Within sociology, the recent publication of Ricca Edmondson's *Rhetoric in Sociology* (1984) is an equally welcome development of the same type. Edmondson examines a variety of sociological treatises to determine how the authors use examples, ideal types, rhetorical deductions, and order within a manuscript for argumentative impact. Though clearly grounded in rhetoric, Edmondson has the advantage of active involvement in the field about which she writes and a sensitivity to how modes of argumentation affect its key issues and topics.

Third, rhetorical scholars inspired by Toulmin's work have sought to conceive of argument itself as an activity of situated social actors. Rather than concern themselves primarily with the claims made by arguers, they have focused on the kind of interaction in which people maintain what they construe to be incompatible positions. The major writer in this vein is Charles Willard, whose early essay, interestingly, is subtitled "Foundations of a Sociology of Argument" (Willard 1978). In this and later works (Willard 1983, 1989) he has maintained that argumentation should itself be studied as a social practice and that argument fields are determined by the construct systems of the interactants. Although it is not Willard's purpose, implicit in his work is a call for sociologists to enter the ranks of students of argument.

So far two directions in contemporary rhetorical studies have been discussed—dramatism and argumentation—which have clear implications for the relationship of sociology and rhetoric. The third approach is even bolder in its proclamation: that rhetoric itself is epistemic. Traditionally epistemology and rhetoric were thought to be clearly distinct. One concerned the means of discovering truth; the other, the means of giving truth artful expression. Not only were they clearly separate enterprises, but the former could be seen as logically prior to the other: *first* one determined what was true; *then* one considered how to present it effectively. This assumption is directly challenged by the rhetoric-as-epistemic movement. Within the literature of rhetorical studies, this view was first espoused by Robert L. Scott (1967, 1976), who suggested that rhetoric actually involved the generation of knowledge and not just its transmission. Subsequent writers, in some cases, have extended this view to suggest that everything we know is only the result of human agreements, or that engagement in rhetorical activity may be the only means of coming to "know."

In an overview of the rhetoric-as-epistemic literature, Leff (1978) distinguishes among four senses in which rhetoric has been described as a means of knowing, arranged from weakest to strongest claim. The weakest version holds that rhetoric is epistemic in that "it allows us to know how particular objects and events relate to fixed, abstract principles," and it is the perception of this relationship that gives meaning or significance to the particular. By relating it to a fixed principle we come to "know" its nature. This is the minimalist position employed by Scott to point out to his critics that there is *some* rhetorical dimension even to seemingly deductive epistemic practices. Concern for how the quality of writing affects interpretation of ideas would also illustrate this first perspective.

A stronger version of the claim marks out a particular *kind* of knowledge obtained through rhetoric. The view is identified most closely with Thomas Farrell (1976), who distinguishes between *technical* and *social* knowledge. The former could be said generally to derive from correspondence with the external world and the latter from inter-subjective agreement among arguers. Social knowledge designates "conceptions of symbolic relationships among problems, persons, interests, and actions, which imply (when accepted) certain notions of preferable public behavior" (Farrell 1976, 4). It refers, in other words, to practical wisdom about the conduct of public affairs, and it is the knowledge—the storehouse of beliefs and values—attributed to the public audience to whom advocates appeal. Since the categories of social knowledge are presumptive and not conclusive, they provide a general frame of reference but not a priori decision rules. As Leff summarizes, "There is almost always a significant margin of ambiguity about how to construe these values, about which values are relevant, and about which have priority. This ambiguity is resolved on a case by case basis in terms of a deliberation about some specific problem" (Leff 1978, 79). Rhetoric produces social knowledge by influencing how a given situation is perceived and the sense of what values or standards should be applied to it.

By either of these first two approaches to viewing rhetoric as epistemic, rhetoric arguably would have little to do with sociology—except in the weak sense that the sociologist's data might be related to fixed principles (were there any) through rhetoric. Clearly, as the science of society, sociology would be seen as productive of technical knowledge about social institutions, claims about regularity that would achieve their force through correspondence with the external world they sought to describe. As a social science, sociology would be concerned with description rather than action; hence it would not be appropriate for discourse that evokes the sense of a public and then summons the public to make decisions about contingent matters that affect their interests. To be sure, individual sociologists may engage in rhetorical discourse to generate social knowledge; they do so whenever they enter the public realm and make policy recommendations. But sociology *as a discipline* would be attuned far more to technical than to social knowledge.

The third and fourth variations on the rhetoric-as-epistemic claim, which seek to broaden rhetoric's epistemic scope, have much clearer implications for sociology. The third perspective is that rhetoric offers a method for choosing between alternative conceptions of reality by securing the first premises of a scientific or philosophical system. In such a system, the first premises are normally unquestioned and may not even be recognized. When they are challenged, though, they cannot be secured by formal means, since argument within a system would presume the very same first principles which are under attack. The easiest way to understand this conception of rhetoric's epistemic function is by reference to Thomas Kuhn's *Structure of Scientific Revolutions* (1970). It is in periods of paradigm shift, or what Kuhn calls revolutionary science, that first principles become contested and must be defended by reference to appeals outside their own system. The conflict in the social sciences between "positivist" and "interpretivist" paradigms is a good case in point. Neither position could be defended to advocates of the other on its own terms, for its defense would rely on just the assumptions at issue. Advocates would need to employ the nonformal method of rhetoric to find the arguments on behalf of either paradigm that the audience would find compelling. Rhetoric hence enters the realm of science by enabling us to "know" as a result of persuasive discourse which of the paradigms or assumptive frameworks ought to be preferred.

The final view of rhetoric's epistemic function is the most ambitious: that rhetoric is fundamentally involved in *all* ways of knowledge, or that *all* knowledge ultimately is rhetorical. This view, somewhat reminiscent of the much-maligned Sophists of old, holds that all knowledge rests on intersubjective agreement, even when we conceal that source of knowledge and claim to rely on objective fact. It maintains that the symbolic context undergirds all knowing because all knowing also involves valuing and doing. In rhetorical studies this view is associated most closely with the work of Barry Brummett (1976), in philosophy of science with that of Walter Weimer (1977).

Scholars who hold this last view have been naturally attracted to "the rhetoric of science," perhaps because it seemingly represents the most difficult case. If even science can be shown to be thoroughly rhetorical, then it should follow that rhetoric infuses all ways of knowing. They then argue that even supposedly precise measurements actually depend on a prior consensus—which must be argued for—as to the unit of measurement and what counts as an instance of the thing to be measured. In a larger sense, the scientific method itself is dependent on a prior consensus that science cannot establish: that controlled verification is a reliable procedure, that under controlled conditions it is relatively unlikely that our senses will deceive us, or even that Hume's paradox ought to be discounted so that we can make predictions about the future based on the experience of the past.

Although rhetorical scholars have flirted with this extreme position, most have been reluctant to embrace it wholeheartedly, perhaps because it would make their own domain so vast and provide little basis for distinguishing between rhetoric and other disciplines. If it were accepted, however, it clearly would capture sociology in its net, holding—to state the obvious—that the very idea of "society" is a rhetorical construct that is worked out in discourse, and that the entire discipline is premised on a consensus, which it cannot establish itself, that the object of its study actually exists.

The convergence of interest between rhetoric and sociology has been described from the perspective of rhetoric. Common concerns range from the rhetorical study of sociological phenomena (social movements) to the sociological study of rhetorical phenomena (argumentation) to the penetration of rhetoric into the domains of social science (rhetoric-as-epistemic). At the same time, sociology, like other human sciences, has taken a rhetorical or interpretive turn. Society, its basic unit of analysis, is increasingly recognized as constituted in important ways through communication. The most sustained argument along these lines has been the work of European social theorists. Habermas (1979), for example, regards communication, along with work and power, as the primary social motives and suggests that it is institutional practices of systematically distorted communication that permit one or another social interest to triumph. Other scholars, influenced heavily by Marx, have treated communication as the means by which elites can maintain ideological hegemony. Recently, Richard Harvey Brown (1987) has suggested that society itself can be viewed as a text and its institutions subjected to the sort of rhetorical analysis normally associated with works of discourse.

This interpretive turn within sociology was prefigured by the appearance in 1966 of Alvin W. Gouldner's *Coming Crisis of Western Sociology.* Though largely a refutation of structural functionalism associated with Talcott Parsons, it offers valuable insight into the relation between sociology and rhetoric. Gouldner calls for a middle ground between a stultifying positivism and the anarchic rejection of theory altogether; rhetorical analysis fills that space. He recognizes that theorizing about society is a form of action that influences audiences. "Any and every statement about the social world," he writes, "as well as the methodologies by which it is reached, has consequences that may be viewed quite apart from its intellectual validity" (Gouldner 1966, 12). Recognizing that sociologists are indeed rhetors in disguise, he urges a "reflexive sociology" in which the field studies its own conventions of thought and practice—anticipating the "rhetoric of inquiry" project discussed above.

Gouldner's work is hospitable to each of the three contemporary developments in rhetoric reviewed here. It recognizes the dramatistic character of the researcher as rhetor in the suggestion, for example, that the norms of "high-science sociology" serve to "defocalize the ideological dimensions of decision-making, diverting attention from differences in ultimate values" and instead providing "a framework for resolving limited differences among the managers of organizations and institutions" (Gouldner 1966, 104–105). The assumption that research yields knowledge of an objective nature is rendered problematic through a focus on the researcher as actor in a dramatic scene. Gouldner concludes that, seen from this point of view, traditional sociology "was using social science as a rhetoric, which might assemble a basis for certainty of belief and might assemble a consensus in society" (114).

Second, Gouldner alludes to the emphasis on argument when he notes that sociological theories differ according to their "deep assumptions" about humankind and society (28). These assumptions represent the unstated premises from which enthymemes are conducted. Social theorizing, on this view, is often seen as a distinct argument field demarcated by autonomous technical criteria. Gouldner's aim, by contrast, is to penetrate the field of sociological argument with the field of moral argument; he is calling for new criteria by which to assess sociology as argument.

Finally, Gouldner explicitly recognizes that rhetoric and epistemology cannot be separated; the act of persuading is bound up in the process of coming to know. It is not the case that theories are verified or disconfirmed and then that adherence to the outcome is automatic. Rather, he writes that theories are accepted or rejected as convincing or not, even before supporting evidence is in hand, based on the consistency between the theory's basic assumptions and those of the listener or reader (30). In other words, the soundness of a theory is not separate from its ability to convince; rather, being influenced is part of coming to know.

In sociology as in other human sciences, the path of the last two decades has been in the directions Gouldner urged. This convergence of interests between rhetoric and sociology, however, has proceeded in an interestingly symmetrical pattern. One of the weaknesses of the rhetoric-as-epistemic literature—as, for that matter, of much of the argumentation literature—is that it tends toward the pontifical and polemical, and is marked by reluctance to get down to cases. After a while, the repeated proclamation that "rhetoric *is* epistemic" comes off as breast-beating, convincing the rhetorical scholar of his or her own importance but not otherwise enhancing understanding of either rhetoric or sociology. The need is to ground abstract theoretical formulations, proving in the doing that they illumine a significant area of behavior. On the other hand, sociologists' concern with rhetoric seems at times to be almost atheoretical. Comments are made about individual discourses without an awareness of the theoretic and philosophic underpinnings of the analysis. The difficulty with a purely *macro* approach is that it may shed no light on particular cases; with a purely *micro* approach the danger is that findings may not be generalizable beyond the specific cases. By joining the general with the particular it may be possible to avoid both difficulties and to break the logjam that can be noticed in both fields. The growing interpenetration of rhetoric and sociology, then, may work to the benefit of both.

Notes

1. Aristotle, *Rhetoric,* ed. and trans. Lane Cooper (New York: Appleton, 1932), p. 7. For an excellent synthesis of classical rhetoric, see George Kennedy, *The Art of Persuasion in Greece* (Princeton: Princeton University Press, 1963); *The Art of Rhetoric in the Roman World* (Princeton: Princeton University Press, 1972). A one-volume survey of the history of rhetoric is now available: George Kennedy, *Classical Rhetoric and Its Christian and Secular Traditions from Ancient to Modern Times* (Chapel Hill: University of North Carolina Press, 1980).
2. Burke's significant works are far too numerous to list. For our purposes the most pertinent are *A Grammar of Motives* (1945; reprint, Berkeley: University of California Press, 1969) and *A Rhetoric of Motives* (1950; reprint, Berkeley: University of California Press, 1969). For an excellent overview of Burke, see William H. Rueckert, *Kenneth Burke and the Drama of Human Relations* (Minneapolis: University of Minnesota Press, 1963).
3. See especially Leland M. Griffin, "A Dramatistic Theory of the Rhetoric of Movements," *Critical Responses to Kenneth Burke,* ed. William H. Rueckert (Minneapolis: University of Minnesota Press, 1969), pp. 456–479. There have been many rhetorical studies of social movements during the past twenty-five years. The entire winter 1980 issue of *Central States Speech Journal* was devoted to issues and problems in the rhetorical study of movements.

References

Aristotle. 1959. *The "Art" of Rhetoric*. Trans. John Henry Freese. Cambridge: Harvard University Press.

Aristotle. 1984 (1954). *Rhetoric*. Translated by W. Rhys Roberts. New York: Random House, Modern Library.

Auer, J. Jeffery and Jerald L. Banninga. 1963. "The Genesis of John Quincy Adams' Lectures on Rhetoric and Oratory." *Quarterly Journal of Speech* 49:119–32.

Bacon, Sir Francis. 1857. *The Works of Francis Bacon, Lord Chancellor of England*. With a Life of the Author by Basil Montagu, Esquire, 3 volumes. Philadelphia: Parry & McMillan.

Barzun, Jacques, and Henry Graff. 1970. *The Modern Researcher*. 2d edition. New York: Harcourt Brace.

Bazerman, Charles. 1981. "What Written Knowledge Does: Three Examples of Academic Discourse." *Philosophy of the Social Sciences* 11:361–387.

———. 1989. *The Shaping of Written Knowledge*. Madison: University of Wisconsin Press.

Becker, Howard S. 1982. *Art Worlds*. Berkeley: University of California Press.

———. 1985. "Telling about Society." Paper presented at the annual meetings of the American Sociological Association, Cooley-Mead Award Session, Washington, D.C.

———. 1986. *Writing for Social Scientists: How to Start and Finish Your Thesis, Book, or Article*. Chicago: University of Chicago Press.

Becker, Howard S. et al. 1961. *Boys in White*. Chicago: University of Chicago Press.

Bellah, Robert N., Richard Madsen, William Sullivan, Ann Swidler, and Steve Tipton. 1985. *Habits of the Heart*. Berkeley: University of California Press.

Bender, Thomas. 1978. *Community and Social Change in America*. New Brunswick, N.J.: Rutgers University Press.

Benkin, Richard L. 1981. *Sociology: A Way of Seeing*. Belmont, Calif.: Wadsworth Publishers.

Bennett, James. 1981. *Oral History and Delinquency: The Rhetoric of Criminology*. Chicago: University of Chicago Press.

Berelson, Bernard, Paul Lazarfeld, and William McPhee. 1954. *Voting*. Chicago: University of Chicago Press.

Berger, Peter. 1963. *An Invitation to Sociology: A Humanistic Perspective*. Garden City, N.Y.: Doubleday.

Bitzer, Lloyd, and Edwin Black, eds. 1971. *The Prospect of Rhetoric*. Englewood Cliffs, N.J.: Prentice-Hall.

Blau, Peter, and Otis Duncan. 1967. *The American Occupational Structure*. New York: John Wiley and Sons.

Bloom, Allan. 1987. *The Closing of the American Mind*. New York: Simon and Schuster.

Bloor, David. 1976. *Knowledge and Social Imagery*. London: Routledge and Kegan Paul.

Booth, Wayne. 1961. *The Rhetoric of Fiction*. Chicago: University of Chicago Press.

Bormann, Ernest G. 1972. "Fantasy and Rhetorical Vision: The Rhetorical Criticism of Social Reality." *Quarterly Journal of Speech* 58:396–407.

———. 1985. *The Force of Fantasy: Restoring the American Dream*. Carbondale: Southern Illinois University Press.

Brewer, John, and Albert Hunter. 1989. *Multimethod Research: A Synthesis of Styles*. Beverly Hills, Calif.: Sage Publications.

Brown, Richard Harvey. 1977. *A Poetic for Sociology*. Cambridge: Cambridge University Press.

———. 1987. *Sociology as Text: Essays on Rhetoric, Reason and Reality*. Chicago: University of Chicago Press.

Brummett, Barry. 1976. "Some Implications of 'Process' or 'Intersubjectivity': Postmodern Rhetoric." *Philosophy and Rhetoric* 9:21–51.

Burke, Kenneth. 1941. *The Philosophy of Literary Form*. Baton Rouge: Louisana State University Press.

———. 1945. *A Grammar of Motives*. Englewood Cliffs, N.J.: Prentice-Hall.

———. 1962. *A Grammar of Motives and a Rhetoric of Motives*. New York: Meridian Books.

———. 1969. *A Rhetoric of Motives*. Berkeley, Calif.: University of California Press.

Calvino, Italo. 1981. *If on a Winter's Night a Traveler*. Trans. William Weaver. New York: Harcourt Brace Jovanovich.

Campbell, Paul Newell. 1974. "The *Personae* of Scientific Discourse." *Quarterly Journal of Speech* 61:391–405.

Cartwright, Nancy. 1983. *How the Laws of Physics Lie*. New York: Oxford University Press.

Chandrasekhar, S. 1987. *Truth and Beauty: Aesthetics and Motivations in Science*. Chicago: University of Chicago Press.

Chicago, Judy. 1975. *Through the Flower: My Struggle as a Woman Artist*. Garden City, N.Y.: Doubleday.

Clark, Burton. 1960. *The Open Door College: A Case Study*. New York: McGraw Hill.

Coleman, James, Elihu Katz, and Herbert Menzel. 1966. *Medical Innovation: A Diffusion Study*. Indianapolis: Bobbs-Merrill.

Collins, H. M. 1981. "Stages in the Empirical Programme of Relativism." *Social Studies of Science* 11:3–10.

———. 1985. *Changing Order: Replication and Induction in Scientific Practice*. Beverly Hills, Calif.: Sage Publications.

Collins, Patricia Hill. 1986. "Learning from the Outsider Within: The Sociological Significance of Black Feminist Thought." *Social Problems* 33:14–32.

Collins, Randall. 1975. *Conflict Sociology: Towards an Explanatory Science*. New York: Academic Press.

————. 1982. *Sociological Insight: An Introduction to Nonobvious Sociology*. New York: Oxford University Press.

Collins, Randall, and Michael Makowsky. 1984. *The Discovery of Society*. 3d ed. New York: Random House.

Coser, Lewis A., Charles Kadushin, and Walter W. Powell. 1982. *Books: The Culture and Commerce of Publishing*. New York: Basic Books.

Cowley, Malcolm. 1956. "Sociological Habit Patterns in Linguistic Transmogrification." *Reporter* 15 (20 September):41.

Cox, J. Robert, and Charles Arthur Willard, eds. 1982. *Advances in Argumentation Theory and Research*. Carbondale: Southern Illinois University Press.

Crane, Diana. 1972. *Invisible Colleges*. Chicago: University of Chicago Press.

Czubaroff, Jeanine. 1973. "Intellectual Respectability: A Rhetorical Problem. *Quarterly Journal of Speech* 59:155–164.

Dantzig, Tobias. 1954. *Number: The Language of Science*. New York: Free Press.

Davis, Murray S. 1971. " 'That's Interesting!' Toward a Phenomenology of Sociology and a Sociology of Phenomenology." *Philosophy of the Social Sciences* 1:309–344.

Deegan, Mary Jo. 1981. "Early Women Sociologists and the American Sociological Society: The Patterns of Exclusion and Participation." *American Sociologist* 16:14–24.

————. 1988. *Jane Addams and the Men of the Chicago School, 1892–1918*. New Brunswick, N.J.: Transaction Books.

Denzin, Norman. 1978. *The Research Act*. 2d ed. New York: McGaw Hill.

Dibble, Vernon. 1972. "Political Judgements and the Perceptions of Social Relationships." *American Journal of Sociology* 79:155–172.

DiTomasso, Nancy. 1982. "Sociological Reductionism: Froms Parsons to Althuser." *American Sociological Review* 47(February) 14–28.

Duncan, Hugh Dalziel. 1962. *Communication and Social Order*. New York: Bedminster.

Dunwoody, Sharon, and Michael Ryan. 1985. "Scientific Barriers to the Popularization of Science in the Media." *Journal of Communications* 35 (Winter):26–42.

Dyson, Freeman. 1979. *Disturbing the Universe*. New York: Harper and Row.

Edmondson, Ricca. 1984. *Rhetoric in Sociology*. London: Macmillan.

Ehninger, Douglas. 1962. "Campbell, Blair and Whately Revisited." *Southern Speech Journal* 28:169–182.

Empson, William. 1938. *English Pastoral Poetry*. New York: W. W. Norton.

Erikson, Kai. 1976. *Everything in Its Path*. New York: Simon and Schuster.

Farrell, Thomas B. 1976. "Knowledge, Consensus, and Rhetorical Theory." *Quarterly Journal of Speech* 61:1–14.

Fischer, Claude. 1982. *To Dwell among Friends*. Chicago: University of Chicago Press.

Fish, Stanley. 1980. *Is There a Text in This Class?* Cambridge: Harvard University Press.

Fisher, Walter R. 1984. "Narration as a Human Communication Paradigm: The Case of Public Moral Argument." *Communication Monographs* 51:1–22.

———. 1987. *Human Communication as Narration*. Columbia: University of South Carolina Press.

Fowler, H. W. 1965. *A Dictionary of Modern English Usage*. 2d ed. rev. Sir Ernest Gowers. Oxford: Oxford University Press.

Fraser, Kennedy. 1981. *The Fashionable Mind*. New York: Knopf.

Friedman, Sharon, and Stephen Steinberg. 1989. *Writing and Thinking in the Social Sciences*. Englewood Cliffs, N.J.: Prentice-Hall.

Fuller, Steve. 1988. *Social Epistemology*. Bloomington: Indiana University Press.

Galison, Peter. 1987. *How Experiments End*. Chicago: University of Chicago Press.

Gans, H. 1979. *Deciding What's News*. New York Patheon.

———. 1982. *The Urban Villagers*. 2d ed. New York: Free Press.

Geertz, Clifford. 1973. "Thick Description: Toward an Interpretive Theory of Culture." In *The Interpretation of Cultures*. New York: Basic Books.

———. 1985. *Local Knowledge*. New York: Basic Books.

Gilmore, Samuel. 1984. "Comparing Tables and Stories." Unpublished manuscript, Center for Urban Affairs and Public Policy Research, Northwestern University, Evanston, Ill.

Glaser, Barney, and Anselm Strauss. 1967. *The Discovery of Grounded Theory*. Chicago: Aldine.

Goffman, Erving. 1959. *The Presentation of Self in Everyday Life*. Garden City, N.Y.: Doubleday.

Golden, James L., and Edward P. J. Corbett. 1968. *The Rhetoric of Blair, Campbell, and Whately*. New York: Holt, Rinehart, and Winston.

Gollin, A. E. 1984. "Publicizing Sociological Activities Serves Important Function for the Discipline." *ASA Footnotes* 12 (December):5.

Gouldner, Alvin W. 1966. *The Coming Crisis of Western Sociology*. New York: Macmillan.

Gusfield, J. 1963. "The 'Double Plot' in Institutions." *Patna University Journal* 18 (January):1–9.

———. 1976. "The Literary Rhetoric of Science: Comedy and Pathos in Drinking-Driving Research." *American Sociological Review* 41(February):16–34.

———. 1975. *Community: A Critical Response*. New York: Harper & Row.

———. 1981. *The Culture of Public Problems: Drinking-Driving and the Symbolic Order*. Chicago: University of Chicago Press.

———. 1986. "Science as a Form of Bureaucratic Discourse: Rhetoric and Style in Formal Organizations." In *Wissenschaft-Sprache und Gesellschaft*, ed. T. Bungarten. Hamburg: Edition Akademion.

Habermas, Jurgen. 1979. *Communication and the Evolution of Society*. Trans. Thomas McCarthy. Boston: Beacon Press.

Hammond, Phillip, ed. 1964. *Sociologists at Work*. New York: Basic Books.

Hawking, Stephen W. 1988. *A Brief History of Time*. New York: Bantam Books.

Hesse, Mary. 1972. *In Defense of Objectivity*. Vol. 57 of *Proceedings of the British Academy*. London: Oxford University Press.

Hillery, George. 1968. *Communal Organizations*. Chicago: University of Chicago Press.

Howell, Wilbur Samuel. 1961. *Logic and Rhetoric in England, 1500–1700*. New York: Russell and Russell.

———. 1971. *Eighteenth-Century British Logic and Rhetoric*. Princeton, N.J.: Princeton University Press.

Howery, Carla B. 1987. "Increasing the Effectiveness of the Public Information Program." *ASA Footnotes* 15 (January):2.

Huizinga, Johan. 1954. *The Waning of the Middle Ages*. New York: Doubleday.

Hunter, Albert. 1974. *Symbolic Communities*. Chicago: University of Chicago Press.

———. 1976. "The Loss of Community." *American Sociological Review* 40:537–552.

Hunter, Albert, and Richard Fritz, 1985. "Class, Status, and Power Structures of Community Elites." *Social Sciences Quarterly* 66:602–616.

Iser, Wolfgang. 1978. *The Act of Reading*. Baltimore: Johns Hopkins University Press.

Janowitz, Morris. 1960. *The Professional Soldier*. New York: Free Press.

Jenkinson, Bruce L. 1949. *Bureau of the Census Manual of Tabular Presentation*. Washington, D.C.: U.S. Commerce Department, Bureau of the Census.

Jones, Mervyn. 1966. "The Sociology Ploy." *New Statesman* 75 (2 September):313.

Kanter, Rosabeth Moss. 1977. *Men and Women of the Corporation*. New York: Basic Books.

Katz, Daniel, and Robert L. Kahn. 1966. *The Social Psychology of Organizations*. New York: John Wiley and Sons.

Kennedy, George. 1963. *The Art of Persuasion in Greece*. Princeton, N.J.: Princeton University Press.

———. 1972. *The Art of Rhetoric in the Roman World*. Princeton, N.J.: Princeton University Press.

———. 1980. *Classical Rhetoric and Its Christian and Secular Tradition from Ancient to Modern Times*. Chapel Hill: University of North Carolina Press.

Kermode, Frank. 1966. *The Sense of an Ending: Studies in the Theory of Fiction*. London: Oxford Univerity Press.

Krieger, Susan. 1983. *The Mirror Dance: Identity in a Women's Community*. Philadelphia: Temple University Press.

Krutch, Joseph Wood. 1963. "Through Happiness with Slide Rule and Calipers." *Saturday Review of Literature* 46 (2 November):69–72.

Kuhn, Thomas S. 1970. *The Structure of Scientific Revolutions*. 2nd ed. Chicago: University of Chicago Press.

Ladd, Everett C., Jr., and Seymour Martin Lipset. 1973. *Professors, Unions and American Higher Education*. Berkeley, Calif.: Carnegie Commission on Higher Education.

Lakatos, Imre. 1976. *Proofs and Refutations: The Logic of Mathematical Discovery*. Vol. 1. Cambridge: Cambridge University Pess.

Lang, Serge. 1981. *The File*. New York: Springer-Verlag.

Laslett, Peter. 1965. *The World We Have Lost*. New York: Scribner's.

Latour, Bruno, and Steven Woolgar. 1979. *Laboratory Life: The Social Construction of Scientific Fact*. Beverly Hills, Calif.: Sage Publications.

Laub, John H. 1983. *Criminology in the Making: An Oral History*. Boston: Northeastern University Press.

Leenhardt, Jacques. 1980. "Toward a Sociology of Reading." In *The Reader in the Text*, ed. Susan Suleiman and Inge Crosman. Princeton, N.J.: Princeton University Press.

Leff, Michael C. 1978. "In Search of Ariadne's Thread: A Review of the Recent Literature on Rhetorical Theory." *Central States Speech Journal* 29:73–91.

Liebow, Elliot. 1967. *Tally's Corner*. Boston Little, Brown.

Lipset, Seymour, and Reinhard Bendix. 1959. *Social Mobility in Industrial Society*. Berkeley, Calif.: University of California Press.

Lofland, John. 1966. *Doomsday Cult: A Study of Conversion, Proselytization, and Maintenance in Faith*. Englewood Cliffs, N.J.: Prentice-Hall.

Lynd, Robert, and Helen Lynd. 1929. *Middletown*. New York: Harcourt, Brace and World.

———. 1937. *Middletown in Transition*. New York: Harcourt, Brace and World.

Lyne, John. 1985. "Rhetorics of Inquiry." *Quarterly Journal of Speech* 71:65–73.

McCloskey, Donald N. 1985. *The Rhetoric of Economics*. Madison: University of Wisconsin Press.

McDowell, Deborah E. 1986. " 'The Changing Same': Generational Connections and Black Women Novelists." *New Literary History* 18:281–302.

McKeon, Richard. 1971. "The Uses of Rhetoric in a Technological Age: Architectonic Productive Arts." In *The Prospect of Rhetoric,* ed. Lloyd Bitzer and Edwin Black, 44–63. Englewood Cliffs, N.J.: Prentice-Hall.

Mandelbrot, Benoit. 1983. *The Fractal Geometry of Nature*. New York: Freeman.

Mannheim, Karl. 1936. *Ideology and Utopia*. Trans. Louis Writh and Edward Shils. New York: Harcourt, Brace and World.

Mead, George Herbert. 1962. *Mind, Self, and Society*. Ed. Charles W. Morris. Chicago: University of Chicago Press.

Mencken, H. L. 1955 (1920). "Abraham Lincoln." In *The Vintage Mencken,* ed. Alistaire Cooke, 179–180. New York: Vintage.

Merton, Robert K. 1938. "Social Structure and Anomie." *American Sociologic Review* 3:672–682.

———. 1949. "Manifest and Latent Functions." In *Social Theory and Social Structure*, 39–72. Glencoe, Ill.: Free Press.

———. 1967. "On Sociological Theories of the Middle Range." In *On Theoretical Sociology: Five Essays Old and New*, 39–72. New York: Free Press.

———. 1973. *The Sociology of Science*. Chicago: University of Chicago Press.

———. 1976. "The Ambivalence of Physicians." In *Sociological Ambivalence*, 65–72. New York: Free Press.

Mills, C. Wright. 1959. *The Sociological Imagination*. New York: Oxford University Press.

Milofsky, Carl. 1974. "Why Special Education Isn't Special." *Harvard Educational Review* 44:437–458.

———. 1976. *Special Education: A Sociological Study of California Programs.* New York: Praeger.

———. 1989. *Testers and Testing: The Sociology of School Psychology.* New Brunswick, N.J.: Rutgers University Press.

Mitchell, W.J.T., ed. 1981. *On Narrative.* Chicago: University of Chicago Press.

Mulkay, Michael. 1979. *Science and the Sociology of Knowledge.* London: Allen and Unwin.

———. 1985. *The Word and the World.* London: Allen and Unwin.

Myers, John H. 1950. *Statistical Presentation.* Ames, Iowa: Littlefield, Adams.

Nelson, John S., Allen Megill, and Donald N. McCloskey, eds. 1987. *The Rhetoric of the Human Sciences.* Madison: University of Wisconsin Press.

Nisbet, Robert. 1976. *Sociology as an Art Form.* New York: Oxford University Press.

Ogburn, William Fielding. 1930. "The Coming Age in Sociology." *Scientific Monthly* 30:300–306.

Orwell, George. 1946. "Politics and the English Language." In *A Collection of Essays by George Orwell,* 153, 156. New York Harcourt Brace.

Perelman, Ch., and Olbrechts-Tyteca, L. 1969. *The New Rhetoric: A Treatise on Argumentation.* Notre Dame: University of Notre Dame Press.

Plato. 1961. *The Collected Works of Plato.* Ed. Edith Hamilton and Huntington Cairns. New York: Pantheon.

Plumb, J. H. 1971. *The Death of the Past.* Boston: Houghton, Mifflin.

Polanyi, Michael. 1958. *Personal Knowledge.* Chicago: University of Chicago Press.

Powell, Walter W. 1985. *Getting into Print.* Chicago: University of Chicago Press.

Reinharz, Shulamit. 1988. "Women and Intellectual Work, or The History of Women's Contributions to American Sociology." In *An Inclusive Curriculum: Race, Class and Gender in Sociological Instruction,* ed. Patricia Hill Collins and Margaret Anderson. Washington, D.C.: American Sociological Association.

———. Forthcoming. *Social Research Methods, Feminist Voices.* New York: Pergamon.

Ricoeur, Paul. 1984. *Time and Narrative.* Chicago: University of Chicago Press.

Rieke, Richard D., and Malcolm O. Sillars. 1984. *Argumentation and the Decision Making Process.* 2nd ed. Glenview, Ill.: Scott, Foresman.

Roch, Itzhah. 1982. *The Rhetoric of News in the Israel Radio.* Bochum: Studienverlag Dr. N. Brockmeyer.

Rossiter, Margaret W. 1982. *Women Scientists in America: Struggles and Strategies to 1940.* Baltimore: Johns Hopkins University Press.

Rueckert, William H. 1963. *Kenneth Burke and the Drama of Human Relations.* Minneapolis: University of Minnesota Press.

Sarason, Seymour B. 1972. *The Creation of Settings and the Future Societies.* San Francisco: Jossey-Bass.

Scott, Robert L. 1967. "On Viewing Rhetoric as Epistemic." *Central States Speech Journal* 18:9–16.

———. 1976. "On Viewing Rhetoric as Epistemic: Ten Years Later." *Central States Speech Journal* 27:258–266.

Selvin, Hanan C., and Everett K. Wilson. 1984. "On Sharpening Sociologists' Prose." *Sociological Quarterly* 25:205–223.

Shils, Edward. 1961. "The Calling of Sociology." In *Theories of Society*, ed. Talcott Parsons et al., 1405–1448. New York: Free Press.

Showalter, Elaine. 1977. *A Literature of Their Own: British Women Novelists from Bronte to Lessing*. Princeton, N.J.: Princeton University Press.

Simons, Herbert W. 1980. "Are Scientists Rhetors is Disguise? An Analysis of Discursive Practices within Scientific Communities." In *Rhetoric in Transition: Studies in the Nature and Uses of Rhetoric*, ed. Eugene White. University Park: Pennsylvania State University Press.

———. 1985. "Chronicle and Critique of a Conference." *Quarterly Journal of Speech* 71:52–64.

———. 1988. *Rhetoric in the Human Sciences*. London: Sage Publications.

Singer, Eleanor, 1986. "Social Science Stories often Report Limited Research as 'Universal Truths.' " *Bulletin of the American Society of Newspaper Editors* (February):16ff.

Skolnick, Jerome. 1967. *Justice without Trial: Law Enforcement in a Democratic Society*. New York: John Wiley and Sons.

Smith, Barbara Herrnstein. 1981. "Narrative Versions, Narrative Theories." In *On Narrative*, ed. W. J. T. Mitchell. Chicago: University of Chicago Press.

Spender, Dale. 1982. *Women of Ideas and What Men Have Done to Them: From Aphra Behn to Adrienne Rich*. London: Routledge and Kegan Paul.

Stinchcombe, Arthur. 1983. *Economic Sociology*. New York: Academic Press.

Suleiman, Susan, and Inge Crosman, eds. 1980. *The Reader in the Text*. Princeton, N.J.: Princeton University Press.

Tompkins, Jane, ed. 1980. *Reader-Response Criticism*. Baltimore: Johns Hopkins University Press.

Toulmin, Stephen. 1958. *The Uses of Argument*. Cambridge: Cambridge University Press.

———. 1972. *Human Understanding*. Princeton, N.J.: Princeton University Press.

Toulmin, Stephen, Richard Rieke, and Allan Janik. 1985. *An Introduction to Reasoning*. 2d ed. New York: Macmillan.

Tuchman, Gaye. 1989. *Edging Women Out: Victorian Novelists, Publishers, and Social Change*. New Haven, Conn.: Yale University Press.

Tuchman, Gaye, and Nina E. Fortin. 1984. "Fame and Misfortune: Edging Women Out of the Great Literary Tradition." *American Journal of Sociology* 90:72–96.

Twain, Mark. 1967 (1883). *Life on the Mississippi*. New York: Dillon Press.

Vidich, Arthur, and Joseph Bensman. 1960. *Small Town in Mass Society*. Garden City, NY: Doubleday.

Walker, Samuel. 1985. "Historians on the Case: Contemporary Crime Policy and the Uses of History." *Organization of American Historians Newsletter* 13 (February):13–15.

Warner, W. Lloyd. 1963. *Yankee City*. New Haven: Yale University Press.

Weaver, Richard. 1953. *The Ethics of Rhetoric*. Chicago: Henry Regnery.

Weber, Max. 1958. "Science as Vocation." In *Max Weber*, ed. H. H. Gerth and C. Wright Mills, 129–156. New York: Oxford University Press.

Weigert, Andrew. 1970. "The Immoral Rhetoric of Scientific Sociology." *American Sociologist* 5:111–116.

Weimer, Walter. 1977. "Science as a Rhetorical Transaction: Toward a Nonjustificational Conception of Rhetoric." *Philosophy and Rhetoric* 10:1–29.

Weiss, Janet. 1987. "Substance vs. Symbol in Administrative Reform: The Case of Human Services Coordination." In *Community Organizations: Studies in Resource Mobilization and Exchange,* ed. Carl Milofsky, 100–118. New York: Oxford University Press.

Wellman, Barry. 1979. "The Community Question: The Intimate Networks of East New Yorkers." *American Journal of Sociology* 84:1201–1231.

White, Hayden. 1981. "The Value of Narrativity in the Representation of Reality." In *On Narrative*, ed. W.J.T. Mitchell, 1–24. Chicago: University of Chicago Press.

Whyte, W. 1942 (1955). *Street Corner Society*. Chicago: University of Chicago Press.

Willard, Charles Arthur. 1978. "A Reformulation of the Concept of Argument: The Constructivist-Interactionist Foundations of a Sociology of Argument." *Journal of the American Forensic Association* 14:121–140.

———. 1983. *Argumentation and the Social Grounds of Knowledge*. Tuscaloosa: University of Alabama Press.

———. 1989. *A Theory of Argumentation*. Tuscaloosa University of Alabama Press.

Wilson, Edmund. 1956. *A Piece of My Mind*. New York: Farrar, Straus and Cudahy.

Wrong, Dennis. 1983. "Professional Jargon: Is Sociology the Culprit?" *University: Academic Affairs at New York University* 2:3–7.

Yates, Frances A. 1966. *The Art of Memory*. Chicago: University of Chicago Press.

Zarefsky, David. 1980. "Causal Argument among Historians: The Case of the American Civil War." *Southern Speech Communication Journal* 45:187–205.

———. 1982. "Persistent Questions in the Theory of Argument Fields." *Journal of the American Forensic Association* 19:191–203.

Zorbaugh, H. 1929. *The Gold Coast and the Slum*. Chicago: University of Chicago Press.

List of Contributors

James Bennett is a research associate at the Center for Urban Affairs and Policy Research, Northwestern University, where he is conducting a study of the social contexts of independent scholars, funded by the Spencer Foundation. He is the author of *Oral History and Delinquency: The Rhetoric of Criminology*.

Marjorie L. DeVault is an assistant professor in the Sociology Department at Syracuse University, where she also teaches Women's Studies. Her book *Feeding the Family: The Social Organizarion of Caring as Gendered Work* is forthcoming from the University of Chicago Press.

Kai Erikson is Professor of Sociology and American Studies at Yale University and is a former president of the American Sociological Association. His most recent book is *Encounters*.

Claude S. Fischer is Professor of Sociology, University of California, Berkeley. He has authored *The Urban Experience* and *To Dwell Among Friends: Personal Networks in Town and City* and is just completing *Person-to-Person: The Telephone, Community, and Modernity, 1880–1940*.

Joseph R. Gusfield is Professor of Sociology at the University of California, San Diego. Among his major publications are *Symbolic Crusade: Status Politics and the American Temperance Movement* and *The Culture of Public Problems: Drinking-Driving and the Symbolic Order*.

Albert Hunter is Professor of Sociology at Northwestern University. He is the author of *Symbolic Communities* and co-author (with John Brewer) of *Multimethod Research: A Synthesis of Styles*.

Lawrence T. McGill has taught in the Department of Sociology and at the Medill School of Journalism at Northwestern University. He is currently manager of News Audience Research at the National Broadcasting Company.

Carl Milofsky is an associate professor in the Department of Sociology, Bucknell University, and author of *Testers and Testing: The Sociology of School Psychology* (Rutgers University Press).

David Zarefsky is Professor of Communication Studies and Dean of the School of Speech, Northwestern University. His books include *President Johnson's War on Poverty: Rhetoric and History* and *Lincoln, Douglas, and Slavery: In the Crucible of Public Debate*.